American Composers of Our Time

Joseph Machlis

American
Composers
of Our Time

Thomas Y. Crowell Company · *New York*

For Leslie, Karen, and Stefanie

By the Author

149950

The Enjoyment of Music: *An Introduction to Perceptive Listening*
Introduction to Contemporary Music

Operas in English (singing versions)

Beethoven: *Fidelio*
Falla: *Atlantida*
Mascagni: *Cavalleria rusticana*
Montemezzi: *L'Amore dei tre re* (*The Love of Three Kings*)
Poulenc: *Dialogues des Carmélites*; *La Voix humaine* (*The Human Voice*)
Prokofiev: *War and Peace*
Puccini: *La Bohème*; *Il Tabarro* (*The Cloak*); *Tosca*
Verdi: *Rigoletto*; *La Traviata*

For Young Music Lovers

Young People's Introduction to the Great Composers: a series
of recordings on the life and music of the great masters
1. Franz Liszt   2. Wolfgang Amadeus Mozart   3. Ludwig van Beethoven
4. Peter Ilyich Tchaikovsky   5. Felix Mendelssohn   6. Franz Schubert
7. Frédéric François Chopin   8. Johannes Brahms   9. Robert Schumann
10. Johann Sebastian Bach   11. Josef Haydn   12. Claude Debussy

Contents

By Way of Introduction

"What we must arrive at is the youthful optimistic vitality and the undaunted tenacity of spirit that characterizes the American man. That is what I hope to see echoed in American music."
—*Edward MacDowell*

Music came to America with the Pilgrims. The first book to be printed in the New World was an almanac; second was the Bay Psalm Book, which was published in Cambridge in 1640. The Pilgrim Fathers, understandably, did not have the leisure to cultivate music as a fine art. Conditions of life in early New England were too harsh for that. The chief function of music, as far as they were concerned, was the singing of psalms and hymns.

Virginia, on the other hand, developed an aristocratic society of planters who tried to recapture, in their new homeland, the social graces they had known in Cavalier England. They looked upon music as a gentle recreation and a necessary part of gracious living. Thomas Jefferson, for example, called music "the favorite passion of my soul." He himself was an amateur violinist and, during his stay at William and Mary College, played string quartets at weekly gatherings in the Governor's palace at Williamsburg. He invented an ingenious violin stand which, when folded, did double duty as an end table.

When he planned his estate at Monticello Jefferson wanted very much to have a little orchestra of his own. To a friend in France he wrote: "I retain among my domestic servants a gardener, a weaver, a cabinet-maker, and a stone-cutter, to which I would add a vine-grower. In a country where, like yours, music is cultivated and practiced by every class of men, I suppose there might be found persons of these trades who could perform on the French horn, clarinet, or oboe, and bassoon, so that one might have a band of two French horns, two clarinets, two oboes, and a bassoon, without enlarging their domestic expenses . . . If there is a gratification which I envy any people in this world, it is to your country its music." There are many references to music in Jefferson's writings. Typical is his observation that music "furnishes a delightful recreation for the hours of respite from the cares of the day, and lasts us through life."

Public concerts were given in such cities as Boston and Charleston in the 1730s. A type of musical play known as ballad opera found great favor with our ancestors. In Boston the city fathers found it necessary to pass a law against such entertainments, stating that they discouraged industry, frugality, and piety (in that order). To get around the law, musical shows masqueraded as "moral lectures" and "readings." By the end of the eighteenth century the Bostonians had succumbed to several dozen ballad operas.

The best known of our early composers was not a professional musician at all, but an aristocratic amateur. Francis Hopkinson (1737–1791) came from the same level of society in Philadelphia as did his friend Jefferson in Virginia. Composing was only one of his many interests, for he was also a lawyer, a writer, a statesman, a signer of the Declaration of Independence, and one of the framers of the Constitution. Hopkinson's most successful song was *My*

Days Have Been So Wondrous Free. In 1788 he published a collection of songs "in an easy, familiar style," for which he also wrote the words. He dedicated the collection to George Washington, to whom he wrote: "However small the Reputation may be that I shall derive from this work, I cannot, I believe, be refused the Credit of being the first Native of the United States who has produced a Musical Composition." To which Washington replied, "I can neither sing one of the songs, nor raise a single note on any instrument to convince the unbelieving. But I have, however, one argument which will prevail with persons of true estate (at least in America)—I can tell them that *it is the production of Mr. Hopkinson.*"

A more substantial composer was William Billings (1746–1800). A tanner by trade, this enthusiastic musician was the product of a pioneer culture. What little he knew about composing was gained from reading the instructions contained in the popular hymn books of his day. Billings is known especially for his "fuguing pieces," in which he treated hymn tunes contrapuntally—that is, he combined them with other voice-parts, so that soprano, alto, tenor, and bass each sang a different melodic line. In this way he produced music that was, he claimed, "twenty times as powerful as the old slow tunes. Each part striving for mastery and victory. The audience entertained and delighted. Now the solemn bass demands their attention; next the manly tenor. Now here, now there, now here again. O ecstatic! Rush on, you sons of harmony!" Billings' psalms, anthems, humorous pieces, and patriotic songs were widely performed in the late eighteenth century. His hymn *Chester* became one of the battle songs of the Revolution. He was rewarded for his efforts with a pauper's grave near Boston Common. His memory lived on, however, to inspire some twentieth-century Americans. William Schuman's *William Billings Overture*, Otto Luening's *Prelude to a Hymn Tune by William Billings*, and Henry Cowell's

Hymn and Fuguing Tune are among the works that pay homage to this extraordinary American "primitive."

A more glamorous figure was the pianist Louis Moreau Gottschalk (1829–1869), who was born in New Orleans, the son of an English Jew and a Creole. Gottschalk was one of the most popular pianists of his time. Handsome and magnetic, he received the same kind of adoration in this country as Franz Liszt did in Europe. He would leave his white gloves on the piano, to be torn to shreds by ecstatic ladies in search of a little souvenir. Gottschalk left behind a number of pieces, such as *The Last Hope* and *The Dying Poet*, which were much played by several generations of piano students. More important were the miniatures he wrote during the 1840s (*Bamboula, Le Bananier, The Banjo*) in which he exploited the local color of New Orleans. By so doing, he set an example for American composers to use specifically American material.

In spite of these and other native-born musicians, music in America for two hundred years was dominated by the European tradition. This was understandable. For ours was a pioneer country whose main efforts had to go into more practical pursuits than the creation of music and art. Nor did we have a hereditary aristocracy such as the princes and dukes of Europe, who had been patrons of music for centuries. Throughout the eighteenth and nineteenth centuries we imported music and musicians from the three great musical cultures of the Old World—Germany, Italy, and France. True, we did produce a great American composer in the years before the Civil War. But he did not issue out of the tradition of Haydn and Mozart. He came out of the humbler realm of the minstrel show, and his name was Stephen Foster.

In the decades following the Civil War a number of trained composers were active in this country. However, most of them had studied in Germany. And when they returned to the United States they tried to compose in the style of Schumann and Mendelssohn or Wagner and Liszt. They thought that if they did this, they would establish in America the same high standards of technique that prevailed in Europe. As a result, their music was hardly typical of our country or its people. And so both they and their compositions were soon forgotten.

At the end of the nineteenth century it was the foreign composer who held the spotlight in this country. Thus, when Carnegie Hall was built, the great Russian composer Tchaikovsky was invited to come to New York in 1891 to take part in the ceremonies that marked the opening of the new hall. A year later, when the National Conservatory of Music was opened in New York City, the Czech composer Antonin Dvořák, then at the height of his fame, was invited to become the director of the new school. Dvořák, who spent three years in the United States, gave his American students some good advice. "Stop trying to compose like Europeans," he told them. "Learn to stand on your own feet. You have beautiful folk songs that express the spirit of your country. Use those as the basis for your music. Only in that way will you become American composers."

With the opening of the twentieth century, our composers began to throw off the European influence. They grew more sure of themselves; they tried more and more to give expression to the life around them. They became aware of a wealth of musical material that was not to be found in any other country: the melodies of the American Indian, Negro spirituals, cowboy songs; the songs of the southern mountaineers; the hymns and religious tunes that had such vivid memories for Americans everywhere; the patriotic songs of the Revolution and the Civil War. There were, in addition, picturesque work songs from every part of the country: songs of sharecroppers, lumberjacks, miners, river men; songs of prairie and railroad, chain gang and frontier. Then there was the folk song of the city dwellers—musical comedy hits, Tin Pan Alley tunes, jazz. All these formed a world of melody, rhythm, and mood that was distinctively American: an inexhaustible treasury of folk and popular material that could inspire our composers to write truly American works.

A nation may build an active musical life by importing famous performers and composers from abroad. Sooner or later, however, if it is going to come of age artistically, it must learn to create its own music and develop its own school of composers. All the same, modern American music did not have an easy time in establishing itself. On the contrary, its path was strewn with obstacles. In the early years of our century, the serious American composer was something of a stepchild in his own country. His music, being modern, did not appeal to the public, which was strongly conservative. And it lacked the made-in-Europe label that carries such weight in our concert halls. He had no powerful publishers to champion his cause. There was no system of awards and fellowships to give him financial assistance. In addition, the conductors of our great orchestras were mostly Europeans who preferred to devote their talents to Beethoven, Brahms, and Tchaikovsky. As we follow the careers of the older members of the modern American school, such as Charles Ives and Charles T. Griffes—composers, that is, who were born between 1870 and 1890—we cannot help feeling that they appeared upon the scene before their country was ready for them.

The middle generation, composers born between 1890 and 1910, had an easier time of it. The gradual victory of modern music in Europe had an influence on our own country. Besides, it became a matter of national pride to develop a strong American school. The era of prosperity in the 1920s encouraged wealthy music lovers to help composers with awards and prizes. American composers found increased opportunities to see their works in print and to hear them performed. The big radio networks began to broadcast modern American music. At this time, too, our composers began to play an ever more important part in our musical life as directors of conservatories, critics on newspapers, and teachers in our colleges and universities. Slowly but surely the tide turned, and the modern American composer came into his own.

In the years after the Second World War our native music made important strides forward. Publishing houses and record companies became more interested in contemporary American music. Our government came to the assistance of deserving musicians through the Fulbright grants. During the 1950s the large philanthropic foundations began to contribute to our musical life in ways that helped composers. Most important of all, the public began to take an interest in modern American music and modern American composers. As a result of these developments, the third generation of the American school, the composers who were born since 1910, have found much more favorable conditions for their work than did their elders.

Once our composers achieved a measure of independence from the European past, they no longer had to emphasize their Americanism. Indeed, certain composers began to feel that the music written in this country did not always have to wear a made-in-America label. They preferred to write in the international idioms that came into fashion in the twentieth century. Others managed to unite both attitudes, using American folk material in certain of their works, but maintaining an international point of view in others. It was gradually realized that Americanism in music was a much broader concept than people had supposed. American music could not but be as many-sided as America itself. A musical composition did not have to quote a Negro spiritual, an Indian harvest song, or a dirge of the prairie in order to qualify for citizenship. As Virgil Thomson summed it up, "The way to write American music is simple. All you have to do is to be an American and then write any kind of music you wish."

The music of the modern American school, therefore, does not follow any single formula. It reflects the contradictory traits in our national character: our humor, and our sentimentality; our idealism, and our intensely practical nature; our rugged individualism, and our desire to look and think like everybody else; our capacity for dreams, and our even greater love of action. No matter which aspect of our character a certain work reflects, American music as a whole has a youthful vitality and bounce. It is energetic, optimistic, virile. It is conceived along big lines. Above all, it is the music of a young, active nation.

In the following chapters you will find the life stories of sixteen modern American composers. Some are outspoken nationalists; others adhere to the international point of view. Some are classicists; others follow the romantic ideal. (For an explanation of these and other terms used in this book, consult the Glossary of Musical Terms at the back of the book.) These composers represent a cross section of the modern American school. They and their comrades have created and are continuing to create America's music.

Each chapter ends with the description of a work that is typical of its composer—a work, moreover, that is available on records. The purpose of this book will be fulfilled only if you make it a point to listen to these compositions. True, it is possible to learn a great deal about a composer by reading about his life. But this is only the first step. For a composer's true story lies not in the external events of his life, but in the sounds that he has created. Only when you have heard his music will you make contact with his inner self. Only then will you really know what his life is about.

American Composers of Our Time

1. EDWARD MAC DOWELL

Edward MacDowell is remembered as the composer of such peren-
nial favorites as *To a Wild Rose* and *To a Water Lily*. More important, he was the first American composer who won fame in
Europe.

Edward MacDowell was born in New York City on December
18, 1861. He came of Scotch-Irish parentage. His father was a
prosperous businessman who encouraged the boy's artistic tend-
encies. Edward began to study the piano at the age of eight. At
first he did not enjoy practicing scales and exercises. He preferred
to dream at the keyboard, making up his own melodies and harmonies. In time, however, he ceased to dream; he developed a
supple technique and became an accomplished pianist. Edward's
gifts showed themselves in a number of directions. He had a remarkable talent for drawing. He wrote poetry. And he made up
fairy tales with a vivid imagination worthy of his Celtic ancestors.

By the time he was fifteen his interest in music had gained the
upper hand over his other pursuits. At that time, gifted young
Americans who could afford it went to Europe to complete their
musical education. Edward, accompanied by his mother, sailed for
Paris in 1876. He passed the examination for admittance to the
Paris Conservatory, one of the most famous schools in Europe.

There he studied piano, harmony, and composition. His mother also engaged a tutor, a gentleman with an extraordinarily big nose, to teach him French. To dispel the boredom of the lessons, Edward secretly began a pencil sketch of his teacher. One day, just as he was completing the portrait, the Frenchman demanded to see what he was drawing and, to Edward's intense embarrassment, examined the sketch. The teacher was so impressed with the drawing that he showed it to an artist friend of his, who immediately offered to give Edward free instruction for three years, so convinced was he that the young man could become a talented painter. For a time Edward was uncertain as to which course he should pursue. In the end music won the day, and he continued his studies at the Conservatory.

However, the French conception of piano playing did not appeal to his temperament. After two years in Paris he went to Germany, where he found an environment more congenial to his taste. He entered the Frankfort Conservatory, worked intensively to perfect his piano playing, and studied composition with Joachim Raff, a composer who was very much admired at that time. Edward made such progress that when his piano teacher left the Conservatory, he was recommended to become his successor. But the other professors objected to his receiving the post. He was much too young, they said.

He began to teach privately. Although he was a painfully shy young man, his gift for arousing the enthusiasm of his pupils made him a remarkable teacher and soon brought him a reputation. In Frankfort he came to be known as "the handsome American" because of his bright blue eyes and fair skin. When he first went to Europe his ambition had been to become a concert pianist. As time passed, he became more and more interested in composing. His teacher, Joachim Raff, encouraged his first creative efforts and spurred him on to continue in this direction. MacDowell taught for a time in the Conservatory of Darmstadt, a town not far from Frankfort. He commuted between the two cities. As all his time was taken up with playing the piano and giving lessons, he spent the hours on the train in writing his music. In this way he composed his first important works.

MacDowell was twenty-one when he completed his First Piano Concerto. Raff urged him to go to Weimar and show his Concerto to the famous composer Franz Liszt. The young man dreaded the prospect of facing one of the outstanding artists of Europe. He finally mustered up enough courage to go to Weimar and play the Concerto before Liszt. The visit was a pleasant surprise. Liszt praised both his music and his piano playing. Even more important, when MacDowell returned to Frankfort he received a most friendly letter from the great man. The letter informed him that a music festival was about to be held in Zurich, and Liszt was recommending that a work by MacDowell should be included in the program. Liszt also suggested that the young American should be invited to Zurich to play his piece. MacDowell had a great success at Zurich. When he finished playing he was greeted with a burst of applause and called out for many bows. A year later Liszt again intervened in behalf of the young composer, by recommending his two piano suites to the most important publisher in Germany. These were the first works by MacDowell to appear in print. In gratitude, he dedicated his First Piano Concerto to Franz Liszt.

At this time a lovely American girl named Marian Nevins arrived in Frankfort to study music. She wanted to take lessons from one of the German professors. Since they were all very busy, she decided to work with MacDowell. She had wrenched her back in a fall, some weeks before. Undaunted by this accident, she turned up for her first lesson on crutches. Marian was as musical as she was pretty. Before long, she and MacDowell were very much in love.

3

When she returned to the United States he followed, eager to marry her. Although he had made a good start with his composing, he realized that he could not earn a living by writing music, especially now when he would have a wife to support. He decided to abandon his aspirations as a composer and to settle down in the United States as a pianist and teacher.

But Marian had other ideas. She believed in MacDowell's gifts, and she was not going to see him sacrifice—because of her—the thing he wanted to do most. She had inherited five thousand dollars (which in those days was a considerably larger sum than it is now). "We'll go back to Europe," she told her fiancé. "There we can live much more cheaply than in the United States. You will have five years in which to make your mark as a composer, without having to worry about earning a living."

MacDowell would not hear of this. "No man should live on his wife," he insisted. "We'll stay right here and I will work for both of us—as a husband should. I certainly won't let you support me!"

"In that case," she replied, "I won't marry you." Marian was a girl who knew her mind. Despite all that MacDowell could say, she stuck to her decision until he gave in. The two young people were married and sailed for Europe shortly after. In Marian, Mac-Dowell found a wonderfully understanding wife and comrade who devoted her whole existence to his well-being.

After a brief honeymoon in England they settled in Frankfort, where MacDowell divided his time between his piano playing and composing. This was a time of quiet joy for the young couple. Their life revolved around his creative work; Marian was determined not to let anything interfere with that. They lived very modestly, in a single room. As a result, Marian had to go out every afternoon so as not to disturb him when he was composing. She would visit friends. As she soon ran through the list of those, she often ended up by visiting acquaintances whom she had not the slightest desire to see. Or she sat alone in the park, which was not very convenient when the weather turned cool. When he finished working they spent happy hours walking in the woods outside the town. In the evening MacDowell would read aloud to her from his favorite poets—Keats, Shelley, Tennyson, Victor Hugo, Heinrich Heine; or from the romantic fairy tales that appealed so strongly to his imagination.

On two occasions MacDowell was recommended for an official post with a conservatory. But his youth was against him, as well as the fact that he was an American. At that time the United States had not yet produced any composer with an international reputation. As a result, American musicians were not regarded highly in Europe.

After a time the MacDowells settled in the pleasant town of Wiesbaden, where they bought a little cottage. After hours of composing, MacDowell would find relaxation digging in his garden or walking in the woods. He had every reason to be satisfied with his existence in Wiesbaden. He was composing steadily, and had completed his Second Piano Concerto. His works were beginning to make their way. As his reputation grew, more and more musicians from America came to visit him. They urged him to return to the United States. They pointed out that it was his duty to play his part in building the musical life of his country. And so the five years of retirement made possible by Marian's generosity came to an end. In September, 1888, the MacDowells sold their cottage and returned to their native land, not without a pang of regret at leaving the place where they had been so happy.

Although both of them were native New Yorkers, they decided to live in Boston, where life was less hectic. MacDowell's fame had preceded him. He was welcomed by the musical world. His appearances as a composer-pianist were extremely successful. He was

5

admired not only in the performance of his own compositions but also when he played the music of Chopin, Liszt, and others. When he performed his Second Piano Concerto with the New York Philharmonic, the newspapers reported "a success such as no American musician has ever won before a metropolitan concert audience. A Philharmonic audience can be cold when it does not like a piece or a player; but Mr. MacDowell had an ovation such as is accorded only to a popular prima donna at the opera."

In 1896 Columbia University received a large gift to be devoted to the founding of a department of music. The committee in charge of the appointment announced that the new professorship was being offered to MacDowell because, in their opinion, he was "the greatest musical genius America has produced." MacDowell felt extremely honored at this offer. All the same, he weighed carefully whether he should accept it. He was having a good career in Boston. He had more piano pupils than he could teach. And he was able in Boston to lead the kind of life that accorded with his retiring disposition. At the same time he realized what a challenge it would be to organize a department of music in a great university. Besides, the appointment at Columbia offered greater financial security than he had achieved during his eight years in Boston. Most important of all, in his new position he would be able to influence the course of music education in America. After balancing the pros and cons, MacDowell decided to accept the offer. That autumn he and Marian moved from Boston to New York; and he took up his duties as the first professor of music at Columbia University.

Although by temperament he was an artist rather than a practical organizer, MacDowell threw himself into his task with all the imagination and energy at his command. He designed a series of courses covering all aspects of music and proved to be a brilliant teacher. One of his pupils left a vivid account of the com-

6

poser in the classroom. "Professor MacDowell never sank into the passionless routine of lecture giving. His were not the dry discourses that students link most often to university professors. They were beautifully illuminating talks, delivered with so much freedom and such a rush of enthusiasm that one felt that the hour never held all that wanted to be said, and the abundant knowledge, in its longing to get out, kept spilling over into the tomorrows."

MacDowell's duties at Columbia ranged from teaching and administering the music courses to the drudgery of correcting student papers. All this took much time and effort. Nevertheless he kept up his composing and piano playing. His summer vacations were spent on a piece of property he had bought at Peterborough, New Hampshire. MacDowell was extremely sensitive to noise and found it very difficult to compose in New York. Even in Peterborough he was disturbed by the noises that came from the household. Marian, unknown to him, had a log cabin built in the heart of the woods, away from the main house, which he could use as a workroom. When the cabin was finished she surprised him with this thoughtful gift. Here, surrounded by the woods and the hills that he loved, he composed some of his finest music. In the last piece he ever wrote, *From a Log Cabin*, he depicted the quiet joy he found in his secluded studio. On the manuscript he inscribed the following lines:

> A house of dreams untold,
> It looks out over the whispering tree-tops
> And faces the setting sun.

MacDowell would go to the studio early in the morning. He took along a lunch basket, so that he would not have to return to the house until he had finished his day's work. There was a fireplace inside the cabin, and on cool days he lit a fire. Mac-Dowell was diffident about his music. It often happened that when he finished a piece, he felt it wasn't worth anything at all. He would crumple the sheet into a ball and throw it into the flames. One afternoon he just missed the fire. The crumpled manuscript lay near the hearth until Marian rescued it. The piece she saved from destruction was *To a Wild Rose,* which became one of America's best-loved melodies.

In planning the music course at Columbia, MacDowell pictured a Division of Fine Arts that would include not only music but also painting, sculpture, architecture, and literature, giving the student a complete experience of the arts. The president of Columbia, Seth Low, was most sympathetic to MacDowell's bold conception. In 1902 Seth Low was succeeded by Nicholas Murray Butler, whose ideas did not coincide with MacDowell's. Butler, a man of practical affairs and an excellent organizer, viewed the arts as a useful tool for teachers rather than as a profound emotional experience. He decided to reorganize the Division of Fine Arts as part of Teachers College, in conjunction with a model kindergarten. For MacDowell the issue was much more than a personal disagreement between himself and President Butler. He saw it as a clash between the artistic and the materialistic view of life. If music was one of the great arts of our civilization, as he believed it to be, then it had to play a leading part in the intellectual life of the university. If it was no more than a pleasant pastime and an accessory to school teaching, as Butler believed it was, then it could just as well be administered by Teachers College. In that case, MacDowell insisted, the Division of Fine Arts acquired "somewhat the nature of a co-educational department store, and tends towards materialism rather than idealism."

When MacDowell saw that Butler was completely unsympathetic to his ideals, he handed in his resignation. The next day "the MacDowell Affair" broke into print. The New York papers seized on the story and came out with headlines quoting Mac-

Dowell: "No Idealism Left in Columbia." Butler issued a statement to the press saying that MacDowell had resigned in order to devote his time to composing. MacDowell issued a counterstatement which said: "President Butler has evidently misunderstood my interview with him when he affirms that my sole object in resigning from Columbia was to have more time to write; he failed to explain the circumstance which led to my resignation. There is certainly individual idealism in all universities, but the general tendency of modern education is towards materialism. For seven years I have put all my energy and enthusiasm into the cause of art at Columbia, and now at last, recognizing the futility of my efforts, I have resigned the chair of music in order to resume my own vocation."

The publicity attendant upon his leaving Columbia was most distasteful to MacDowell. Yet he had to take a firm stand where his convictions were concerned. Embittered by the failure of his bright hopes for Columbia, he sought refuge in the peace and quiet of his home at Peterborough. But he was not destined to enjoy for long the solitude of his cabin in the woods. Years of overwork, of trying to carry on his career as a composer along with his teaching and piano playing, finally took their toll. He was mentally and physically exhausted. On top of this had come the tension and irritation of his struggle with President Butler. A year after he resigned from Columbia, MacDowell developed alarming nervous symptoms. Shortly thereafter he suffered a mental breakdown.

He was found to be suffering from a brain lesion that was incurable. His mind became like the mind of a child. He would sit staring before him for hours, or gaze down at a book of fairy tales that had once given him so much pleasure. In vain he tried to recognize the friends who flocked to his side. He lingered for two years in this condition. Despite Marian's devoted care, despite all that the doctors could do, he failed to rally. He died in New

9

York City on January 23, 1908, at the beginning of his forty-seventh year. His body was taken to Peterborough. He was buried on an open hilltop where he and Marian had often come to watch the sunset. A bronze tablet on his grave bears the lines he wrote about his "house of dreams untold."

MacDowell was at his best in the short lyric pieces that he wrote for the piano. These show his gift for appealing melody, the charm and tenderness of his poetic imagination. His most widely played set of piano pieces, the *Woodland Sketches* (1896), includes not only *To a Wild Rose* but also *At an Old Trysting Place, From an Indian Lodge, To a Water Lily,* and *From Uncle Remus.* Popular too are the *Forest Idyls* (1884), *Sea Pieces* (1898), *Fireside Tales* (1902), and *New England Idyls* (1902). His songs are among the most attractive that this country has produced. Among them are such favorites as *Thy Beaming Eyes, The Swan Bent Low to the Lily,* and *As the Gloaming Shadows Creep.* MacDowell also cultivated the large forms of music. His two piano concertos (1882, 1885) and four piano sonatas—the *Tragica* (1893), *Eroica* (1896), *Norse* (1900), and *Keltic* (1901)—reveal a romantic tone poet. Of his orchestral works, the best known, dating from 1897, is the Second (*Indian*) Suite.

MacDowell's career unfolded at a time when it was of crucial importance for composers in this country to find their way as Americans. He took a broad view of nationalism in music. On the one hand he was deeply attached to the European heritage, especially to the tradition of German romanticism. On the other, he believed that American composers ought to reflect their environment and to interpret the spirit of their country. Yet they had to do this, he maintained, on a deeper level than by merely quoting an Indian tune or a Negro spiritual. He felt that if our composers truly loved their country and were identified with its spirit, their music would be American even without their consciously striving to make it so. He expressed this conviction with remarkable clarity: "Before a people can find a musical writer to echo its genius it must first possess men who truly represent it—that is to say, men who, being part of the people, love the country for itself: men who put into their music what the nation has put into its life."

MacDowell knew from his own experience how difficult it was for an artist to find the peace and quiet necessary for creative work. He wished that other artists could enjoy the same ideal conditions which he had found at Peterborough. He dreamed of a group of artists—musicians, painters, writers—living and working together, each deriving stimulation from the company of the others. During his last years, when he was no longer able to compose, he kept wishing that someone else could make use of his log cabin. When he died, Marian was left heartbroken, for she had found in him the great love of her life. She was wholly dedicated to his memory and his art. And so she resolved to make his dream come true. Thus was born the idea of the MacDowell Colony. She decided to convert the estate at Peterborough into a colony where writers, composers, and painters could come for four months every summer and create under ideal conditions, undisturbed by material cares or by the distractions of the outside world. It would take a lot of money, she realized, to transform the dream into a reality. She set out bravely to raise it. She traveled all over the country, giving recitals of MacDowell's music and trying to interest people in her plan. A woman of indomitable spirit, she let no obstacles deflect her from her goal. As a result of her efforts there sprang up MacDowell clubs throughout the country to help her with her work. Before long the MacDowell Colony was able to receive its first group of artists.

The Colony embodies the New England ideal of "plain living and high thinking." Each colonist is assigned a studio in the woods where he can work undisturbed. Approximately twenty-five studios have been erected in the course of the years. A basket lunch is delivered to each studio, so that the occupant does not have to interrupt his work in the middle of the day. Dinner is served in the common dining room; the evenings are spent in conversation, games, listening to music, or walks to the village. Mrs. MacDowell succeeded, after years of effort, in raising a substantial endowment fund for the Colony; the artists who go there are required to pay very little for their keep. Those who cannot afford even a little pay nothing at all. Many young musicians, painters, and writers receive fellowships at the Colony. This gives them an opportunity to live for a summer in close contact with artists who already have achieved a reputation in their field. As time went on, an impressive list of works came out of the MacDowell Colony. Here—to mention only a few—Thornton Wilder wrote *The Bridge of San Luis Rey*, DuBose and Dorothy Heyward wrote *Porgy*, Elinor Wylie produced *The Venetian Glass Nephew*, and Edwin Arlington Robinson wrote his beautiful poem *Tristram*. Most of the composers whom we will discuss in the following chapters found a haven at one time or another at the MacDowell Colony.

Mrs. MacDowell, during its first years, played a most active part in running the Colony. A woman of exquisite tact, she knew how to remain in the background. She encouraged the artists, she helped them and served them. But she never interfered either with them or their work. One afternoon, as she was working in her garden, a car drew up, the driver asked for directions. Suddenly the lady in the car asked her if she was one of the help. Mrs. MacDowell thought a moment and replied, "Yes. That's exactly what I am." She guided the enterprise for many years. On her ninety-fifth birthday she received greetings from all over the country and was hailed as one of the remarkable women of her time. She died three years later, having lived to see the MacDowell Colony established as a unique institution in our cultural life—a monument to her husband more enduring than marble or bronze. She lived also to see the triumph of her husband's ideas about the place that music should occupy in a university. Today the music departments of our colleges play a vital role in the artistic life of our country. The art of music is considered to be as important as other academic subjects, and is taught at our colleges in all its branches—history, theory and esthetics, harmony and counterpoint, ear-training and sight-singing, analysis, orchestration, and composition. Columbia University has made amends for its ungracious treatment of its first professor of music. The most important member of its music department is known as the Edward MacDowell Professor of Music.

The best introduction to MacDowell's music is through piano pieces such as *To a Wild Rose* and *To a Water Lily*. These amply show his heartfelt lyricism. Equally enjoyable is his *Indian Suite*, which he based on melodies of the Iroquois, Chippewa, and other Indian tribes. He used the Indian tunes freely, changing them according to his fancy and giving them the imprint of his own style. The work is broken up into five parts: I. *Legend*. The introduction is marked "Not fast; with much dignity and character." A dark orchestral tone sets the scene for a tale of ancient times. The movement itself is marked "Twice as fast, with decision," and sings of brave warriors and heroic deeds. It is based on a ceremonial song of the Iroquois. II. *Love Song*. "Not fast. Tenderly." Here we encounter MacDowell's gentle lyricism and romantic ardor. He took as his point of departure a love song of the Iowas. III. *In War Time*. "With rough vigor, almost savagely." A war dance of the Iroquois Indians leads into a traditional melody associated with their Scalp Dance. The movement works up to an exciting climax. Suddenly a slow passage intervenes to break the mood. It forecasts the lament of the next movement. The war dance returns and mounts in fury until the end. IV. *Dirge*. "Slowly, mourn-

13

fully." The theme previously announced in the middle of the war dance is now expanded into a song of mourning. A horn plays off-stage, with an effect of mystery and remoteness. "Of all my music," wrote MacDowell, "the *Dirge* in the *Indian Suite* pleases me most. It affects me deeply and did when I was writing it. In it an Indian woman laments the death of her son; but to me, as I wrote it, it seemed to express a world-sorrow rather than a particularised grief." V. *Village Festival.* "Swift and light." This is a lively, strongly rhythmic finale that brings the suite to a rousing conclusion.

The composer of this work was one of America's first tone poets. His art announced to the world that our country—musically speaking—had come of age, and was ready to take its place among the nations that create their own music.

2. CHARLES IVES

The story of Charles Ives is one that is not uncommon in the annals of modern art. His music was ignored for decades. Then, at the very end of his life, he was hailed everywhere as the first truly American composer of the twentieth century.

Ives was born on October 20, 1874, in Danbury, Connecticut, not far from where his ancestors had settled soon after the landing of the Pilgrims. His father had been an army bandmaster in the Civil War. When the war was over George Ives continued as a bandmaster in Danbury. He was an extraordinarily progressive musician who was interested in exploring the nature of sound. On holidays such as the Fourth of July, when his own band was augmented by other bands from the surrounding countryside, he would divide the players into groups and station them in different places, one in the church steeple, another on the roof of a building, a third on the village green, each in turn playing a variation on a tune that he had specially arranged, so that he could test the effect of the sound coming from all directions. His son never forgot "the echo parts from the roofs played by a chorus of violins and voices." Or he would make his family sing *Swanee River* in the key of E-flat while he played the accompaniment in the key of C, "in order," as Charles Ives wrote later, "to stretch our ears and strengthen our musical minds."

Despite his love of experiment, George Ives believed that a musician ought to have a solid foundation. He taught his son to play a number of instruments, and introduced him to the music of Bach and Beethoven. In addition, he saw to it that Charles did the necessary exercises in harmony (the science of chords) and counterpoint (the art of combining several melodies simultaneously). When Charles was thirteen he was playing the organ at the West Street Congregational Church in Danbury. A year later, when he was hired by a larger church, he was described in the *Danbury News* as "the youngest organist in the state." Charles had already begun to compose. His *Holiday Quick-Step* was performed by his father's band and won the unanimous approval of Danbury. All the same, Charles was slightly ashamed of his interest in music. "Most boys in the country towns of America, I think, felt the same way," he stated many years later. "When other boys on Monday morning in vacation were out driving the grocery cart, riding horses or playing ball, I felt all wrong to stay in and play the piano." To make up for this he took care to be a regular fellow and excelled in sports, especially baseball and football. When people made much of his musical talent and asked him what he liked to play, he would reply defensively, "Shortstop!"

After Charles was graduated from Danbury High School he went on to the Hopkins Preparatory School in New Haven and entered Yale University at the age of twenty. There he studied composition with Horatio Parker, a conservative composer who, as his pupil pointed out, was entirely governed by the rules he had learned in Germany. "Parker's course," Charles wrote, "made me feel more and more what a remarkable background and start Father had given me in music. Parker was a composer and Father was not; but from every other standpoint I should say that Father was by far the greater man. After the first two or three weeks in Freshman year I did not bother Parker with any of the experimental ideas that Father had been willing for me to think about and try out."

Shortly after Charles entered Yale, George Ives died. This was a severe loss for Charles, who had found in his father both an inspiring teacher and a sympathetic friend. He always felt that if he accomplished anything worth while in music, it was primarily because of his father. He was grateful not only for what his father taught him about music but also, as he wrote when he was a man, for "his influence, his personality, character and open-mindedness, and his remarkable understanding of the ways of a boy's heart and mind."

Charles was active in music throughout his four years at Yale. Nevertheless, when he had to choose a career he decided against becoming a professional musician. "Father felt," he explained, "that a man could keep his music interest stronger, cleaner, bigger and freer if he didn't try to make a living out of it. Assuming a man lives by himself and with no dependents, he might write music that no one would play prettily, listen to or buy. But—but if he has a nice wife and some nice children, how can he let the children starve on his dissonances? So he has to weaken (and if he is a man he *should* weaken for his children), but his music more than weakens—it goes 'ta-ta' for money! Bad for him, bad for music!" Thus Charles Ives from the beginning suspected that the unconventional kind of music he wanted to write was not the kind that would ever bring him any money. He was right.

Ives moved to New York and shared an apartment on the West Side with several friends; they called it Poverty Flat. At this time he entered the field of life insurance. The young man was ambitious to get ahead and, after a few years as a clerk, went into business for himself. Together with a friend he formed the firm of Ives and Myrick, which eventually became the largest insurance agency in the country. Shortly after the beginning of his business career

Ives fell in love with Harmony Twichell, daughter of a New England minister who had been a friend of Mark Twain, John Greenleaf Whittier, and other famous writers. Harmony was very beautiful, and Charles was afraid that he would never win her for his wife. For a while things were very tense in Poverty Flat. Soon, however, Ives and Harmony were married. Some years later they adopted a baby daughter named Edith. The marriage was an extremely happy one. During the long years when the world refused to accept Ives's music, it was his wife who sustained him with her encouragement and understanding.

Ives's career as a composer was carried on simultaneously with his career as a successful businessman. He wrote his music at night, during week ends, and in his summer vacations. His busy life did not allow him much time to go to concerts and listen to the music of other composers. But he did not regard this as a disadvantage, for it encouraged him to be original and to put down on paper only the sounds that he heard in his head. As he said, "I felt I could work better and liked to work better if I kept to my own music and let other people keep to theirs."

Ives found inspiration in his New England heritage, in the tradition that came to flower in the idealism of Ralph Waldo Emerson and Henry Thoreau, of Nathaniel Hawthorne and the Alcotts. His thinking had been nourished by Emerson's faith in man, by Thoreau's belief that nature is good, and by his own conviction that, as he expressed it, "the soul is each man's share of God." At a time when American composers were still guided by the musical traditions of Europe, Ives turned to his roots—to the world of his childhood. He based his musical language on the melodies he had grown up with: the hymn tunes and popular songs he had learned in Danbury, the sound of the town band at parades, the lively square dances and reels of the fiddlers at Saturday night dances, patriotic songs and parlor ballads, the melodies of Stephen Foster, the medleys that he had heard in small theaters and at country fairs.

Other composers had been attracted to this wealth of American music. But they had weighed everything according to European standards. And so they proceeded to smooth out and "correct" the popular tunes according to the rules they had learned in Leipzig or Munich. Ives, on the other hand, disregarded the European tradition in music exactly as Walt Whitman had done in poetry. His keen ear caught the sound of untrained voices in a village church singing a hymn, some straining a little and sharping the pitch, others just missing it and going flat; so that in place of a single tone there was a cluster of tones that made a wonderfully dissonant chord. Some were a trifle ahead of the beat, others lagged behind; so that the rhythm sagged and swayed, and turned into a mixture of different rhythms all going on at the same time. He retained in his mind the exciting sound when two bands in a parade, each blaring a different tune in a different key, came close enough together for the two melodies to overlap and clash. He remembered the effect when fiddlers at a country dance, in order to heighten the excitement, played just a little off pitch or added off-beat accents to the music. He never forgot the sound of the wheezy harmonium at church that was slightly out of tune as it accompanied the hymns. All these sounds, Ives realized, were not "mistakes" that had to be corrected. They were the heart and soul of American musical speech. To correct the popular melodies of America according to the rules taught in European conservatories would be the same as correcting the speech of a Yankee farmer according to the rules of grammar taught at Yale. It would deprive our folk songs of their flavor, their tang, their special American quality. And so he wrote down the melodies, harmonies, and rhythms exactly as he remembered them, exactly as he heard them in his mind.

But in the early years of our century no one was writing in several keys at the same time (polytonal music), or in no definite key at all (atonal music). No one was using a variety of rhythmic patterns simultaneously (polyrhythms). Nobody was building chords by using all the tones of the scale together (cluster chords), or combining melodies that met head-on in clashing intervals (dissonant counterpoint). These things became fashionable many years later in the music of Stravinsky, Schoenberg, Bartók, Milhaud, Hindemith, and other European composers. Yet here was a pioneering American, isolated from his fellow composers as well as from the public, finding his way to these daring innovations all by himself. It was only because Ives was so intent on expressing the truth as he felt it, and because he was so fiercely independent of European traditions, that he was able to explore new realms of expression and to forecast the direction in which twentieth-century music was going to move. In so doing, he created something entirely new.

Ives wanted to reach people. He hoped that they would understand what he was driving at. But he was so far in advance of his time that when he showed his music to others they could make neither head nor tail of it. Some of them smiled, convinced that such strange scores could come only from someone who had never properly learned the rules of composition. Others assured him that the music he was writing was absolutely impossible to play. Still others came away persuaded that the man was cracked. "Said I to myself: Why do I like to work in this way and get all set up over what just upsets other people? No one else seems to hear it the same way. Are my ears on wrong? I began to feel that if I wanted to write music that was worth while (that is, to me) I must keep away from musicians."

In his heart he had only contempt for those who clung to the traditions of the past, fearful of the present and the future. On one of his scores he scribbled: "Don't mind the soft ears a-lolling around in the hall—knock 'em over the ropes! Make 'em work their ears like real men!" Many years later, when a piece of his was performed at a concert, some people in the audience began to boo and jeer at his music. Ives sat quietly by. But when they did the same to a work by another modern composer, he sprang to his feet and cried, "Don't be such a sissy! When you hear strong music like this, get up and try to use your ears like a man!"

As the years passed, Ives realized that he would not be able to interest conductors and performers in his music. He gave up showing his manuscripts, and continued on his own along the path he knew he must follow. Yet at times he felt a great need, as every composer does, to hear his music and to find out whether it sounded the way he thought it did. On such occasions he would engage a group of musicians to run through one of his scores. Needless to say, these were altogether inadequate performances, as a number of instruments were missing; but at least they gave Ives some idea of the sound of his music. When he hired men from a theater orchestra they were able to make their way through the score, for they were accustomed to playing all sorts of popular music. But when he picked musicians from the New York Symphony Orchestra they were completely baffled by the unconventional harmonies and rhythms, for they were hidebound by tradition. Except for these rare performances, Ives never heard his music save in his imagination. He persevered, piling up one score after the other in his barn in Connecticut. His friends urged him to write the kind of music that people were accustomed to; then it would be performed. But he would answer, "I can't do it—I hear something else!" There was only one person who unfailingly encouraged him—his wife. She kept telling him to remain true to his inner vision, and never to allow himself to be deflected from his course by those who failed to understand him.

The twenty years that it took Ives to achieve his success in the business world—roughly, from the time he was twenty-two to forty-two—were also the years when he wrote all his music. The most important compositions in his output were his four symphonies. He worked on the First Symphony from 1896 to 1898, a period when he was still developing his style. The Second, a romantic work in five movements, occupied him from 1897 to 1902. Concerning this piece Ives stated: "The part suggesting a Steve Foster tune, while over it the old farmers fiddled a barn dance with all of its jigs, gallops and reels, was played in Danbury on the old Wooster House bandstand in 1889." In his Third Symphony, on which he worked from 1901 to 1904, Ives quoted the old hymn *Take It to the Lord* as well as the Welsh battle song known as *All Through the Night*. The Fourth Symphony for orchestra and two pianos, written in the years 1910–1916, contains the hymn tune *Watchman, Tell Us of the Night*. During these years Ives also wrote *A Symphony: Holidays*, based, as he said, on "the recollections of a boy's holidays in a Connecticut country town." The four movements are entitled *Washington's Birthday, Decoration Day, Fourth of July*, and *Thanksgiving Day*. In several other works Ives went back to the memories of his New England childhood; as in *Hallowe'en* (1911) for string quartet and piano, which he called "a kind of April Fool's piece for a Hallowe'en Party." This became the first of *Three Outdoor Scenes*, the others being *The Pond* (1906) and *Central Park in the Dark* (1898–1907).

The most important of Ives's piano pieces is the Sonata No. 2, which he named *Concord, Mass. . . . 1840–1860*. The four movements, on which he worked from 1909 to 1915, reflect four aspects of the flowering of New England. The first movement, *Emerson*, evokes Ives's favorite writer, whom he imagines "standing on a summit, at the door of the infinite where many men do not dare to climb, peering into the mysteries of life, contemplating the eternities, hurling back whatever he discovers there—now thunderbolts for us to grasp, if we can, and translate—now placing quietly, even tenderly, in our hands, things that we may see without effort —if we don't use them, so much the worse for us." The composer took for his basic theme the opening four notes of Beethoven's Fifth Symphony, which he identified with the spiritual message at the heart of Emerson's philosophy—as Ives described it, "the Soul of humanity knocking at the door of the Divine mysteries, radiant in the faith that it *will* be opened and the human become Divine!"

Second is *Hawthorne,* the kind of light, rapid movement which is known in music as a *scherzo* (sker'-tso). This part is supposed to suggest, Ives explained, some of Hawthorne's "wilder, fantastical adventures into the half-childlike, half-fairylike phantasmal realms." Third is *The Alcotts,* a gentle, slow movement inspired by the family of the beloved author of *Little Women.* "As one walks down the broad-arched street," Ives wrote, "he comes presently to the old elms overspreading the Alcott house. It seems to stand as a kind of homely but beautiful witness of Concord's common virtue. Within the house, on every side, lie remembrances. There sits the little old spinet piano on which Beth played the Fifth Symphony . . ." The movement is meant to evoke "the memory of that home under the elms—the Scotch songs and the family hymns that were sung at the end of each day . . . a conviction in the power of the common soul which, when all is said and done, may be as typical as any theme of Concord and its transcendentalists." (The transcendentalists were the New England idealists who believed in the philosophy of Emerson and Thoreau.) The last movement is called *Thoreau*—"as it might be a day with Thoreau alone at Walden Pond, with an echo over the water . . ." The *Concord Sonata* is a powerful work that shows Ives's style at its noblest.

Ives wrote many songs and choral pieces; works for orchestra; and chamber music, such as string quartets and sonatas for violin and piano. However, his double life as a big-business executive by day and composer by night eventually undermined his health. In 1918, when he was forty-four years old, he suffered a physical breakdown that left his heart permanently damaged. The years of protracted toil without recognition, without encouragement or reward of any kind had taken more out of him emotionally than he had suspected. Although he lived almost forty years longer, he did not have the energy to produce anything further of importance. His work was done.

When Ives recovered from his illness, he realized that the world of professional musicians was closed to his compositions and would remain closed. He felt that he owed it to his music to make it available to those who might be interested in it. Accordingly, he had the *Concord Sonata* printed at his own expense, along with a little book he had written which he called *Essays Before a Sonata* —a kind of program note that not only explained what the music meant but also expressed his views on life and art. These two volumes were followed by a third, *114 Songs*, which contained all the songs he had written between 1896 and 1916. The three books were to be distributed free of charge to libraries, music critics, or anyone else who asked for them. Ives wrote an explanatory note for the *114 Songs* that is characteristic of his way of expressing himself: "Some have written a book for money; I have not. Some for fame; I have not. Some for love; I have not. Some for kindlings; I have not. I have not written a book for any of these reasons or for all of them together. In fact, gentle borrower, I have not written a book at all—I have merely cleaned house. All that is left is out on the clothes line—but it's good for a man's vanity to have the neighbors see him on the clothes line."

The three volumes were completely ignored by the musical world. But they came to the attention of a few discerning souls who became Ives's enthusiastic supporters. One of these was the music critic Henry Bellamann, who later gained fame as the author of the novel *King's Row*. He did everything in his power to obtain performances of Ives's compositions and to draw attention to the man and his music. The volumes also reached a few experimental composers who were struggling to make their way in an unheeding world. One of them, Nicolas Slonimsky, conducted three movements from *Holidays* in Paris, Budapest, and Berlin. The European critics were astonished to hear such modern music written by an American composer. Ives began to see that he was not as alone as he had thought. There were others who grasped what he was driving at and who were engaged in the same struggle as he.

As the 1920s wore on, new conceptions came to the fore in the art of music. The techniques that Ives had experimented with twenty-five years earlier, which had so puzzled those to whom he showed his scores, now became part of the vocabulary of music. The world was catching up with him. His day came at last when the *Concord Sonata* received its first performance, almost a quarter-century after Ives had written it. The piece was played by the American pianist John Kirkpatrick at a concert in Town Hall, in New York, in January, 1939. When Kirkpatrick repeated the Sonata several weeks later, it scored a triumph. Ives's dream came true: an audience responded spontaneously to the sounds he had heard in his mind, and understood all that he was trying to say. Those present at the concert never forgot the sense of excitement that filled the hall. The next morning the famous critic Lawrence Gilman described the *Concord Sonata* as "the greatest music composed by an American." Ironically enough, Ives was not present to witness his victory. He was then sixty-five, a semi-invalid living in retirement on his Connecticut farm. Kirkpatrick had played the Sonata to him privately, but he did not feel up to attending the concert.

Now Ives was "discovered" by the public and hailed as "the

father of American music"—the first composer, that is, who drew his inspiration exclusively from the American scene without relying in the least on European sources. The season 1944–1945, which marked his seventieth anniversary, witnessed several important performances of his music. A year later Ives was elected to the National Institute of Arts and Letters. In 1947 his Third Symphony was performed for the first time, more than forty years after he composed it. The piece won a Pulitzer Prize. "Prizes are for boys—I'm grown up," Ives commented wryly when he was told the news.

Here certainly was a story to capture the imagination. It was carried by newspapers throughout the country. Ives awoke at seventy-three to find himself famous. Four years later Leonard Bernstein and the New York Philharmonic presented the premiere of his Second Symphony, exactly fifty years after Ives had written it. Bernstein offered to set a rehearsal at Ives's convenience, and to arrange for the composer to be alone in Carnegie Hall. But the prospect of hearing his work at last strangely agitated the old man, and he attended neither the rehearsals nor the performances. He did listen to the radio broadcast of the piece, and realized that the symphony which had once been pronounced unplayable and crazy was now giving pleasure to millions. In the remaining years of his life Ives was recognized as one of the most original artists this country had produced. Thus, by remaining true to himself, he won the fame and admiration that had been withheld from him—and won them on his own terms. He died in New York City in 1954, at the age of eighty.

As an introduction to Ives's music, listen to the recording of *Three Places in New England*, one of his best-known works. This set of orchestral pieces was written between 1903 and 1911. The first piece evokes the famous statue by Saint-Gaudens in Boston Common—a monument to Colonel Shaw and his Colored Regiment. The piece opens very softly, in a mood of solemn dedication. The melody conjures up the world of the Stephen Foster songs and the emotional atmosphere of the Civil War. Gradually the music builds to a powerful climax in which the woodwinds, in high register, are thrust against the brass in the low. Ives's keen ear for rhythm shows itself in an observation he wrote in the score: "Often when a mass of men march uphill there is an unconscious slowing up. The drum seems to follow the feet, rather than the feet the drum." The piece ends, as it began, very softly.

The second number in the set is called *Putnam's Camp, Redding, Connecticut*. It is marked *allegro* (fast), "in Quick-Step Time." Ives explained what he wanted to express in this piece. "Near Redding Center is a small park preserved as a Revolutionary Memorial, for here General Israel Putnam's soldiers had their winter quarters in 1778–1779. Long rows of camp fireplaces still remain to stir a child's imagination." Ives imagined a Fourth of July picnic in a small American town. The music suggests the gay crowds, the shouting and the horseplay, the two bands in the parade whose sounds overlap and clash. During the picnic, one little boy wanders off by himself into the woods. He remembers the stories he has so often heard about Putnam's soldiers and the hardships they endured, and how they wanted to break camp and abandon their cause, but were recalled to their duty when Putnam came over the hills to lead them. Amid the silence of the old trees he dreams of those stirring times. "The little boy awakes," Ives wrote. "He hears the children's songs and runs down past the monument to 'listen to the band' and join in the games and dances." All this is told in the music. There is one passage where two march rhythms clash, four measures of one equaling three measures of the other. The ending is loud and dissonant—an exciting close for a holiday celebration.

Third and last is *The Housatonic at Stockbridge*. This piece, the

27

composer recalled, "was suggested by a Sunday morning walk that Mrs. Ives and I took near Stockbridge the summer after we were married. We walked in the meadows along the River and heard the distant singing from the Church across the River. The mist had not entirely left the river bed, and the colors, the running water, the banks and trees were something that one would always remember." The piece opens with a rippling current of sound set up by the string instruments. A serene melody emerges, which suggests the hymns at the prayer meetings that Ives recalled from his boyhood. The music of this lovely nature-piece flows calmly and steadily to a climax marked *fortissimo* (very loud). Then it subsides to a quiet ending, even as the river flows off quietly in the distance.

A deep love for all things American lies at the heart of this music. *Three Places in New England* springs from our native soil and could have been written nowhere else. Certainly no other composer captured so eloquently the spiritual quality of his heritage. Like Emerson and Thoreau, the two writers whom he admired above all others, Charles Ives has become an American classic.

3. CHARLES T. GRIFFES

Charles Tomlinson Griffes was one of the most poetic composers that this country has produced. He appeared upon our musical scene just a little too soon, before the public was ready to understand the subtle beauty of his art.

Charles was born on September 17, 1884, in Elmira, New York. He showed musical talent as a boy. For example, he would listen intently to the birds and whistle an accurate imitation of their calls. Or he would pick out on the piano a melody he had heard. When he was eight years old his sister Katherine tried to give him piano lessons. But he lost interest in music when he had to practice scales and exercises. Instead he turned to painting, and showed a sensitivity to color that remained with him throughout his life.

It was not until he was eleven that Charles developed a real interest in music. While he was convalescing from an attack of typhoid fever he listened to his sister practicing a piece by Beethoven, and was filled with a desire to be able to play it himself. Piano lessons were begun as soon as he got well. Now he regretted the time he had wasted, and applied himself to his music with so much energy that before long his sister did not have anything more to teach him. She turned him over to her own teacher at Elmira College, Mary Selena Broughton, a cultivated Englishwoman who quickly recognized the remarkable talent of her new pupil. Miss

Broughton gave him extra lessons, tried to improve his mind by recommending books for him to read, took an interest in everything he did, and became, indeed, a second mother to him.

Charles took part in the musical life of Elmira. He played the organ at the Lutheran Church, accompanied the Y.M.C.A. chorus, and performed at Miss Broughton's concerts. All the same, he did not have many friends among the boys at the Elmira Free Academy, where he spent his high-school years. He was a dreamy, sensitive lad who lived in a world of his own—a world that consisted of his music, his books, and long walks in the woods. He was a lonely wanderer from the start, and a lonely wanderer he remained.

Miss Broughton eventually decided that she had nothing further to teach her protégé. She wanted him to continue his studies in Germany, where she herself had studied when she was young. Since Charles's family could not afford the expense, Miss Broughton decided to send him abroad herself. He was a good investment, she said, and would pay back the money when he had become a successful musician. Charles was graduated from the Academy in 1903. That summer, at the age of nineteen, he set out on what is one of the most exciting experiences that can befall a young American musician—the journey to the rich musical culture of the Old World.

Charles enrolled at the Stern Conservatory in Berlin, where he studied piano, theory, and composition with German musicians who gave him a thorough grounding in his art. He learned to speak German fluently and read the classics of German literature. He met other music students who were as eager for musical knowledge as himself. He attended concerts and operas, and heard artists of international fame. He came to admire the operas of Richard Wagner, the symphonic poems and operas of Richard Strauss. He made friends with several music-loving Berliners who opened up a new world to the young man from Elmira. Most important of all, he was stimulated by an environment where music was not a specialty or a sideline, as it had been back home, but an essential part of daily living. In one of his letters he wrote that in America music "is generally used to give people's tongues a little time to rest, and often not even that." He could not listen to the songs of Schubert, Schumann, and Brahms without realizing their superiority to what he had heard in Elmira. "I must say," he wrote, "that most of the American songs seem pretty empty and shallow after the German ones."

The most important thing that happened to Charles during his four years in Berlin was that his interest gradually turned from piano playing to composing. This change is reflected in a letter he wrote to his mother during his second year abroad. "Last year I began to realize what a lot there was for me to know besides the piano, especially if I wanted to do anything with composition and the other branches. I feel this almost more in the composition than in the piano playing. For instance, I am beginning orchestration now and by June will have finished an overture and have learned a good deal. But in this short time and this one thing I shall not have gained enough facility in writing for the orchestra so that I could go ahead and attempt anything alone."

He realized the handicaps that his environment had imposed upon him. "A composer nowadays has to be able to write for the orchestra. The Americans are under a great disadvantage; unless they happen to live in New York where things are given and have money enough to take them in, they generally know only their own instrument and its literature, at most. With me, who never heard an orchestra in my life but three times in Philadelphia and twice in New York and who didn't know one instrument from another, it takes a long time to get even a slight knowledge of the different instruments and of what can be done with the orchestra."

31

Charles already saw in what direction his future lay. "I don't want to become merely a piano teacher. And I feel sure that I shall never become a great concert player and virtuoso, for I realize now that to be such one has to begin much earlier than I did and has to devote much more time to it than I ever did at home. So I want to be an all-round musician who can do something else besides teach and play the piano. I want to know music in general, especially if I want to do anything with composition." Charles returned to this point in a subsequent letter. "It is rather a fault of piano students," he wrote, "and especially of Americans that they know nothing except the piano and its music. They practice it all the time and go principally to piano concerts and in the end never learn anything except just that."

Charles's father died that year. He came home to spend the summer with his family. But he desperately wanted another year abroad. Miss Broughton had given him all the help she could. Assistance came unexpectedly from another source. A young German who had become a devoted friend of his and who believed in his gifts offered to pay for his fourth year of study. By now, too, he was able to earn some money himself by giving lessons and accompanying singers. And so Charles returned to Berlin. During his final year abroad he took some lessons in composition with Engelbert Humperdinck, the celebrated composer of the opera *Hänsel und Gretel*. He played in a few concerts. Most important of all, he performed his first compositions in public, and they were quite well received. The year went by as swiftly as had the others. In the summer of 1907 Charles Griffes, immeasurably enriched by his stay in Europe, returned to America to begin his career as a professional musician.

Through a teachers' agency he obtained a position at the Hackley School in Tarrytown, New York. This was a school that prepared the sons of well-to-do families for college. Griffes was expected to give piano lessons to the boys who desired them. He had to accompany the singers and violinists who occasionally played at the school. He trained the choir and took charge of the musical services in the Chapel. And he gave informal piano recitals for the students on Sunday nights. These duties would not have been too heavy for someone who wanted to be only a teacher. For a creative artist they were a grievous burden.

There were many things wrong with the job. To begin with, music occupied an inferior position at Hackley. The main emphasis was on sports and on those subjects that would help the boys get into the university of their choice. The pay was low and the hours were long. When he came there Griffes was paid $1,300 a year —that is, thirty-six dollars a week with room and board. Even more depressing was the fact that the duties he was called upon to perform fell far short of his abilities. In all his years at Hackley he never once had a really talented pupil, as far as piano playing was concerned (although he did meet a few thoughtful boys who appreciated what he had to offer). But the worst thing was that his work took up so much of his time. The precious hours that might have been spent in composing had to be sacrificed to all sorts of unimportant tasks. Griffes often rebelled against the drudgery of his post. But he was trapped by his own feeling of insecurity, as well as by his obligations to his family; he was his mother's chief support. Besides, there were not many opportunities open to an aspiring composer at that time.

He continued to compose in spite of all interruptions: at night, during week ends and holidays, and in the all-too-short summer vacations. Also on the train during the one-hour journey from Tarrytown to Manhattan. More and more he was attracted to the exciting atmosphere of New York. "Life isn't worth living anywhere else," he wrote to a friend. As the years went on, his trips to New York became more frequent. Apart from the pleasure he found in getting away from Hackley, these visits were necessary for his career as a composer. He would play his music for

33

singers, pianists, dancers, publishers, and fellow composers, trying to interest them in his work. But he would often come back discouraged, because those who controlled the musical world in the first quarter of our century were not eager for compositions that were fresh, new, and off the beaten track. At the end of a typical day, during which he had played his manuscripts to various people, Griffes wrote in his diary: "Took the 12:35 train back and had to walk up the hill in the pouring rain. It wasn't worth while."

Griffes gradually acquired a circle of friends in New York who believed in his gifts and lost no opportunity to further his cause. He came to know Alice and Irene Lewisohn, founders of the Neighborhood Playhouse, and wrote the music for some of their productions. He found an enthusiastic ally in the critic Paul Rosenfeld, who championed the cause of modern music. He met Rose Pastor Stokes and others who were active in the labor movement. Under their influence Griffes, who had always felt a deep sympathy for the underprivileged, began to take an interest in social problems. During the strike of the New York garment workers in 1916 he played the piano at some of their rallies. This brief excursion into the labor movement had one musical result—a choral piece called *These Things Shall Be,* on a poem by John Addington Symonds, which Griffes wrote for a friend who conducted the New York Community Chorus. This was his only attempt to write in a popular style. The song found its way into the Army and Navy Songbook during the First World War.

Griffes reached maturity as a creative musician at a time when composers were turning away from the major scale, that is, the familiar *do-re-mi-fa-sol-la-ti-do* on which European music had been based for the better part of three hundred years. His delicate, dreamlike art reflected an imagination that was stimulated by faraway places and far-off times. He found inspiration in the exotic scales of Oriental music—the music of India, China and Japan, Java

34

and Bali—and in ancient scales that had existed long before the major-minor. "Modern music," he declared, "tends more and more toward the archaic, especially the archaism of the East. The ancient Greek modes, the five-tone scales of China and Japan are much used. In the dissonances of modern music the Oriental is more at home than in the consonance of the classics."

Griffes came to admire the composers who at that time were attracting the attention of progressive musicians, such as Modest Musorgski and Alexander Scriabin, Igor Stravinsky and Arnold Schoenberg. In several of his compositions he was influenced by the French impressionist composers, Claude Debussy and Maurice Ravel, who captured in music the misty coloring and fluid rhythm that marked the canvases of painters such as Claude Monet, Auguste Renoir, Édouard Manet, and Édouard Degas. Griffes became the leading American impressionist composer. Yet he took from the Europeans only what fit in with his own way of expressing himself. "If I have written into my score Oriental sounds and Slavic themes," he stated, "it is only because those tonal combinations and melodies have said and expressed the things I wanted to say."

Griffes's music, with its exotic atmosphere, borrowed nothing from American folk song. He represents that group among our composers which was most responsive to foreign influence. He stood at the opposite end from those who were trying to create a homespun American music. This came out during a visit to Boston when a friend took him to see the American composer Henry F. Gilbert, who at that time was a leading figure among our nationalist musicians. Griffes played some of his piano pieces; Gilbert was filled with admiration for their refined workmanship. However, it soon became clear that the two men disagreed violently as to the proper course for American music. Gilbert insisted that our composers must base their works upon Indian and Negro

35

melodies, folk songs, and similar Americana. Griffes maintained that the artist's first duty is to express sincerely what he feels in his heart, and to create beauty, no matter what its nationality. There was absolutely no meeting ground between the two points of view. But as Griffes left, his host exclaimed in wonderment, "How can such hypersensitive art and technique exist in an American carcass?"

Griffes's relations with the music publishers well illustrates the plight of the American composer in the first decades of the twentieth century. They accepted his early songs, for those were written in a familiar style and would sell well. Editors were far less willing to take a chance on the works in which he found his true musical language. In 1912 Griffes, in a letter, described himself as "in a bad humor all day" because his publishers had refused to accept three of his new piano pieces. "It takes away one's confidence," he commented. "Am I on the right track or not?" Five years later he had answered that question to his own satisfaction, having decided to stick to his course no matter what anyone else thought. To a young composer he wrote: "Keep your conscience even if the publishers have none—in fact, just because they have none. Somebody must have one, you know."

Griffes's efforts finally bore fruit. The more progressive musicians began to present his works. Artists such as the singer Eva Gauthier and the flutist Georges Barrère became champions of his art. His scores, whether in published form or in manuscript, were arousing ever greater interest. But in 1916 his royalties totaled only sixty-two dollars and forty-nine cents, the highest they were ever to be in his lifetime.

He continued to be torn between his duties in Tarrytown and the precious moments in New York; between his teaching and his composing. Increasingly he felt that he must break loose from Hackley. America's entry into the war in 1917 made such a step impossible. "There is a great deal of hardship," he wrote to a friend, "among smaller musicians just now. Concert engagements are few and not so well paid as usual. I am glad for my steady job, as dull and uninteresting as it is. Between you and me, it is a deadly bore, but I have stuck it out for quite a sum of years and shall not give it up in these uncertain times." He decided finally that he wanted to join the war effort, and was on the point of enlisting in Military Intelligence, where he could use his knowledge of French and German, when the Armistice was signed.

The fall of 1919 saw Griffes finally on the road to fame. To his old teacher Miss Broughton (to whom he had paid back the money she had advanced for his education), he wrote proudly: "The Boston Symphony is to give the first performance of my symphonic poem *The Pleasure-Dome of Kubla Khan* on Nov. 28, the Philadelphia Orchestra gives the first performance of a set of four pieces for orchestra this fall, and the New York Symphony gives for the first time on Nov. 16 a new *Poem* for solo flute and orchestra. All these things have to be put into final shape and parts prepared. What a nuisance lessons are!"

A composer writes his orchestral works in a score, that is, on a page containing a number of staffs, each of which represents another instrumental part. On top of the page are the parts of the woodwind instruments (piccolo, flutes, oboes, English horn, clarinets, bass clarinet, bassoons, and contrabassoon). Immediately below are the staffs representing the brass instruments (horns, trumpets, trombones, and tuba). In the middle of the page are the parts of the percussion (kettledrums, bass and side drum, glockenspiel, celesta, xylophone, triangle, cymbals, tambourine, castanets, and similar instruments). The staffs representing the string group (first and second violins, violas, cellos, double basses) are at the bottom. By looking straight down the page at a certain measure one sees what is going on in the whole orchestra at that point. In other

37

words, all these separate lines are really one line—the full orchestral sound produced by all the different instruments playing together. When the work is about to be performed by an orchestra, all the lines in the score that represent the flute part have to be copied out on a separate sheet of music that is given to the flute players; the same for the oboes, clarinets, bassoons, and all the other instruments. This is a dull, laborious task that is done by a copyist. Griffes, in order to save money, did a good deal of the copying himself, working late every night after the long day at school was over. One of his students found him engaged in this task, and asked why he did not have someone else do it for him. Griffes replied that it would take more money than he could afford.

The *Poem* for flute and orchestra won a resounding success in New York. Griffes was called out seven times to take a bow. He went to Boston for the premiere of *The Pleasure Dome of Kubla Khan*. It had taken him four years to obtain a performance of this work, which was now received with enthusiastic applause. He returned to give his lessons at Hackley. A week later he had his final triumph when the Bostonians repeated *Kubla Khan* in New York. Griffes sat in a box at Carnegie Hall and received the plaudits of the crowd.

A few days later the accumulated strain of years took its toll at last. Griffes collapsed. The doctors diagnosed his illness as pleurisy and pneumonia. The deeper cause was total exhaustion of the physical and nervous system. After several weeks in bed the composer, accompanied by his mother, entered a sanatorium for the tubercular in the Catskill Mountains. He lingered for a few months, oppressed more and more by the fear that he would not recover. He was brought back to New York for an operation on his lungs, and failed to rally. He died in the New York Hospital on April 8, 1920, at the age of thirty-six.

Suddenly everyone was sorry. *The New York Times* declared in an editorial: "We speak with pity or scorn of a public that could

38

let a Mozart or a Schubert die and think that those bad old days are gone, but from time to time something uncomfortably like them and of the same sort is revealed in the present." A long eulogy in the magazine *Musical America* carried the headline: "Charles T. Griffes Cut Down in His Prime, a Victim of Our Barbarous Neglect of Genius," with the subcaption: "American Composer whose Art was Blossoming into Glorious Fruition Died as the Result of Overwork." His publishers, in a paid advertisement, mourned the loss that American music had sustained, and said how privileged they had been to publish the work of one "to whom, during his lifetime, musicians, critics, and public denied the appreciation so necessary and precious to a composer of lofty ideals."

Griffes's fame rests on a comparatively small number of works. He did not favor the large forms of music like the symphony and concerto. His style was at its best in the short lyric forms—the picturesque piano piece and the song—or the symphonic poem. (For an explanation of this and other musical terms see the Glossary.) He was a lyricist of exquisite sensitivity who commanded the intimacy of mood and spontaneous emotion that make up the subtle world of the art song. His three songs to lyrics by Fiona MacLeod —*The Lament of Ian the Proud*, *The Rose of the Night*, and *Thy Dark Eyes to Mine* (1918)—rank with the finest that this country has produced. Equally distinguished are such songs as *By a Lonely Forest Pathway; Symphony in Yellow*, on a poem by Oscar Wilde; and his setting of Henley's *We'll to the Woods and Gather May*.

Griffes was just as successful with the short piano piece. He brought into American piano music a poetry that had hitherto been found only in the writing of French composers like Debussy and Ravel. Characteristic of his picturesque style are the *Three Tone Pictures* of 1910–1912: *The Lake at Evening*, *The Night Winds*, and *The Vale of Dreams*; the *Fantasy Pieces* of 1912–1914: *Barcarolle* (Boat Song), *Notturno* (Nocturne or Night Song), and *Scherzo*. The most famous set of Griffes's piano pieces is the *Four*

39

Roman Sketches of 1915–1916, consisting of *The White Peacock, Nightfall, The Fountain of Acqua Paola,* and *Clouds.* Griffes later arranged *The White Peacock* for orchestra. Along with *The Pleasure Dome of Kubla Khan,* which he wrote in 1912 and revised in 1916, it has remained the most popular of his orchestral works. We should mention also the *Two Sketches on Indian Themes* for string quartet, the *Poem* for flute and orchestra, and the impassioned Piano Sonata, which revealed Griffes to be standing on the threshold of new developments in his art.

When you listen to the music of Charles Griffes you will find that tone color plays a very important part in his art, especially in his imaginative use of such woodwind instruments as the flute, oboe, and clarinet. This sensitivity to color is to be expected from one who always responded strongly to painting. "A beautiful color is lovely in itself," he wrote, "quite aside from any part it plays in the design of the picture." He associated certain keys with colors: E-flat for him was yellow or golden, A-flat was bright red, C major was the most brilliant key of all, a blazing white. It is worthy of note that when he described the music of his dance-drama *Sho-Jo,* he did so in terms of painting: "The orchestration is as Japanese as possible: thin and delicate, and the muted string organ-points serve as a neutral-tinted background, like the empty spaces in a Japanese print." (Organ-points are tones that are held in the bass while the harmonies change above them.)

The White Peacock offers a splendid introduction to the music of Charles Griffes. The orchestral score, which dates from 1919, carries a quotation from a poem by Fiona MacLeod (the Celtic pen name of the Scottish poet William Sharp):

Here where the sunlight floodeth the garden,
Where the pomegranate reareth its glory of gorgeous blossoms;
Where the oleanders dream through the noontides—

· · · · · ·

Here as the breath, as the soul of this beauty
Moveth in silence, and dreamlike, and slowly,
White as a snowdrift in mountain valleys
When softly upon it the gold light lingers:
Moves the white peacock, as tho' through the noontide
A dream of the moonlight were real for a moment,
Dim on the beautiful fan that he spreadeth—

. . . .

Pale, pale as the breath of blue smoke in far woodlands,
Here, as the breath, as the soul of this beauty,
Moves the White Peacock.

The music conjures up an image of the proud, graceful bird as he moves languidly through the golden light. A solo oboe introduces a little motive that recurs throughout the work; a flute follows with the langorous melody that symbolizes the White Peacock. Dreamlike impressionistic harmonies caress the ear with their fluid rhythms. Flute, oboe, and clarinet are used in such a way that their melodies stand out as single strands of color against the orchestral web. There is an upsurge of sound at the climax, when the bird spreads his feathers. A beautiful passage follows, in which a solo violin soars high above the orchestra.

The creator of this haunting music did not live to fulfill the rich promise of his gifts. But he captured in his art a vision of beauty that was of prime importance to the musicians who came after. The popularity of his music after his death made amends for the neglect he suffered during his lifetime. Charles Tomlinson Griffes remains one of the most appealing figures in the history of American music.

4. DOUGLAS MOORE

Douglas Moore advocates a wholesome Americanism in music. "The particular idea," he explains, "which I have been striving to attain is to write music which will reflect the exciting quality of life, traditions, and country which I feel all about me." He has adhered to this goal throughout his career.

Moore was born on August 10, 1893, at Cutchogue on Long Island. His ancestors on his father's side came to this country from England before 1640 and settled in Southold Town on Long Island, the first English-speaking settlement in New York State. His mother was a descendant of both Miles Standish and John Alden. Moore's older daughter married into a family as illustrious as his own, for her husband is a descendant of Governor Bradford.

The composer's father was the publisher of *Ladies' World,* one of the earliest women's magazines, of which his mother was the editor. She was an ardent music lover and presided over the local choral society, which frequently held its rehearsals and concerts in the spacious music room of the Moore home in Brooklyn. As a child Douglas loved to hear his mother play the piano. His interest in music went hand in hand with a passion for dramatics, which he shared with his brothers. They produced a melodrama entitled *The Bride's Fate* in the family attic. Douglas, who was seven years old at the time, not only wrote the play but also acted the leading role and managed the enterprise. The price of admission was one penny. Considering that the box office took in five cents, the production was regarded as a huge success by all concerned.

Douglas's pleasure in music took a sudden turn for the worse when he began to take piano lessons and had to practice scales and exercises. His dislike mounted steadily until his mother promised to stop the lessons. But when the time came for him to go away to school—he was thirteen then—she changed her mind and insisted that he must continue to study the piano. "I felt very bitter about it at the time," he recalls, "as if I'd been betrayed." However, he began to take a more friendly view of the piano when he was allowed to make up his own melodies. Indeed, during his years at the Hotchkiss School he recaptured something of his earlier love of music. During one summer vacation, when he was fifteen, Douglas and one of his brothers put on a musical show at their father's clubhouse. He composed the score, which made such a hit that he proudly informed his mother, "Now I can write any kind of music I want."

At Hotchkiss Douglas found a congenial friend in his classmate Archibald MacLeish, who later became one of America's best-known poets. MacLeish was always scribbling verses. When Douglas saw these, he decided to set them to music. Thus began a collaboration that continued through the years, after both of them had achieved fame.

Douglas Moore looks back to his schooling with a certain regret. "At that time," he says, "I should have been sent to a conservatory." This remark reveals the difficult choice that many young musicians have to make. If they go to college they receive a general education as well as a musical one; but the music course is apt to be less intensive than at the conservatory, where the whole curriculum revolves around music. Besides, at a conservatory the student specializes in music from the beginning, whereas at college he has to devote the better part of his first two years to his required subjects, which have nothing to do with music. It took Douglas Moore many years to receive a thorough grounding in the technique of composition. For this reason he feels that it would have been better for him to attend a conservatory. Today, of course, the two types of institution have drawn closer together. Our conservatories offer a much broader academic education than they used to, and our colleges give the music student a more intensive training in his chosen field.

Douglas was eighteen when he was graduated from Hotchkiss and entered Yale University. His gift for turning out a good tune was already in evidence. During his freshman year he wrote a number of songs, one of which, *Good Night, Harvard,* became Yale's favorite football rally. It was not until he reached his junior year that Douglas decided to become a musician. He was asked to write background music for a college production of Walter Scott's *Quentin Durward.* Up to this time he had written only songs. Music for a play involved much more, for he had to compose a series of orchestral numbers that would connect the different scenes and create the proper atmosphere for each. Douglas had no experience in this direction, but he didn't let that stop him. He tackled his new task with enthusiasm and turned out a highly satisfactory score for the play.

One afternoon, seated at the piano, he was going over the music for *Quentin Durward* with some classmates. He played for them one of his favorite bits, the march. Suddenly the door opened and the senior professor of music walked in. It was the composer Horatio Parker, who was something of a legendary figure at Yale. Douglas had seen him before, but had never dared to approach him. The professor turned to Douglas. "Did you write this?" he asked. "I did, sir," the young man answered timidly. Parker sat down at the piano and played the march from beginning to end. He had picked it up by ear at one hearing. "It's not at all bad," the professor said. From this meeting there sprang up a friendship that was of the greatest importance for Douglas Moore. He became Parker's pupil and threw himself heart and soul into the study of composition, working with redoubled zeal to make up for his late start.

After he finished the course at Yale Moore stayed on for two more years to do graduate work with Parker, who wanted him to teach at the university. By this time the United States had entered the First World War, and Moore enlisted in the Navy. He continued to write songs while he was in the service. One of these, called *Destroyer Life*, became extremely popular with his shipmates. At this time the ballad singer John Jacob Niles was collecting material for a book of folk songs. He thought that *Destroyer Life* was a folk tune, and decided to include it in his book. When he was told that the song was by Douglas Moore, Niles looked up the young composer to find out if this was really so. The two young men quickly became friends and collaborated on a book which appeared under the intriguing title *Songs My Mother Never Taught Me.*

When the war was over Moore was faced with an important decision. His father had died. His older brother had taken over the management of the magazine and wanted Douglas to enter the business. "You've fooled around with music long enough," his brother told him. "It's time you settled down to something practical." But Moore could not abandon his dream of becoming a composer, even though it seemed to promise a far less practical career —as far as financial gain was concerned—than the publishing business. He turned to his schoolmate Archibald MacLeish for advice. Moore set three of MacLeish's poems to music and asked the poet what he thought of them. MacLeish and his wife praised Moore's songs to the skies. "But am I good enough to make my way as a composer?" Moore wondered. There was only one way to find out: to try.

He did not have to worry about making a living for the time being, for he had inherited some money from his father. He felt that he needed further study and, like so many young American artists after the First World War, decided to go to Paris. Moore was vastly stimulated by the year he spent in the French capital, studying composition and the organ. Of the many new friendships he made, the most important was that with the poet Stephen Vincent Benét, many of whose poems he subsequently set to music.

Moore interrupted his studies to come home and marry Emily Bailey, in whom he found a devoted wife. Emily was most sympathetic to his aspirations as a composesr. Moore took her back to Paris for what he remembers as "a second marvelous year," during which he continued his studies. When they returned to the United States, a splendid opportunity opened up for Moore. The Cleveland Museum was looking for someone who could give organ recitals and organize concerts. Archibald MacLeish suggested him for the post, and the young composer was appointed curator of music at the Cleveland Museum of Art.

The Moores spent four happy years in Cleveland. They had two daughters, Mary and Sarah. Moore obtained valuable experience as an educator and organizer of musical events. He also had an opportunity to indulge his old love of dramatics, by acting in the plays that were put on by the Cleveland Playhouse. Most important of all, he came in contact with a group of talented young musicians who were studying with the composer Ernest Bloch. Moore decided to follow their example, and in Bloch he found the best teacher he had ever had.

While he was at Yale Moore had spent an exciting summer at the MacDowell Colony in Peterborough, New Hampshire. He now returned to the Colony and wrote his first serious work, a suite called *Four Museum Pieces* (1922), in which he expressed in music his impressions of four art treasures at the Cleveland Museum: *Fifteenth Century Armor*, *A Madonna of Botticini*, *The Chinese Lion and the Unhappy Flutist*, and *A Statue by Rodin*. Moore originally wrote this composition for the organ, but later orchestrated it and conducted the first performance with the Cleveland Symphony Orchestra. In his next work Moore struck out toward his future path as an American nationalist. *The Pageant of P. T. Barnum* (1924) is an orchestral suite in five movements that evokes the composer's childhood memories of the circus. From the first note until the roistering *Circus Parade* at the end, this piece vividly captures the flavor of the American scene.

Not long afterward Moore won a fellowship that freed him for one year from the duties of his job, so that he could devote himself completely to composing. Although he already had two successful works to his credit, he felt that he needed further study. He went to Paris and began to take lessons from Nadia Boulanger, a brilliant musician who taught a number of our important composers. Mlle. Boulanger made him go back and master certain fundamentals that had been neglected in his early training. She insisted, for example, that he learn to read the different clefs with ease. In this country most of us learn only the treble and bass clefs. Abroad, where sight-reading in the different clefs is taught in the early grades, musicians learn the soprano, alto, and tenor clefs as well. As a result, they achieve a facility in sight-singing which American musicians do not ordinarily possess. Moore had to work hard to master what he should have been taught at the beginning of his studies. As a result of this experience, he believes that *solfeggio* (ear-training and sight-reading in the different clefs) should be taught to every pupil in public school; for it is much easier to learn this when one is young.

When Moore returned from Paris, he was invited to join the

music department of Columbia University. There he found a sympathetic atmosphere for his activities. He was a kindly, warm-hearted teacher with a special knack for explaining music to non-musicians. He was able to put himself in the place of the student who had no musical training, and explained the fundamentals of his art in simple terms that could be understood by all. Moore's courses in music appreciation at Columbia and Barnard College became popular. He organized the material of his lectures into two books, *Listening to Music* (1932) and *From Madrigal to Modern Music* (1942), which offered the layman a simple and attractive introduction to the art. In time Moore received the Edward Mac-Dowell Professorship at Columbia University and became head of the music department.

In his development as a composer Moore realized that he would find his own style only if he shook off the foreign influences to which he had subjected himself during his years abroad. He felt that he must go back to his roots. The European styles of composition, he maintained, were all very well for Europeans. "I cannot believe," he wrote, "that they are likely to be appropriate or becoming for us." Just as the European composers found inspiration in the writings of their national poets and dramatists, Moore found inspiration for his music in American literature. His orchestral piece *Moby Dick* (1928) came out of his enthusiasm for Herman Melville's great novel. His *Overture on an American Tune* (1931) conjures up the boisterous world of Sinclair Lewis's *Babbitt*. The American scene is further evoked in such works as *Village Music* (1941), a suite for orchestra in four movements: *Square Dance, Procession, Nocturne,* and *Jig. Farm Journal* (1947), for chamber orchestra, suggests four rural pictures: *Up Early, Sunday Clothes, Lamplight,* and *Harvest Song.* When he sets the verse of our poets—his favorites are Stephen Vincent Benét, Vachel Lindsay, and Archibald MacLeish—Moore's me-

48

lodic line follows the rhythms and inflections of American speech in the most natural way. As a result, the melody is characteristically American in its shape and character. Even his abstract works, such as the lively Quartet for Strings (1933), the tuneful Symphony in A (1945), and the Quintet for Clarinet and Strings (1946), have an unmistakable American flavor.

Moore's music is tuneful and unpretentious. It reflects the simplicity and optimism of the composer; his sincerity, and his love for his homeland. Moore's most important trait is his gift for melody. His music has an abundance of appealing tunes. He is a romantic at heart. As far as he is concerned, the romantic attitude is ingrained in the American character. "We are incorrigibly sentimental as a race," he points out. "The best of what we accomplish is usually achieved by dint of high spirits, soft-heartedness, and a great deal of superfluous energy." He realized that many of our composers in the 1920s were being influenced by the new styles of composition that held sway in Paris. But he was convinced that such a course would only lead them into ways of expression that were alien to them. In their desire to sound modern and advanced our composers, he felt, were giving up the best part of their heritage. "If we happen to feel romantically inclined, if we like a good tune now and then, if we still have a childish love of atmosphere, is it not well for us to admit the fact and try to produce something which we like ourselves?"

"I've always liked setting words better than any other form of composition," Moore declared fairly early in his career, "and I've always had a passion for the theater." A composer who loves to set words and who has a passion for the theater inevitably ends by writing operas. Moore leaves us in no doubt as to his favorite type of composition. "I love to write operas. To me it is the most spontaneous form of expression. The music writes itself if the book is good." His early love of dramatics gave him a keen feeling for

49

what is effective in the lyric theater. As a result, he has been able to pick stories that make good operas.

Moore's most ambitious work for the lyric stage, *The Ballad of Baby Doe* (1956), is based on an American legend that really happened: the rise and fall of Horace Tabor, who struck silver in Leadville, Colorado; became one of the wealthiest men of his time; and was ruined when the United States abandoned the silver standard for gold. The action takes place in a stormy period of American history, against the lusty background of a Colorado mining town. The love story involves Augusta, Horace's domineering and strait-laced wife, who accompanied him from his humble beginnings to power and riches; and Baby Doe, as she was known among the miners, a twenty-year-old beauty for whose sake the middle-aged millionaire divorced his wife. Before his death Horace made Baby Doe promise that she would never sell the Matchless Mine which had made his fortune. She kept her word. She guarded the abandoned mine, a solitary eccentric dressed in castoff men's clothing, with gunny sacks wrapped around her feet, until she was found frozen to death on the floor of her shack in March, 1935.

The Ballad of Baby Doe received a gala premiere in Central City, Colorado, not far from where the drama of Horace and Baby Doe took place. As a matter of fact, there were people in the audience who still remembered them. The opera won a huge success, and rightly so. Moore's music for *Baby Doe* is rich in feeling and atmosphere. It is both lyric and dramatic. It contains some enchanting melodies. The opera evokes a turbulent era in our country's past, and makes first-rate theater.

Equally attractive is Moore's one-act opera *The Devil and Daniel Webster* (1938), which offers an excellent introduction to his music. Stephen Vincent Benét wrote the libretto, basing it on his celebrated short story which tells how Daniel Webster matched his wits against the Devil's. In discussing the piece Moore declared: "Mr. Benét and I have classified *The Devil and Daniel Webster* as a folk opera because it is legendary in its subject matter and simple in its musical expression. We have tried to make an opera in which the union of speech, song and instrumental music will communicate the essence of the dramatic story." Even though no folk tunes are actually quoted in the opera, both the libretto and the music vividly capture the spirit of American folklore.

Be sure, when you listen to *The Devil and Daniel Webster,* to follow the music with the text that comes with the records. In this way you will not have to strain to catch the words, especially when the chorus sings. The action takes place at the home of Jabez Stone in New Hampshire, during the 1840s. The inhabitants of Cross Corners are celebrating the wedding of Jabez and Mary. Jabez had always been poor; but in the past few years he has prospered in an amazing fashion, and is now a state senator. There is even talk of his running for governor. Everybody at the wedding is in a festive mood; and the occasion is made even more festive with the arrival of Daniel Webster, the great orator and Secretary of State, who is the pride of New England. Webster receives a real New Hampshire welcome.

The gay mood is dispelled with the arrival of an unexpected guest—a Boston lawyer named Scratch. "He is, of course, the Devil, a New England devil, dressed like a rather shabby attorney, but with something just a little wrong about his clothes and appearance, possibly his gloved hands, certainly his air. He carries a large black tin box, like a botanist's collection box, under one arm." The bridegroom is strangely upset when he catches sight of the unbidden guest. Scratch sings a devilish ditty that terrifies the neighbors. The village fiddler opens the Devil's box. Out flies a lost soul in the shape of a moth. Then the guests realize that Jabez Stone has sold his soul to the Devil. Horrified, they denounce Jabez and run away.

Mary remains. She loves Jabez and will not abandon him. He

51

confesses to her that, in his eagerness to raise himself from poverty and win her love, he had indeed made a pact with the Devil. Daniel Webster too has remained. He is not the kind who runs away. He decides to help the young couple. When Mr. Scratch arrives to claim his due—Jabez's soul—Webster demands a trial for his client. Scratch summons from the depths of Hell a jury of famous American traitors and renegades. (Daniel Webster inquires why Benedict Arnold is not among them, but the Devil explains that Arnold is busy on another assignment.) Presiding is the infamous Judge Hathorne of the Salem witch trials. This jury of damned souls is hardly likely to give Jabez a fair deal. Yet the impossible happens. Webster is so eloquent an orator that he turns the tables on the Devil, and persuades the jury to set Jabez free. "The neighbors rush in to drive the Devil out of New Hampshire, and the case ends with pie breakfast, as it should."

From the square-dance atmosphere of the opening scene you will find this folk opera a sheer delight. The action unfolds in both speech and song. In the sung parts Benét's text moves toward the lyricism of poetry. The spoken parts that explain the action are in a simpler style. The highlight of the opening scene is the tender duet between the bride and groom, and the sinister ballad of the Devil, "Young William was a thriving boy . . ." (That is, he was thriving until the Devil got hold of him.) The second scene contains a rousing song by Daniel Webster, "I've got a ram, Goliath"; also Mary's touching song of faith and hope, "Now may there be a blessing and a light betwixt thee and me, forever." The climax of the play is, of course, Webster's speech to the jury. This is spoken against a musical background, which gives special eloquence to the words. The work ends with a jubilant chorus that sings the praises of New England virtue and New England pie.

Benét's libretto is a beautiful piece of writing, and Moore has set it with affection and understanding. You will hear people say that they like opera better in a foreign language because English is not easy to sing. You have only to listen to a work such as this to realize how singable is our language when it is properly set. *The Devil and Daniel Webster* is suffused with love for our country, her past, her legends, her people. You will feel proud of being an American when Daniel Webster's ringing speech to the jury reaches its culminating point: "They have broken freedom with their hands and cast her out from the nations, yet shall she live again while man lives. She shall live in the blood and in the heart, she shall live in the earth of this country, she shall not be named in vain. When the whips of the oppressors are broken and their names forgotten and destroyed, I see you, mighty, shining, liberty, liberty! I see free men walking and talking under a free star! God save the United States and the men who have made her free."

The Devil and Daniel Webster has established itself as an American classic. Its composer expresses American feelings in a sincere and convincing way. For this reason Douglas Moore has become one of our leading nationalist composers.

5. WALTER PISTON

Walter Piston differs in a fundamental way from composers like Charles Ives and Douglas Moore, who tried to create a distinctly American music. He believes that a composer's first duty is to write down what he hears in his mind and feels in his heart, without worrying whether this is especially American or not. Consequently he is one of our internationally minded composers, and a most distinguished member of this group.

He was born in Rockland, Maine, on January 20, 1894. His grandfather, an Italian sailor named Antonio Pistone, came to this country as a young man, settled in Maine, and, when he became Americanized, dropped the final "e" from the family name. As a boy Walter showed no inclination for music. His parents did not even have a piano in the house. When he was ten the family moved to Boston, where Walter attended the Mechanic Arts High School. At this time he was interested mainly in painting. It was only when he was around seventeen that he began to take an interest in music. He studied the violin, taught himself the piano, and worked his way through school by playing in bands in dance halls, restaurants, and theaters. His ambition was still to become a painter. With that end in view he enrolled in the Massachusetts Normal Art School, which he attended for four years.

When he was graduated from art school he was torn between painting and music. His mind was made up for him by external events: the United States entered the First World War. Walter enlisted in the Navy because, ever since his childhood on the coast of Maine, he had loved the sea. But he never saw the ocean while he was in service. "The only battle I took part in," he recalls, "was the 'Battle of the Charles River'!"

As he was a musician, Walter naturally wanted to play in the Navy Band. "What instrument do you play?" he was asked at his enlistment. Walter hesitated. The only instruments he played were piano and violin, neither of which would make him eligible for a brass band. So he put down, "Saxophone." On his way home he bought a saxophone, stopped in at the public library, and borrowed a book on how to play it. All that day and far into the night he proceeded to become acquainted with the instrument. When he reported for duty the next morning he was on the way to becoming a saxophonist. His technical rating in the Navy was "second-class musician," a designation, he feels, that accurately described his playing. During the time he spent in the Navy Band he learned to play most of the wind instruments. "They were just lying around," he explains, "and no one minded if you picked them up and found out what they could do."

By the time the war was over he had made up his mind to become a musician. He went back to the violin and became so proficient at it that he was able to play in a symphony orchestra. But was this, he asked himself, what he really wanted to do? A violinist, he reflected, spends his life playing what other men have written, and has to play it as the conductor directs him to. Piston realized that this would never give him the opportunity to assert his own personality. He had to have the kind of work in which he would be on his own. He had already begun to compose a little and had discovered what an exciting challenge creative work can be. Accordingly, although he already was twenty-seven years old —a late age for a man to begin the serious study of composition—

he enrolled in the music course at Harvard University. It was a gamble, he knew; for if he failed, it would be too late to turn to something else. But he was willing to take a chance.

During his years in art school he had met a lovely girl named Kathryn Nason, who was in the same class as he. Piston fell in love with her. During his second year at Harvard they were married. Kathryn subsequently became a well-known painter. Piston is convinced that his wife's talent at painting had very much to do with his becoming a composer. "She painted so much better than I did," he says, "that I had to give up art and become something else—a musician, or a plumber!" Kathryn encouraged her young husband in his desire to become a composer. Through the years she enthusiastically shared in Piston's career, even while she found the time and energy to continue her own.

At Harvard Piston made rapid progress and gained a thorough grounding in the fundamentals of his art. He was graduated with the highest honors and won a fellowship that enabled him to study abroad. Soon after his graduation Piston and Kathryn set sail for Paris, which at that time was the Mecca of all aspiring musicians. He wanted to study at the Paris Conservatory, but he had already passed the age limit for admittance to that famous school. Some friends advised him to work with Nadia Boulanger, who had won the reputation of being the most brilliant teacher in Paris. Piston could not get used to the idea of studying with her. How could a woman possibly teach composition, he wondered. But when he met Mlle. Boulanger he was so impressed by her tremendous grasp of music that he immediately began to take lessons from her, and he found her to be an inspiring teacher.

When he returned from Paris he was faced with the problem of earning a living. He would have been delighted to stay at home and spend all his time composing. But writing serious music, he well knew, was not going to bring him enough to live on. He felt that, of all the ways open to composers to gain a livelihood, teaching was the one most congenial to his temperament. It was also the occupation least likely to interfere with his creative work. He therefore joined the music department of Harvard University, where he spent the major part of his career. For several years he served as chairman of the department. In time he was made a full professor and resigned the chairmanship, so as to free himself from the duties of an administrator. Piston gradually established his reputation as one of America's outstanding composers. Harvard was very proud of him. Ultimately he taught only a few hours a week, which left him all the time he needed for writing his music.

As professor of composition at Harvard University, he influenced many composers of the younger generation. His pupil Elliott Carter has given us a vivid picture of Piston as his students saw him. "In class Piston is affable, tolerant, and reserved. Though quiet, he is far from the dry professor because he casts over his subject a penetrating wit or a thoughtful seriousness that comes from a deep concern with the subject at hand. Usually willing to talk about his music to someone who is seriously interested, he is not inclined to talk about himself. When he does, it is with a dignified modesty. These traits seldom fail to command the respect and liking of his students, especially those who share his concern for the art." In his teaching Piston tried to give his students a thorough grasp of the musical traditions inherited from the past. At the same time he interspersed these with modern concepts, so that the young musicians under his guidance would feel at home in the music of the twentieth century. Out of his experiences as a teacher came four books, *Principles of Harmonic Analysis* (1933), *Harmony* (1941), *Counterpoint* (1947), and *Orchestration* (1955), that are used as textbooks in colleges throughout the country.

The art of music has alternated, through the ages, between two attitudes. The classical ideal exalted beauty of form and elegance of manner, even as the romantic ideal favored the expression of intense personal emotion. The classical composers of the late eighteenth century, such as Haydn, Mozart, and Beethoven, favored "pure" or absolute music—music that has no outside meanings attached to it in the form of a story, a title, or a scene of nature. On the other hand, the romantic composers of the nineteenth century, such as Franz Liszt and his followers, favored program music—music that carries a poetic title and is associated with a definite story or scene. (Mozart's symphonies, concertos, and string quartets are examples of absolute music; Liszt's *Les Préludes*, Tchaikovsky's *Romeo and Juliet* Overture, and Smetana's *The Moldau* are examples of program music.) In other words, the classical composers liked to present and to develop abstract musical ideas, while the romantic composers tended to associate musical ideas with a specific mood, scene, or story. Classicism dominated the thinking of the eighteenth century; romanticism was in the ascendant throughout the nineteenth century. In our own time many composers began to feel that romanticism had run its course and that it was necessary to return to the principles of the eighteenth century. Walter Piston became one of the leading representatives of the New Classicism.

His talent found its natural expression in the large forms of instrumental music—symphonies, concertos, sonatas, string quartets, and the like. His main concern has been to create beautifully designed forms and to develop abstract musical ideas; he does not believe that music should be used to tell a story or describe a scene. "Musical thought," he writes, "is not a translation into music of what can be or has been expressed in some other medium such as poetry or photography." For this reason he does not like to say what any one of his compositions means. He feels that when a composer attaches a specific title to a piece, it limits the listener's imagination. If there is no title or explanation, you are free to listen to a composition in your own way and to read your own meaning into the music.

In accordance with this point of view, Piston does not favor a specifically American music. He does not feel that composers born in the United States have to limit their inspiration to American folk songs, or that they have to tie in their music with American history and literature. As a result, he advocates the broadest possible interpretation of what is American: "The plain fact is that American music is music written by Americans. Ours is a big country and we are a people possessing a multitude of different origins. If a composer desires to serve the cause of American music, he will best do it by remaining true to himself as an individual and not by trying to discover musical formulas for Americanism."

What Piston feared was that American composers would fall into stereotyped patterns if they all tried to express the spirit of the prairie or based their works on cowboy tunes. "Is the Dust Bowl more American," he asked, "than, say, a corner in the Boston Athenaeum? Would not a Vermont village furnish as American a background for a composition as the Great Plains?" He was afraid that if our composers tried to be American all the time, they would end by writing all alike instead of each developing his own style. "The self-conscious striving for nationalism," he points out, "gets in the way of the establishment of a strong school of composition and even of significant individual expression. The composer cannot afford the wild-goose chase of trying to be more American than he is."

This does not mean that Piston's music bears no relation to the American scene. As a matter of fact he has absorbed into his style certain elements of American popular music, especially the jazz idiom that he came in contact with as a young man. But these elements are not his main purpose. He refines them and uses them to express musical ideas that are not tied down to any specific place. Piston speaks the international language of the New Classicism, which is understood with equal readiness in Paris, London, Vienna, or New York. Having assimilated the most important trends in the musical art of our time, he has combined them into a style that bears the imprint of his own personality. He is a meticulous craftsman. "Each new work," he writes, "is for me the start of a new problem, a new adventure the outcome of which I am never able to predict. It is in a sense another study towards the perfect balance between expression and form."

The advocates of Americanism in music argue that Piston's music lacks the earthiness which comes from contact with the native soil. By the same token it gains, in the eyes of the internationalists, a dignity and universality of outlook. Piston's music is elegant, polished, witty, controlled. The grace and ease of his writing are much admired by other composers. Aaron Copland has written: "Piston's music, if considered only from a technical viewpoint, constitutes a challenge to every other American composer. It sets a level of craftsmanship that is absolutely first-rate in itself and provides a standard of reference by which every other American's work may be judged." Coming from a fellow composer, this is praise indeed.

Typical of Piston's early period is the brilliant Concerto for Orchestra (1933) and the witty Concertino for piano and orchestra (1937). As the years passed, he moved toward greater simplicity of speech, a more melodious style, and, above all, a more personal lyricism. Seven symphonies form the central item in Piston's output. The First was composed in 1937, the Seventh in 1960. The Third (1947) brought him a Pulitzer Prize. The list of his works includes three string quartets, two orchestral suites, the Violin Concerto of 1939, and a Quintet for piano and strings (1949) that is a distinguished addition to contemporary chamber music.

These works show Piston's preference for absolute music. All the same, his most popular piece belongs to the category of program music. It is the orchestral suite from his ballet *The Incredible Flutist* (1938) and offers a charming introduction to his music. The action of the ballet takes place in a Spanish village during carnival time. The siesta hour is over. The Merchant's Daughters reopen their father's shop and display its wares to the customers. Various village characters appear. Suddenly a march is heard, announcing the arrival of the circus. The grand parade files past amid great excitement. The circus band is followed by the Barker, the Jugglers, the Snake Charmer, the Monkey Trainer, the Crystal Gazer, and the star attraction of the show, the Incredible Flutist, whose playing charms even the circus animals. He charms also the prettiest of the Merchant's daughters. She agrees to meet him that evening in the village square.

When she arrives, the Flutist is waiting for her. But they are not alone in the square, as other couples have been lured out by the romantic night. The Merchant courts a rich widow who has resisted his wooing for years. Love is in the air; the Widow suddenly yields and grants the Merchant a kiss. Alas, they are discovered by their prying neighbors. The lady swoons from embarrassment, but is revived by a little music from the Incredible Flutist. The enchanted moment is over; the circus must be on its way. The band strikes up. The Incredible Flutist, so gay, so debonair, is off on new adventures.

The suite consists of eight sections: 1. *Introduction* and *Dance of the Vendors*. A languid melody establishes the Spanish atmosphere and suggests the siesta hour in the market place. The *Dance of the Vendors* has a tartly dissonant flavor. 2. *Entrance of the Customers* and *Tango of the Merchant's Daughters*. The *Tango* is a graceful tune in 5/8 time that shows off Piston's flair for appealing melody. 3. *Arrival of the Circus* and *March*. The villagers greet the circus with shouts of joy. In these noisy measures we hear the expectancy of the crowd and the excitement that attends the arrival of a circus. The *Circus March* is properly brassy and bright. 4. *Solo of the Flutist*. The hero of the ballet weaves his spell with trills and roulades whose silvery tones display the magic of his instrument.

61

5. *Minuet.* The Widow and the Merchant mark their rendezvous in the village square with a lovely minuet. 6. *A gay Spanish waltz.* 7. *Siciliano Duet.* The Flutist and the Merchant's Daughter have their romantic moment to the tender strains of a siciliano (a dance of Sicilian origin, generally in 6/8 time taken at a very moderate tempo, featuring a soft lyrical melody of pastoral character). 8. *Polka Finale.* For the brilliant conclusion of the ballet Piston uses a polka, a lively dance in quick 2/4 time. In this number Piston introduces a device that is always effective: he presents a catchy tune which is repeated over and over again, each time a little faster.

This music is tender and gracious. It has the feel of the theater, the suggestion of ballet movement and gesture. You will be enchanted by its catchy melodies, lilting rhythms, and sparkling orchestral color.

In a period of great experimentation and rapid change, such as the age we live in, composers tend to be divided into a number of camps. There are the conservatives, who want to hang on to tradition. There are the radicals, who adhere passionately to the newest trends. And there are those who follow the middle of the road, striving to combine what is best in the old with what is most valuable in the new. Piston throughout his career has been a mediator between the two extremes. "It is not one of my aims," he has said, "to write music that will be called modern, nor do I set out to compose according to any particular style or system. I believe my music is music of today in both manner and expression, since I am inescapably influenced by the art, thought, and daily life of the present."

Walter Piston has fully achieved his aim of reconciling the values of tradition with twentieth-century ways of thinking and feeling. He is in the fullest sense of the term a modern classicist.

6. HOWARD HANSON

Howard Hanson's importance in our musical life extends far beyond his activities as a composer. It is no exaggeration to say that during the 1920s and '30s no one in the United States did more for the cause of American music than he.

Hanson was born on October 28, 1896, in Wahoo, Nebraska. His grandparents had emigrated from Sweden and settled in the town because it had a thriving Swedish community. Howard had the advantage of growing up in an environment where music was appreciated. The Lutheran Church had a large chorus that performed the oratorios of the masters at annual music festivals. Howard's love for music was further stimulated by the beautiful old Lutheran chorales that were sung by the congregation. His mother played the piano and began to give him lessons when he was six. Soon afterward he began to compose. "At the age of eight," he recalls, "I turned out my Opus 1, a little trio of doleful melodies very much under the influence of Grieg, who was at that time and who remained for some years my musical idol."

Howard soon began to take part in the musical life of the town. From the beginning he displayed the qualities of leadership that marked his later career. At the age of nine he organized a string quartet. "I was given the job of learning to play the cello, as none

63

of our group could play that instrument." Howard excelled in sports and games; but best of all he enjoyed playing with the string quartet. "We also had a creditable little orchestra," he recollects, "which afforded great experience for all of us and a great deal of fun." Howard's musical talent attracted the attention of the teachers at Luther College, which was the cultural center of the town. Shortly after he entered high school he was allowed, as a special privilege, to study harmony and counterpoint at Luther College, even though he was much younger than the other pupils.

On looking back upon his career, Hanson feels that he received an excellent start in Wahoo. For this reason he objects strenuously when he hears people say that the musical life of small towns is inferior to that of the big cities. "It always riles me a little to read the glib accounts of the Main Streets of the Middle West, for if that little town where I was born didn't have as much appreciation of good music per square foot as some of our large eastern cities, I should be willing to eat the town, paved streets and all! People who are brought up on Handel, Mozart, Beethoven, Grieg and Lutheran chorales can hardly be considered musically illiterate."

Howard's natural ability as a leader asserted itself as soon as he came to high school. By the time he was fifteen he was conducting the school orchestra. (Ever since then, conducting has been as important a part of his life as composing.) He had already written a considerable amount of music. Now he had an opportunity to rehearse it with the orchestra and to find out how it really sounded.

When he was graduated from high school the superintendent warned him against a musical career. "Music is not a man's job!" he told Howard. "With your ability you could make a first-class success in some important position." But Howard had already decided to devote his life to music, and was not to be dissuaded. He had been studying piano, cello, and composition at Luther College throughout his high-school years, and he now finished the music course there with the highest honors. He had to obtain special permission to graduate, as he was not yet seventeen.

Howard had no money with which to continue his musical studies. But at this point his knowledge of the cello stood him in good stead. For the next six months he played one-night stands that took him from Colorado to New York and from Minnesota to Texas. During this tour he gained what he called "an almost too intimate acquaintance with the United States." The money that he saved enabled him to go to New York. There he enrolled at the Institute of Musical Art (which later became the Juilliard School), and finished the course in one year. His piano teacher urged him to practice hard, as he had the gift to become a concert pianist. But the head of the composition department made Howard realize that his real talent lay in composing.

Another summer of touring as a cellist brought him the money to complete his college education. With this in mind he went to Northwestern University at Evanston, Illinois. The dean of the music school quickly recognized Howard's ability and allowed him, while he was still a student, to teach the classes in harmony. "I was in my nineteenth year and most of my pupils were older than I, but they were courteous and friendly and we got along beautifully." At the end of the year a visitor came to Northwestern, looking for a teacher of theory and composition. This was President Seaton of the College of the Pacific in California. He was very much impressed with Howard Hanson's brilliant record and with the young man's forceful personality. There was only one drawback: Hanson looked so young. "How old are you?" he asked. "I'll be twenty next fall," Hanson replied. "You're rather young to be a college professor. But," the president added with a smile, "that's a fault which time will take care of. I'll take a chance."

The following September Hanson moved to California and took

65

up his duties at the College of the Pacific. His energy and enthusiasm made him an ideal teacher, and he soon was one of the most
popular professors on the campus. Three years later he was appointed to an even more responsible post: he became dean of the
music school, the youngest dean in the annals of American education.

It was during his years in California that Hanson wrote his
first three compositions for orchestra: *Symphonic Poem* (1916),
Legend (1917), and *Symphonic Rhapsody* (1919). These works
came to the attention of the director of the Los Angeles Philharmonic Orchestra, who invited Hanson to Los Angeles to conduct his *Symphonic Rhapsody*. This was the most important event
that had happened to the young composer, and in later years he
looked back to it with great affection. "I have conducted many
excellent orchestras since that time, but I never hope to get in this
world the thrill which I had in hearing the first chord of my own
music from a great orchestra."

Hanson continued as dean of the College of the Pacific for two
more years. Then there came to him an even more important opportunity. The American Academy in Rome had been giving its
annual Prix de Rome (Rome Prize) to painters and sculptors.
That year the Academy decided to include composers as well, and
instituted a competition for the prize. Hanson submitted his fourth
symphonic poem, *Before the Dawn,* and shortly thereafter received a telegram informing him that he had won the prize. This
meant that he would be able to spend three years in Rome, utterly
free to compose. Hanson had never been to Europe, and he had
never before had an opportunity to devote himself completely to
writing music. It was an excited young man indeed who, in January, 1922, set sail for Italy.

At this time most young composers, eager to free themselves
from the heritage of nineteenth-century romanticism, were at-

tracted to an ultramodern style of writing that was based on dissonant harmony. The new classical school cultivated a type of music in which the composer was more interested in exploring the possibilities of his material than in expressing personal emotion. Hanson at first tried to write in this style. But he was a romantic at heart, and found his true path by following in the footsteps of such composers as César Franck, Johannes Brahms, and Jean Sibelius. In his First Symphony, the *Nordic* (1922), he paid homage to the heroic sagas of his Scandinavian ancestors. The first movement, he explained, "sings of the solemnity, austerity and grandeur of the North, of its restless surging and strife, its somberness and melancholy." The gentle second movement he inscribed, "To My Mother." The third movement, based on sturdy Swedish folk songs, he entitled "To My Father." In this way he acknowledged the gift his parents had bequeathed to him—a heritage of manly effort and devotion to ideals.

Hanson wrote several other works in Rome: the symphonic poems *North and West* (1923) and *Lux Aeterna* (Eternal Light, 1923), as well as a string quartet. He also began *The Lament for Beowulf*, a work for chorus and orchestra. After two and a half years at the Academy in Rome, Hanson returned to America in order to conduct *North and West* with the New York Symphony Orchestra. He also conducted his *Nordic Symphony* with the Rochester Symphony Orchestra. The visit to Rochester proved to be the turning point in Hanson's life. For there he met George Eastman, the Kodak millionaire who had just endowed a new music school at the University of Rochester. Eastman and the president of the university, Rush Rhees, were looking for someone to direct the new music school. They were deeply impressed with Hanson's dynamic personality, with his confidence and enthusiasm. "When I returned to Rome," Hanson relates, "I received a letter from Dr. Rhees, offering me the directorship of the Eastman

67

School of Music. Realizing the tremendous opportunities of this school, I was quite willing to leave the quiet haven of Rome for the arduous duties of the direction of a great organization."

Thus, in 1925—before he was yet thirty—Howard Hanson took over the direction of the school which, under his imaginative leadership, became one of the most important musical institutions in the United States. Until that time the important music schools in our country were headed by performers. The pianist Josef Hofmann directed the Curtis Institute in Philadelphia, and was succeeded by the violinist Efrem Zimbalist. The pianist Ernest Hutcheson was president of the Juilliard School in New York; the pianist Ossip Gabrilowitsch directed the Chicago College of Music. Under their influence our major conservatories concentrated on turning out performers—pianists, violinists, cellists, singers—who hoped to achieve success as concert artists (a goal which, naturally, only very few of them attained).

Now, for the first time in this country, the destiny of a great music school was entrusted to a composer. Hanson realized from the beginning of his career as an educator that it is the composer who is the central figure in a musical culture. For if he did not write the music, instrumentalists and singers would not have music to perform. Under Hanson's guidance the Eastman School became a center of training for composers; and he himself, in his composition classes, helped to train a generation of young creative musicians. "I have a profound conviction," he stated, "that the creative artistic life in American music is all-important, more important than orchestras, operas or any other form of musical activity." Hanson realized that our country would never come of age musically if our musicians devoted themselves exclusively to playing over and over again the works of the great European masters. Only by encouraging our native composers could we hope to build a truly American musical culture. His aim, consequently, was to create in Rochester, as he put it, "a center of musical composition that would serve the needs of the young American composer."

Since he was a composer himself, he knew exactly what those needs were. He was aware from his own experience how valuable it is for a composer to hear his works played, for only in this way can he judge whether the effects he heard in his imagination really work. Hanson realized only too well that the American composer did not receive the proper opportunity to hear his music. As we saw in our opening chapter, the famous conductors were mostly Europeans and naturally favored the European classics which they knew best. If they did play a twentieth-century work, it was apt to be by a Frenchman or German rather than by an American. Hanson's first care, therefore, was to give the American composer a fair hearing. To this end he inaugurated at Rochester a series known as the American Composers' Orchestral Concerts, presented under the auspices of the Eastman School. "What seemed to be necessary," he writes, "was the creation of a laboratory for composers, a place where the young composer might come and hear his works performed by a competent orchestra under conditions sufficiently sympathetic to give his compositions a fair test." On May 1, 1925, the first American Composers' Concert was given in the Eastman Theater. With these concerts, Hanson realized, he would also help to educate the public and create a receptive audience for American music. The public reacted favorably. "Listeners began to discover for themselves the fascinating adventure of hearing new music. Sometimes they suffered, but they came again and again, and in increasing numbers."

It was in Hanson's nature to throw himself wholeheartedly into everything he did, as though it were a magnificent adventure. Yet even with his infectious enthusiasm, he could not hope to convince everybody of the rightness of his course. "Some felt that this 'coddling' of the young composer was a waste of money. After all, was it not a tradition of good composers to starve in the garret and be 'discovered' after they were dead?" Fortunately Hanson had the backing of George Eastman, who never wavered in his support of the enterprise. "One ultraconservative critic," Hanson relates, "remarked to Mr. Eastman that the concerts had been going on for five years and he had not yet observed that we had discovered any Beethoven. George Eastman's answer was characteristic of the man. 'If we discover one Beethoven in fifty years I shall consider this venture an enormous success.' "

The Composers' Concerts were soon supplemented by an annual spring festival of American music that was presented by the Rochester Symphony Orchestra under the direction of Howard Hanson. At these concerts some of the most significant American compositions of our time were given their first performance. Indeed, a number of American composers who subsequently achieved fame owe their start to Hanson. During these years more new American music was presented in Rochester than by all the other orchestras of the United States put together. In time Hanson widened the sphere of his activities. He conducted orchestras throughout the country, always featuring new American works. Ultimately he carried his crusade abroad. He gave concerts of American music in the music centers of Europe, and revealed to the world what our native composers were achieving.

Hanson realized that a single performance of a new work is not enough to establish it in the repertory. He therefore adopted the enlightened policy of repeating the works he played. It was also important that the work be published, so that other musicians would be able to study the score. Besides, once a piece was published, conductors would be more likely to consider it for performance with their orchestras. Yet—as we learned from the careers of Charles Ives and Charles Griffes—at that time our big publishing houses were not very hospitable to new American music. They could make more money by concentrating on the established masterpieces. Hanson therefore saw to it that many new American works were published under the auspices of the Eastman School.

Even more important was the recording of a work. When a new piece is played at a concert, this one hearing of it is hardly enough to leave a lasting impression on the listener. However, if it is made available on records, the work can be played over and over again until the listener is familiar with it. Of the many enterprises initiated by Hanson, perhaps none was more significant than his series of recordings with the Rochester Symphony Orchestra, in which he made available to the public many striking new works by American composers.

Hanson's activities proved that the new American music could make its way with the public if it was presented by a conductor who believed in it with all his heart. Once Hanson set the example, many other conductors began to find a place on their programs for American music. In this way Hanson's activities had far-reaching results. He had the vision to become a champion of American music at a time when it desperately needed a champion. His efforts on its behalf bore rich fruit.

Hanson's many duties took him away from composing. Only a man with his enormous capacity for hard work could have found the time to go ahead with his own creative efforts. His composing was often done at night, after an arduous day at the school and the concert hall. It meant that he had to give up, for long periods of time, the pleasure of social evenings and the relaxation of seeing his friends. As he always said, "In the creative field it is necessary to fight for every bit of leisure." For many years he remained a bachelor. He was so busy, he explained, that he simply did not have time to think of marrying. However, in 1946 he married Margaret Elizabeth Nelson, a girl of charm and taste who centered her life around his needs and shared in all his activities with true

71

wifely devotion. She built him the kind of home a composer needs in order to be able to pursue his work. Hanson found, to his astonishment, that after his marriage he had more time for composing than he had ever had before.

His five symphonies form the most important item in his substantial list of works. The most popular of these is the Second (1930), which he named the *Romantic*. "My aim in this symphony," he declared, "has been to create a work that was young in spirit, lyrical and romantic in temperament, and simple and direct in expression." In this piece Hanson took his stand against those who wished to lead music away from romantic expression. He affirmed his belief that "romanticism will find in this country rich soil for a new, young and vigorous growth." The Third Symphony was completed in 1938. The Fourth, the *Requiem* (1943), in memory of his father, brought Hanson a Pulitzer Prize. Fifth is the *Sinfonia Sacra* (Sacred Symphony, 1955), a work suffused with mystical feeling.

Hanson never forgot the beauty of the choral singing in the little town where he grew up. He has written a number of choral pieces and has done some of his best work in this medium. The most important of his choral pieces are *Three Songs from "Drum-Taps"* and *The Lament for Beowulf*. Hanson's opera *Merry Mount* was produced at the Metropolitan Opera House in 1934. He has written a variety of orchestral pieces, chamber music, piano and organ music, and songs. In these works Hanson upholds the romantic point of view, which regards music as the language of the emotions. "Though I have a profound interest," he states, "in theoretical problems, my own music comes 'from the heart' and is a direct expression of my own emotional reactions." He wants music to convey its message to as many people as possible. "There is music for everyone, music for every mood, music for laughter and tears, music frivolous and music serious, music for joy and music for hope and faith. Let no one deprive us of any of its beauty, for we need it all."

You could have no better introduction to Hanson's music than through *Three Songs from "Drum-Taps,"* for baritone solo, mixed chorus, and orchestra. The work is based on three poems by Walt Whitman (1819–1892), who is considered by many to be the leading poet of American democracy. Hanson's piece takes on a special eloquence because of the fiery character of Whitman's lines. *Drum-Taps* communicates Whitman's intense reaction to the drama and the urgency of the Civil War.

> 1. Beat! beat! drums!—blow! bugles! blow!
>   Through the windows—through doors—burst like a ruthless force,
>   Into the solemn church, and scatter the congregation;
>   Into the school where the scholar is studying;
>   Leave not the bridegroom quiet—no happiness must he have now with his bride,
>   Nor the peaceful farmer any peace, ploughing his field or gathering his grain,
>   So fierce you whirr and pound you drums—so shrill you bugles blow.
>   Beat! beat! drums!—blow! bugles! blow! . . .

The orchestral introduction captures the immense excitement of these lines, which were written in 1861 in the heat of the struggle. Drums and trumpets create an atmosphere of travail and terror. The entrance of the voices piles tension upon tension. The music surges forward, relentless in its advance, its frenzied and persistent rhythms driving all before it as the composer captures in sound the terrifying images of the poet's vision. (Be sure to follow the music with Whitman's text before you. The poem is given in its entirety on the back of the record cover.)

2. By the bivouac's fitful flame,
A procession winding around me, solemn and sweet and slow
—but first I note
The tents of the sleeping army, the fields' and woods' dim
outline,
The darkness lit by spots of kindled fire, the silence . . .

O tender and wondrous thoughts
Of life and death, of home and the past and loved, and of
those that are far away;
A solemn and slow procession there as I sit on the ground,
By the bivouac's fitful flame.

A baritone voice sings these words, written in 1865, against a background of strings, in a mood of lyric sweetness and sorrow. Presently the chorus is heard in the background, singing no words but humming or vocalizing on the syllable *Ah*, setting up a curtain of sound behind the solo voice. The mood is one of solemn remembrance, which the music encompasses with a strangely stirring eloquence.

3. To thee old cause!
Thou peerless, passionate, good cause,
Thou stern, remorseless, sweet idea,
Deathless throughout the ages, races, lands,
After a strange sad war, great war for thee,
(I think all war through time was really fought, and ever
will be really fought, for thee.)
These chants for thee, the eternal march of thee.

In these lines of Whitman, written in 1871, emotion is "recollected in tranquility." The poet becomes the voice of his people, hymning the ideal of freedom for which the nation had fought so bitterly. The music rises to a great climax on the words *Deathless throughout the ages, races, lands.* It reaches its final affirmation —a statement that is positive, unflinching, fulfilled—on the last line of the poem.

The creator of this deeply felt, moving piece has been a vital force in America's artistic life. As composer and conductor, educator, administrator, and organizer of musical events, Howard Hanson has played a key role in our musical coming of age.

7. VIRGIL THOMSON

The two most important cities in Virgil Thomson's life are Kansas City, where he was born, and Paris, where he found his spiritual home. These two places are far away from each other in every possible way. Yet Virgil Thomson regards his art as a link between them. "I wrote in Paris," he says, "music that was always, in one way or another, about Kansas City. I wanted Paris to know Kansas City, to understand the ways we like to think and feel on the banks of the Kaw and the Missouri."

Virgil Thomson was born on November 25, 1896. His father's ancestors came to this country long before the Revolution. On his mother's side he is descended from one of the first settlers of Jamestown, Virginia. Virgil was interested in music from his early childhood. Two of his cousins played the violin and piano. He was so excited when he heard them play that, he recalls, he "rolled on the floor in ecstasy." He began to take piano lessons when he was five years old, and before long was known as a child prodigy. All the same, his immediate forebears were anything but musical. "My father and his mother before him," he writes, "were what used to be called 'tone deaf.' They never sang or whistled or paid any attention to musical noises. The four to six hours a day piano practise that I did for some years in my father's house never fazed either of them. They would read or sleep while it was going on as easily as I read or sleep in a railway train."

By the time he was twelve Virgil was giving piano recitals and playing the organ in the Calvary Baptist Church in Kansas City. Although he spent hours every day in practicing, he still found time to do his school work. He went through grammar and high school with a string of A's, and was graduated from Central High School at the age of eighteen. It looked as if he had come to the end of his schooling, for his father could not afford to send him away to college, and there were no institutions of higher learning in his home town. Fortunately for him, that very year the Kansas City Junior College opened its doors. Virgil enrolled immediately as a member of its first class.

He soon gave evidence of the literary gift which, in later years, made him one of the most widely admired critics of our time. He formed a literary society and before long, together with a few classmates who shared his artistic interests, founded a little magazine devoted to the newest trends in the arts. "We are a group of young men," he wrote in the first issue, "organized ostensibly for mutual benefit. We are interested in anything that can be known. Like Bacon, we take all knowledge to be our province; and like a good governor, we hope to get acquainted with our province."

Young Thomson's carefree life in Kansas City was interrupted when the United States entered the First World War. He went into the Army in February, 1917, and ultimately reached the rank of second lieutenant in the Military Aviation Corps. He received some of his training as a radio officer at Columbia University in New York. Thomson took full advantage of the opportunity offered by the city's theaters and concerts. In September, 1918, he received his orders to go overseas. But the Armistice was declared just before his troop ship was to sail.

Thomson returned to Kansas City to complete his studies at the

77

Junior College. His experience in the Army had given him a confidence in himself that he had never possessed before. It had broadened his experience, brought him into contact with all kinds of people, and made him realize that he was able to take care of the practical details of life. Besides, two important decisions had taken shape in his mind. He was determined to become a musician. And he was going to study at Harvard University.

He lost no time in pursuing both goals. One of the churches in Kansas City maintained a fund to help promising young people. Thomson applied for a loan and was soon in Cambridge, Massachusetts. During his first year at Harvard he was granted a scholarship and an assistant instructorship. He also held a job as an organist in Boston. He studied philosophy, languages, and English composition along with his courses in harmony, counterpoint, and orchestration. And he became a member of the famous Harvard Glee Club. Harvard offered him a more exciting intellectual atmosphere than he had ever known before.

The year 1921 was an eventful one for Thomson. He was chosen one of the fifty members of the Harvard Glee Club who were to go on a summer tour of Europe. And he won a fellowship that gave him a year's study in Paris. The Harvard Glee Club made its first European appearance in Paris. Thomson fell in love with the city. Then came performances throughout France, Italy, and Germany and in Geneva. When the rest of the group sailed for the United States, Thomson remained.

His year in France brought him into contact with an old culture to which he responded wholeheartedly. He also achieved a new awareness of himself as an American, because he was able to see his homeland and his heritage from the outside. He made many friends in artistic circles and worked hard at his music.

While in Paris, Thomson studied with the famous teacher Nadia Boulanger. Although she was very strict when it came to such basic disciplines as harmony, counterpoint, and fugue, she nonetheless gave him a freedom in composing such as he had never enjoyed previously. At Harvard he had been made to feel, when he wrote a piece, that he was competing with the great masters of the past, and that compared to them he had little that was worth saying. Mlle. Boulanger, on the other hand, was able to make him feel that what he had to say was very much worth saying as long as he said it clearly and sincerely. A young composer, she insisted, was not supposed to imitate the classics but to develop his own powers of musical expression.

After his return to Harvard in 1922, Thomson became assistant conductor of the Glee Club. He taught in the music department, played the organ at King's Chapel, and gave concerts of modern French music at the Harvard Musical Club. After his graduation from Harvard, there came a year of study in New York. He then returned to Harvard as an assistant instructor. That year saw an important new development in his career. He began to write articles about music for the magazine *Vanity Fair*. He revealed such skill in writing about music that his friends were convinced he ought to become a music critic. To which Thomson replied, "My business is making music, not talking about it."

In 1925 Thomson was offered a job teaching music in a university and a post as organist of a large church in Kansas City. But he had a much better idea. With five hundred dollars in his pocket and a third-class ticket, he sailed for France. He was going back to Paris to try to establish himself as a composer. As he put it, if he was going to starve, he "preferred to starve where the food was good."

Paris in the mid-twenties was one of the most stimulating spots in the world. Here were gathered representatives of the modern movements in painting, poetry, and music. Thomson soon found his way into the most advanced intellectual circles of the French

79

capital. During the fifteen years that he spent in Paris, he became friends with such artists as the novelist André Gide, the painter Pablo Picasso, the poet Jean Cocteau, and the American novelists Ernest Hemingway and F. Scott Fitzgerald. He acquired a knowledge of literature and painting most unusual for a musician. This breadth of view was apparent in the articles he wrote for such periodicals as *Vanity Fair*, the *New Republic*, and the *American Mercury*. During his years abroad Thomson carried out his intention of letting Paris know how people felt back home in Kansas City. In his *Symphony on a Hymn Tune* (1928) he combined the advanced musical techniques of Parisian musicians with the hymns and folk songs he remembered from Missouri.

An event of far-reaching importance was his meeting with the American writer Gertrude Stein. Miss Stein was famous for a special kind of writing: she used words for their sound and color rather than for their meaning, combining them in the most unexpected ways. She achieved thereby the same effects of shock and surprise that Picasso and other Cubist painters achieved by breaking up familiar objects and combining them in new patterns. Thomson had admired Miss Stein's remarkable prose-poetry while he was still in Harvard and had set some of her poems to music. Now that they were friends, it occurred to them that they might unite their talents. The result was the opera *Four Saints in Three Acts*, which created a sensation when it was presented in 1934, first in Hartford, Connecticut, then in New York.

The remarkable acting, singing, and dancing of the Negro cast; the imaginative costumes and stage sets—a fantasy of cellophane, crystal, and feathers—by the painter Florine Stettheimer; the combination of Gertrude Stein's disconnected lines and Thomson's flowing melodies made for a musical show of the most extraordinary originality. Nobody quite knew what the opera was about except the Stein experts (and there weren't many of those!). The opening chorus, a vigorous waltzlike movement, was sung to the following mysterious lines:

To know to know to love her so.
Four saints prepare for saints.
It makes it well fish.
Four saints it makes it well fish.
For saints prepare for saints it makes it well well fish prepare for saints. . . .

No less mystifying was Miss Stein's famous "Pigeons on the grass alas. . . . Shorter longer grass short longer longer shorter yellow grass. Pigeons large pigeons on the shorter longer yellow grass alas pigeons on the grass. . . ." All this set to perfectly simple tunes, as if it were the most sensible material in the world. The surprise, the vitality and freshness of the production enchanted its audiences. *Four Saints in Three Acts* made operatic history. It ran up sixty performances in one year, a record for American opera. It was broadcast, it was recorded, it was performed in Europe. And it made Virgil Thomson famous.

In the next years he divided his time between Paris and New York. This period in his life came to an end in 1940, when Hitler conquered France. Thomson left the beautiful city on the Seine shortly before the Nazis marched in. His return to the United States opened a new chapter. He became chief music critic for the *New York Herald Tribune* and soon established himself as one of the most penetrating chroniclers of the musical scene. He was outspoken in his judgments and, a great virtue in a critic, he was not afraid to be wrong. In other words, he was not afraid of taking a stand as to what he believed, instead of hedging and trying to play it safe. He had his prejudices and his blind spots. But even those musicians who disagreed with his columns could not resist reading them.

There were several reasons for Thomson's success as a critic. In the first place, he complimented his readers by never writing down to them. In the second, he approached his task with enormous gusto. In the third, he brought into his writing the spirit of a brilliant performance. As he himself said, writing a review "is something like giving a concert. Of course there is no Carnegie Hall glamor and that sort of thing, but there is a certain resemblance. It is a 'quick' thing like a concert. In the space of two or three hours you hear some music, you rush off to your office and (in solitude and silence, to be sure) you write your piece about it; presently the paper appears—and there you are! It is really a kind of performance."

Early in his career as a critic Thomson let it be known that he considered a concert to be news only if it offered some new artist or some new music. In this way Thomson rendered a great service to the cause of contemporary music. Many pianists, violinists, cellists, singers, and conductors who for years had been repeating the same pieces over and over, went looking for new material in the hope of luring him to their performances. Many of them commissioned new works: that is to say, they asked a composer to write a piece specially for their New York concert, and paid him for it.

His first book, *The State of Music* (1939) was followed by three others: *The Musical Scene* (1945); *The Art of Judging Music* (1948); and *Music Right and Left* (1951). These show his personal blend of seriousness and wit. Almost any page communicates the special flavor of his prose. For example, in reviewing a concert by the New York Philharmonic he reported that the conductor, Dimitri Mitropoulos, "for the most part did everything to the orchestra but conduct it. He whipped it up as if it were a cake, kneaded it like bread, shuffled and riffled an imaginary deck of cards, wound up a clock, shook an umbrella, rubbed something on a washboard and wrung it out. There were few moments when a film taken of him alone, without sound, would have given any clue to the fact that he was directing a musical composition." Of the French composer Claude Debussy: "He did not sculpt in music or build architectural monuments. He only painted. And no two of his canvases are alike. That France, classically the land of freedom, should have produced a model of musical freedom is only natural. All the same, Debussy, even for France, is something of a miracle. His music is not only an ultimate, for our century, of sheer beauty. It is a lesson to us all in how to make use of our liberty." Of the celebrated operetta *La Vie parisienne* (Parisian Life) by Jacques Offenbach: "It is a crown of waltzes picked out with polkas and quadrilles and interwoven with melodies that distill the tender sentiment, the whole tied up with a great big lacy ribbon in the form of a cancan. And the melodies are as fresh as the day they were picked; the rhythm pops like champagne."

Thomson belongs to that group among American artists who found themselves through contact with French civilization. Paris revealed to them the clarity and directness of the Latin spirit in art, its fine taste and wit, its careful avoidance of everything that is overblown and pretentious. Paris freed them from provincialism and forced them to measure themselves against the craftsmanship of a great tradition. Yet, like Aaron Copland and Ernest Hemingway, who also served their apprenticeship in Paris, Thomson at heart remained an American. His music is rooted in the hymns and folk tunes, the Civil War melodies and popular waltzes amid which he grew up. His direct, forthright melodies, supported by plain harmonies, are altogether American in character. Thus Thomson's music represents an unusual mixture of Parisian sophistication and good American homespun.

When Thomson first came to Paris, modern composers, in their need to leave behind the outworn ways of nineteenth-century romanticism, were emphasizing emotional detachment, technique, and objective forms rather than personal expression and lyricism. Thomson embraced this trend. However, as the years passed his warm lyrical nature impelled him in another direction. He found his true path in the camp of a new romanticism which, as he explains, aims "to express sincere personal sentiments with a maximum of directness and spontaneity." Music, he felt, had been taking itself too seriously; it had become too complex, too intellectual. Now it had to learn to relax. Accordingly, he wrote music that was simple and elegant, that would entertain and please, and that would not be above spoofing itself occasionally. He had talent as a humorist to begin with. He developed a gift for parody and satire that endeared him to those listeners who enjoy a good musical joke.

The list of Thomson's compositions shows his activity in all branches of his art. The *Symphony on a Hymn Tune* (1928) was followed in 1931 by a Symphony No. 2 which, like its predecessor, is based on American folk material. Two symphonic "landscapes" pay homage, respectively, to Paris and Missouri: *The Seine at Night* (1947), and *Wheat Field at Noon* (1948). To these the composer added *Sea Piece with Birds* (1952). A melodious Concerto for Cello and Orchestra (1950) has been widely played. Among his piano compositions are four short sonatas. His chamber music includes two string quartets. His four sets of Variations and Fugues on Gospel Hymns, for the organ, are a worthy addition to the literature of that instrument, which is so neglected nowadays.

Thomson has produced much vocal music to French and English texts. His ear is remarkably sensitive to the inflections of American speech. He sets our language with great felicity, letting the words float on the music without ever submerging them. Thomson's association with Gertrude Stein resulted in a second opera, *The Mother of Us All* (1947), based on the life and career of the feminist leader Susan B. Anthony. Characters from different decades of American history are brought together in this work. General Grant declares gravely, in excellent Steinese, "As long as I sit I am sitting." Miss Anthony sings with conviction, "You're entirely right but I disagree with you," and is informed that "a Cause is a Cause because." Thomson's collaboration with Miss Stein came to an end with her death. One wonders what their next opera would have been like.

Thomson is particularly vivid in his film music. The concert suites that he fashioned from his music for *The Plough That Broke the Plains* (1936), *The River* (1937), and *Louisiana Story* (1948) are among his most widely played works. *Louisiana Story,* which was written for Robert Flaherty's documentary film, offers a fine introduction to Virgil Thomson's music. The film deals with the coming of the oil industry to the bayou country, as seen through the eyes of a boy. It shows what happens when modern industrialization invades a rural area where simple folk have lived quietly for generations. The concert suite consists of four pieces.

1. *Pastoral* (The Bayou and the Marsh Buggy). This is a descriptive piece which, in the film, accompanies the boy as he paddles his canoe through his beloved bayou. The music evokes a quiet, lonely landscape of giant trees, sky, and water. The mood is projected through an old Louisiana folk tune played by the English horn. The music becomes louder and faster—what is known as a *crescendo* and *accelerando*—as the boy's canoe approaches the marsh buggy (an amphibious tractor used in oil prospecting). The swell of the water almost overturns the canoe.

2. *Chorale* (The Derrick Arrives). A chorale is a hymn tune, or a melody-and-chords in the style of a hymn. The stately chorale in this piece is associated with the derrick that is used in pumping the oil. It is preceded by a lively folk song; the two themes are used in alternation. The chorale expresses the boy's wonder as

85

he gazes at the lofty mesh of steel that thrusts against the sky.

3. *Passacaglia* (Robbing the Alligator's Nest). A passacaglia—pronounced *pah-sa-cah'-lya*—is a piece of music in which a short melody or theme in the bass is repeated over and over while the voices above it weave a pattern of countermelodies, that is, melodies against the theme. Thomson's Passacaglia accompanies the exciting scene in which the boy decides to steal the alligator's eggs and is suddenly confronted by the angry beast. The theme, announced *pianissimo* (very soft) by the violas, cellos, and double basses, builds suspense as it is repeated again and again, while the other instruments trace ever-fresh patterns against it.

4. *Fugue* (Boy Fights Alligator). A fugue is a polyphonic composition (see Glossary) which is generally in three or four voices. The theme or subject of the fugue is stated at the outset in one voice—say, the soprano—then in the other voices, such as the alto, tenor, or bass. The theme reappears throughout the fugue, now in one voice, now in another, against counterthemes in the other voices. The Fugue from *Louisiana Story* accompanies the dramatic struggle that forms the climax of the film. The alligator tries to drag the boy into the swamp. He is finally rescued by his father. The theme is announced by bassoons, trombones, and tuba, and is then imitated by the other instruments of the orchestra, with steadily mounting tension. The harmonies communicate the excitement of the scene as the boy fights for his life.

The creator of this thoroughly attractive work played an important part in our musical life at a time when the battle for American music still had to be won. Despite his being a citizen of the world, he has retained his affection for his American background, for his homeland and its past.

His music is pervaded by a great longing and tenderness. Longing is one of the prime traits of the romantic artist. Virgil Thomson is in every sense of the term an American romantic.

86

8. ROY HARRIS

Roy Harris burst upon our musical scene in the 1930s as a home-spun, outspoken young man from the West who boldly upheld his American heritage. When he appeared on the stage to take a bow he looked, as one commentator put it, "like a mid-western farmer in city clothes." With his spare frame, soft drawl, and inexhaustible energy, he captured the imagination of his countrymen and was soon hailed everywhere as the most American of our composers.

Harris was born on Lincoln's Birthday, 1898, in Lincoln County, Oklahoma. "Ever since," he says, "the shadow of Abe Lincoln has remained with me." He came of pioneer stock. His parents, who were of Scotch-Irish extraction, had traveled by ox-cart and staked out their claim to a homestead. They cut down the trees, built the log cabin in which the future composer was born, and went into farming. When Roy was five years old his mother's health began to fail. His parents moved to Southern California, where life was easier, and established themselves near Los Angeles.

Great changes were taking place in California in the early years of our century. Roy witnessed, as he later wrote, "the end of the pioneer days and the beginning of commercial standardized America." The Harris home contained the only piano in the neighborhood. Roy would listen to his mother play and was fascinated by the sounds she drew from the instrument. His mother gave him his first lessons. "Then a teacher came to the house each week. Soon I was performing in public." But the boys with whom he attended the Covina Public School felt that only sissies were interested in music. "I became very sensitive," the composer recalls, "about the disapproval which my schoolmates showed after each concert." It became important for him to prove to his friends that he was a regular guy, so he gave up the piano and played football. Then he broke his arm and permanently injured one of the fingers of his right hand—which ended his career as a pianist.

When he reached high school his interest in music reawakened. He became a member of a small group that met every week to discuss literature and art, music and philosophy. He and his new friends took long walks together. They often went into Los Angeles to hear a concert or an opera. Through this band of kindred souls Roy found, as he described it, "faith in beauty, peace of mind, ideas, spiritual aspirations, and individuality." Yet he grew more and more aware that his friends lived like exiles in their little town. Their interests had nothing in common with the practical, everyday life that surrounded them. "As I finished high school my world was dividing into two parts. Music, philosophy, poetry, the wonder of clouds, mountains, bird songs and sunsets— all belonged to a beckoning, unknown world; while the farming and bank account belonged to a very sure, well-known world which laughed at the other and slept and worked and ate between the Fourth of July, Thanksgiving and Christmas."

Roy tried to follow in his father's footsteps and became a farmer. At this time our country entered the First World War. Roy enlisted in the artillery and spent an unhappy year trying to adjust to army life. When the war was over he found it just as difficult to adjust to civilian life. He could not decide what to do; he was driven by a strange restlessness. He wanted to see things and to find out about life for himself. For a time he drifted from place to place, bumming his way across the country. He slept in haystacks and on park benches, did odd jobs to keep body and soul together. On one occasion he worked as a gatekeeper for a rodeo. Finally he decided to study at the University of California in Los Angeles. "I turned to college to search for the truth," he relates. But the things he learned there failed to satisfy him.

Roy was now twenty-two, and felt that he was getting nowhere. He decided to leave college and took a job as a truck-driver for a dairy company, delivering milk, eggs, and butter. His interest in music was growing by leaps and bounds. He wanted to hear as much of it as possible. As he could not afford to buy tickets to concerts, he worked at night as an usher in the Los Angeles Auditorium. Those years were not very eventful outwardly. Yet, he remembers, "they were years crowded with enthusiasms. Each new harmony, each new melody, each composer I discovered was a milestone for me."

But it was not enough for him to listen to the music that other men had written. He felt within himself a desire—vague and obscure at first, yet more and more insistent—to create melodies and harmonies of his own. He was twenty-four when he finally decided to become a composer. He studied with various musicians in Los Angeles until he found the teacher who was right for him. Arthur Farwell, a composer himself, gave Harris a thorough grounding in the fundamentals of composition. Farwell believed in Harris's talent, encouraged him in every way, and was convinced that he had a brilliant career ahead of him.

Harris's first attempts at composition were crude and halting. But he made up in ambition for what he lacked in experience, and went from one piece to the next in a roughhewn style that had in it an elemental power all its own.

When Harris finished his first composition for orchestra, an

89

Andante, his teacher was so enthusiastic about it that he persuaded the conductor Willem van Hoogstraten to perform it at one of the concerts in the Hollywood Bowl. The manuscript was so poorly written that when Hoogstraten received it he almost decided not to play the piece. However, he soon came to like it so much that he not only presented it in Hollywood but repeated it that summer with the New York Philharmonic Orchestra at the Lewisohn Stadium.

Meanwhile the Andante for Orchestra had come to the notice of Howard Hanson, the dynamic conductor of the Rochester Symphony. Hanson decided to play it with his orchestra and wrote Harris a letter inviting him to Rochester to hear the work. Harris left California thinking that he would be gone for two weeks. He stayed away for five years. The Andante made a deep impression upon all who heard it. Suddenly the musical world became aware of a new voice from the West. Harris, who had no money to live on, was invited to stay at the MacDowell Colony. At the end of the summer, through the generosity of some wealthy music lovers, he was given the opportunity to continue his studies in Paris.

His friends had advised him to study with the famous Nadia Boulanger. Harris lost no time in presenting himself at her studio. He was not an easy pupil to work with, for he had definite ideas on how he should go about improving his technique. He was convinced that the best way to do this was not through exercises in harmony and counterpoint, but through actual composition—by writing down the music that he felt was in him. Mlle. Boulanger, he confesses, "had the patience of an angel." Although she believed wholeheartedly in the value of discipline, she did not try to force him into a mold that did not suit his personality. Instead she allowed her unruly pupil to develop in his own way. In time he came around to her point of view. He discovered the string quartets of Beethoven from which he learned, he tells us, "about the passion and discipline of uninterrupted eloquence." He studied these great works day and night. As a result he became, as he says, "a profound believer in discipline and form."

During his first year abroad Harris wrote the Concerto for Piano, Clarinet, and String Quartet, which added greatly to his reputation. The piece brought him a Guggenheim Fellowship. Harris was one of the first musicians to benefit from these fellowships, which made it possible for him to remain in Paris for two more years. His stay abroad was cut short by an accident: he slipped on a stairway and fell on his back, breaking three vertebrae. He was brought back to the United States on a stretcher and was operated on in a New York hospital. For six months he lay flat on his back in a plaster cast, but he continued to compose. In later years Harris looked upon this accident as a blessing in disguise, for it taught him to write music without relying on a piano. As a result, he achieved a freedom he could not have found in any other way.

When he returned to California he had to face the fact that he was not going to be able to support himself by composing. A composer, Harris realized, was supposed to earn a living by teaching in a school, or playing in an orchestra, or working as an arranger. He was expected to compose in his spare time, as though writing music were a hobby or a luxury. "Of course, if I could have the energy left to write a few little piano pieces and songs or even some choruses not too difficult to perform, that would boost my value as a teacher." Harris was determined not to accept this state of affairs. He had decided that composing would be his main activity, not a sideline. At this juncture his problem was solved for him in a most opportune way. He was awarded a fellowship of two thousand dollars by a group of art-loving citizens of Pasadena, which made it possible for him to throw himself into creative work.

Yet he was not satisfied with this stroke of luck. He was deeply troubled by the fact that composing serious music was not looked upon in America as a profession. He had worked just as hard to become a composer as did a doctor or lawyer when they prepared for their professions; yet so far he had never received any money for his music. He had been taught to believe that a composer stood above money, relying—if he was lucky—on fellowships or the generosity of patrons. But Harris did not want to be supported any more by grants and fellowships. He wanted to practice his profession just as a doctor or lawyer did. He gave up his fellowship and came to New York with five dollars in his pocket. At last he understood what was wrong with the composer's position in our society. "I walked the streets watching the janitors, the cops, the garbage men. It suddenly occurred to me that I was living in a twentieth-century civilization where cops and janitors and everyone else got paid for being what they were. Everybody except composers. So I decided never to write again except for a fixed sum of money agreed upon in advance." It took courage to reach such a decision, and even greater courage to stick to it. But he did. "I have proved that a composer of serious music can get paid for his work." Roy Harris considers this to be one of his main achievements.

In the early 1930s Harris became *the* American composer. The time was ripe for him. Performances, broadcasts, commissions, and awards came to him from all sides. Part of his popularity was due to the fact that he was the first of our composers to bridge the gap between modern music and the general public. At that time many composers were writing an advanced kind of music which only a select minority of music lovers could understand. But Harris was trying to produce works that, even though they remained on a high level, would have meaning for the country at large. Besides, he was able to talk about his aims in down-to-earth language that made sense to the man in the street. "If nobody bought corn and wheat it meant that the corn and wheat were bad. Music wasn't much different. To buy music people had to like it. For them to like it, it had to be good. If it weren't good no one would buy it." His countrymen enjoyed knowing that, even though he had achieved fame and success, deep down in his heart Roy Harris was still "the Oklahoma farm boy who gave up chickens for music."

Yet there was another side to Harris's complex personality. He could also write about his art in altogether different terms, with an almost mystical exaltation. "The creative impulse is a desire to capture and communicate feeling. Call that feeling what you will. Call it romantic fervor—call it a longing for Truth . . . Always it is a lonesome hunger that gnaws within the human heart, forcing us to search for understandable expression." When an artist, Harris explained, translates his creative impulse into a work of art, he gives shape to all the wonderful forces that lie hidden in the human spirit. "It is small wonder then that humanity regards the creative impulse as sacred."

Harris's wife Johana is an accomplished pianist. She has played her husband's piano pieces in concerts and has recorded them. Roy and Johana Harris have been very happy together, for they share their musical as well as their personal interests. For several years they presented an educational series on the radio, "Let's Make Music," that attracted wide attention. They have three children, Paddy, Sharen, and Daniel. Harris and his family have moved from place to place, as he has been connected with a number of colleges—Cornell University, Colorado College, Utah State College, Peabody College for Teachers, and other institutions. Harris does not like to become a regular member of a college faculty, as this might involve him in all kinds of duties that would interfere with his composing. He prefers to serve as "composer-in-residence": a kind of visiting professor who guides a few advanced pupils without becoming a full member of the staff. For a time he tried out an interesting experiment in education. He had a few gifted pupils live with him and his wife. They helped him by doing all kinds of musical chores, such as copying out the parts of his scores; in other words, they served as apprentices. It was precisely in this way, of course, that the great painters of the Renaissance taught their pupils.

Harris is a spontaneous artist who yields completely to his inner impulse. His music is extremely lyrical and owes its appeal to its freshness and enthusiasm. There is a certain roughness in his style that is part and parcel of his way of expressing himself, like the roughness in the poetry of Carl Sandburg or in the prose of Theodore Dreiser. His music is American in its buoyancy and drive, its expansiveness and manly strength. It has zest and emotional sweep; it is warm and compassionate.

Harris is clear about his direction as an artist. "I am trying," he states, "to write a music which expresses our time and period in America and which is serviceable to our musical life. By serviceable I mean music which effectively uses the instrumental and choral and other resources available at present." For example, he wrote his *Folksong Symphony* "so that the adults and young people of our cities could sing and play the folk songs of our nation for pleasure. I wrote the choral parts for the range of good high school choruses, with the thought in mind that such choruses might have a work to prepare with the symphony orchestras of their cities." He maintains that there are many ways of being American in music. An American artist has to express the spirit of our country according to the region from which he comes and which he knows with every fiber of his being. "What I am trying to say in music is related principally to the region of the West where I was born and where I understand life best."

Harris is at his most effective in the large forms of instrumental music. In this he is a classicist. His seven symphonies occupy the central position in his output. The First was written in 1933. The

Third (1938) is one of the finest symphonies yet written by an American. The final passage strikes the epic tone in its power and majesty. As one critic wrote, it echoes "the dark fastness of the American soul, its despair and its courage, its defeat and its triumph." The Fourth is the *Folksong Symphony* (1940), a fantasy for chorus and orchestra on American popular tunes. In his Fifth Symphony (1942), which was written in time of war, Harris tried to portray "the qualities of heroic strength—determination—will to struggle—faith in our destiny" which struck him as the essence of the American character. The Sixth (1944), based on Lincoln's Gettysburg Address, was dedicated to "the Armed Forces of Our Nation." Both the Fifth and Sixth Symphonies were broadcast to our armies in Europe and Africa during the Second World War. Harris received many letters of appreciation from soldiers and sailors who were moved by his music. He treasured these letters, for they made him feel, more than anything else could possibly have done, that he had truly reached his audience. His Seventh Symphony was written in 1951.

Chamber music occupies an important place in Harris's output. Among his chamber works are the Quintet for Piano and Strings (1936) and Third String Quartet (1937). His piano music includes the suite *Children at Play* (1942), which has been recorded by Johana Harris. Two major choral works, the *Song for Occupations* (1934) and *Symphony for Voices* (1935), are on texts by Walt Whitman, a poet to whom Harris feels very close. Whitman's poetry also inspired *American Creed* (1940) and *Walt Whitman Suite* (1944). Harris has written music for the stage, films, and ballet; but his imagination does not take to the kind of music that evokes specific images and situations. He is at his best in the realm of "pure" or absolute music—music that is concerned primarily with the statement and development of musical themes, without trying to suggest a specific story, scene, or mood.

The *Folksong Symphony* offers a fine introduction to Harris's music. In discussing this work the composer stated, "I was brought up with simple folk attitudes by my pioneer parents. Folk music was as natural to our way of life as corn bread and sweet milk. My mother played the guitar and we hummed along with her after supper on the front porch or in the kitchen. We whistled folk songs as we worked on the farm. When I began to study music, I decided that composers were folk singers who had learned to write down the songs that took their fancy; and that therefore folk songs could be recast to suit a composer's purpose, and that they could be legitimately used to generate symphonic forms." Harris goes on to say: "I wrote my *Folksong Symphony* in 1940, when our nation was deeply committed in World War II, and I conceived a form that reflected the feelings of the time." Because he wanted his listeners to share these feelings, he picked famous folk songs from different parts of the country that are known to all. Here is the composer's description of his symphony:

"First Movement. *The Girl I Left Behind Me.* This is a Civil War song which is sung in the spirit of bravado to keep up the courage of both the young men and the young women whom war has parted. It should be sung in the gayest of moods."

If ever I travel this road again and tears don't fall and blind me,
I'm goin' back to Tennessee, to the gal I left behind me.
    Oh the pretty little gal, the sweet little gal, the gal he left behind him;
    With rosy cheeks and curly hair, the gal he left behind him.

If ever I travel this road again and angels they don't blind me,
I'll reconcile and stay awhile with the gal I left behind me.
    Oh the pretty little gal, the sweet little gal, the gal he left behind him;
    With rosy cheeks and curly hair, the gal he left behind him.

I'll cross Red River one more time, if tears don't fall and drown me;

A-weepin' for that pretty little gal, the gal I left behind me.
(Refrain)
I'll build my nest in a hollow tree where cuckoos they won't find
me,
I'll go right back to see that gal, the gal I left behind me.
(Refrain)

"Second Movement. *Western Cowboy*. This movement uses
three well-known Western folk songs: *Oh Bury Me Not on the
Lone Prairie*, *The Old Chisholm Trail*, and *Laredo*. These three
songs characterize the lonesomeness, hilarity, and tragedy which
the early Western cowboys lived with every day."

"Oh, bury me not on the lone prairie."
These words came low and mournfully
From pallid lips of a youth who lay
On his lone bed at break of day.

He wailed in pain till o'er his brow
Death's shadows fast were gath'ring now.
He thought of home and his lov'd ones nigh
As cowboys gather'd to see him die.

As I recall the well-known words
Of free wild wind and the song of birds,
I think of home in the shady bower
And scenes I've loved in childhood's hour.

It matters not, I've oft been told,
Where the body lies when the heart grows cold.
Oh bury me not on the lone prairie
In a narrow grave six foot by three,
Where buffalo paws o'er prairie sea;
Oh bury me not on the lone prairie. . . .

. . . .

97

As I walked out in the street of Laredo,
As I walked out in Laredo one day,
I spied a poor cowboy wrapped up in white linen,
Wrapped up in white linen as cold as the clay.

"I see by your outfit that you are a cowboy;"
These words he did say as I boldly stepped by.
"Come sit down beside me and hear my sad story
I'm shot in the breast and I know I must die. . . .

Oh, beat the drum slowly and play the fife lowly,
Play the dead march as you carry me along;
Take me to the valley and lay the sod o'er me;
I'm a young cowboy and know I've done wrong."

"Third Movement. First Interlude for String Orchestra and Percussion. This is a dance for fiddles and is naturally made from a combination of many fiddle tunes of the early pioneer days.

"Fourth Movement. *Mountaineer Love Song*. A love song from the life of the mountain folk of the South, based on the tune *He's Gone Away*, possessing both the pathos and the savage wildness which characterizes these passionate people."

I'm goin' away for to stay a little while.
But I'm comin' back if I go ten thousand miles.
Oh, who will bind your hair, and who will glove your hands,
And who will kiss your ruby lips when I am gone?
Oh, Pappy'll tie my shoes, and Mammy'll glove my hands,
And you will kiss my ruby lips when you come back.

"Fifth Movement. The Second Interlude for Orchestra. A gay work using the folk song *Jump Up My Lady*, and a dance tune which is a composite of many fiddle tunes.

"Sixth Movement. Negro Fantasy. Two Negro Spirituals, *Little Boy Named David* and *De Trumpet Sounds It In My Soul*, from the deep South of long-standing tradition, are used in this movement."

> De trumpet sounds it in my soul.
> Lawd! Lawd! De trumpet sounds it in my soul.
> I ain't got long to stay here.
> De trumpet sounds it in my soul.

"Seventh Movement. *Johnny Comes Marching Home*. This is, of course, the famous song that came out of the Civil War. In it I hoped to capture the spirit of exhilaration and joy which our people would feel when the men came home from war."

> When Johnny comes marching home again, Hurrah! Hurrah!
> We'll give him a hearty welcome then, Hurrah! Hurrah!
> The men will cheer, the boys will shout,
> The ladies they will all turn out.
> And we'll all feel gay when Johnny comes marching home. . . .

The creator of this rousing work has succeeded remarkably well in capturing in his music the spirit of the American scene. Roy Harris has played a significant role in the development of our country's music.

9. GEORGE GERSHWIN

George Gershwin has become something of a legend. He is the most widely played among modern American composers; and not even his most enthusiastic admirers could have foreseen that, a quarter-century after his death, he would become a world figure.

He was born in Brooklyn, New York, on September 26, 1898, the son of Russian-Jewish immigrants. The family moved to Manhattan; George grew up on the lower East Side. He was a restless, dynamic boy who loved games and sports. School he regarded as a bore, and he was frequently taken to task for failing to do his homework, misbehaving in class, or getting into scrapes. He showed no interest in music when he was young, especially since the boys of his neighborhood regarded anybody who studied music as a sissy. Yet on the rare occasions when he heard music, he found himself drawn to it almost against his will.

One day, when he was ten, he heard a schoolmate play Dvořák's *Humoresque* on the violin. "It was to me," he remembered in later years, "a flashing revelation of beauty. I made up my mind to get acquainted with this fellow, and I waited outside from three to four-thirty that afternoon, in the hopes of greeting him. It was pouring cats and dogs, and I got soaked to the skin." The boy, Max Rosen, who later won fame as a violinist, opened up the world of music for George. They became inseparable companions.

Under the influence of this friendship George was soon trying to make up his own melodies. He brought one of these to Max, who told him with an air of certainty: "You haven't got it in you to be a musician, George. Take my word for it. I know."

Despite this admonition, George was not to be dissuaded. Soon afterward a piano arrived at the Gershwin household on Second Avenue. Mrs. Gershwin had bought it for George's older brother Ira, who was a quiet, studious boy. Ira soon tired of the piano lessons, but George was fascinated by the instrument from the start. He amused himself by picking out tunes on the keyboard. Then he began to take lessons. He threw himself into his musical studies with an intensity that he had shown, till then, only in his games and sports. He learned not only by practicing, but also by going to concerts. By the time he was fourteen he was a devoted concert-goer. "I listened not only with my ears," he recalled in later life, "but also with my nerves, my mind, my heart. I listened so earnestly that I became saturated with music. Then I went home and listened in memory. I sat at the piano and repeated the motives." Before long he outgrew the neighborhood teacher. When he was fourteen a friend took him to the studio of Charles Hambitzer, a dedicated musician who was impressed by George's talent and gave him a firm foundation in all branches of the art.

At this time George entered the High School of Commerce. He appeared as a pianist at the school assemblies. The following summer he took a job at a summer resort in the Catskill Mountains, playing the piano for the munificent sum of five dollars a week. That year he wrote his first song, *Since I Found You*, which was never published. George was fascinated by popular music. He was a passionate admirer of Irving Berlin, whose first big hit, *Alexander's Ragtime Band*, was sweeping the country. "This is American music," he told his teacher, who looked down on popular music and jazz. "This is the kind of music I want to write."

George was determined to find a job in Tin Pan Alley. This was the name given to the neighborhood in New York City where the publishers of popular songs had their offices. Tin Pan Alley originally was off Broadway on Twenty-Eighth Street. Later it extended roughly from Forty-Eighth to Fifty-Second Street along Seventh Avenue, in the Times Square district. The song publishers located in this area were building a powerful industry based on the sale of sheet music throughout the country. This sale reached impressive figures at a time when millions of homes had pianos. Tin Pan Alley was the natural goal of every aspiring song writer. George felt that if he could work for a publisher of popular music he would learn his profession from the ground up.

His mother wanted him to finish high school and then enter the fur business. Again and again she pointed out to him the un-certainties that every musician faced. But George had made up his mind. He left the High School of Commerce when he was fifteen. A friend of the family introduced him to the manager of Remick's, one of the most enterprising song-publishing houses of the day. George was given a job and became the youngest song-plugger (or "piano-pounder") in Tin Pan Alley, at a salary of fifteen dollars a week.

Today it is the disc jockey who helps to make a song popular. In those days it was the song-plugger, whose duty it was to play the songs published by his company for those who could make it popular—singers, actors, vaudeville stars, leaders of dance bands and restaurant orchestras, singing waiters, managers of theaters, and the owners of the stores that sold sheet music. During his years at Remick's George was able to learn the song-publishing business in all its aspects. Most important, he was establishing his reputation in a world where he knew he belonged. He carefully studied the songs of Irving Berlin and Jerome Kern, the two com-posers he admired most, then tried to write his own songs. But when he showed them to his employer at Remick's, he received no encouragement. "You're paid to play the piano, not to write songs," he was told. "We've plenty of song writers under contract." He persevered, however, and before long his first song was published. It was called *When You Want 'Em, You Can't Get 'Em,* and it brought him exactly five dollars.

During his first attempts as a song writer, George diligently continued to study the piano, harmony, theory, and orchestration. He realized that the popular song in this country was entering upon a new era. The older generation of song writers had been men like Irving Berlin, who possessed no formal musical training. They were essentially folk singers who had only their talent to guide them. Now, however, the time was ripe for a new type of song writer: a trained musician who could bring to his tunes all the techniques and resources of classical music. One day, in his cubicle at Remick's, George startled the other song-pluggers by practicing a Prelude and Fugue from Bach's *Well-Tempered Clavier.* "Are you studying to be a concert pianist?" he was asked. "No," he answered. "I'm studying to be a great popular-song composer."

In 1917 George left Remick's. He had learned all that Tin Pan Alley could teach him. His next objective was Broadway. He found a job at Fox's City Theater where he was supposed to accompany the vaudeville acts during the supper hour when the orchestra went out to eat. George reported for work in a hopeful mood. He did quite well for the first few acts, particularly since some of the numbers were Remick songs. But when the headline act came on, he had to read at sight from a manuscript—and missed his cue. He suddenly realized that he was playing one song while the chorus was singing another. The comedian made some wisecracks about the piano player; the audience began to laugh; and George fled from the pit, overwhelmed by embarrassment.

He then became a rehearsal pianist for the musical show *Miss 1917* and enjoyed close contact with his idol, the composer Jerome Kern, who had written several numbers for the show. Often, after rehearsal, he would remain at the piano, playing his own songs, while the members of the cast listened, spellbound. He had a wonderful sense of rhythm when he played; and he introduced all kinds of unexpected melodies and off-beat rhythms in the bass, which he made up on the spur of the moment to embellish the main tune in the right hand. Those who heard him at these impromptu recitals felt that it was only a matter of time before this talented young man made his mark.

The manager of *Miss 1917* was so impressed by George that he introduced him to Max Dreyfus, head of the publishing house of T. B. Harms and the most powerful man in the popular-song business. Dreyfus listened carefully while the young composer described the kind of song he hoped to write. Then Dreyfus came forth with an unusual offer. George was to receive thirty-five dollars a week as a drawing account. All he had to do in return was to continue writing songs and to submit them to Dreyfus. In later years Dreyfus was often pointed out as the man who discovered George. Dreyfus's comment is illuminating: "A man with Gershwin's talent did not need anybody to push him ahead. His talent did all the pushing."

It was in 1919 that George Gershwin's career hit its stride. He was twenty-one; he had just completed the score for *La La Lucille*, his first Broadway show; and he produced his first song hit. *Swanee* was introduced at the Capitol Theater in New York by Arthur Pryor's band. Night after night Gershwin and Irving Caesar, the author of the words, stood outside the theater to watch the sale of the sheet music in the lobby. Only a few copies of the song were sold. Caesar was so discouraged that he was willing, one evening, to sell his rights to the lyrics for two hundred dollars to anyone who would buy them. But Gershwin dissuaded him.

That same night Al Jolson, the famous singer, gave a party to which he had invited Gershwin. In the course of the evening Gershwin played his new song. Jolson liked it so much that he decided to sing it at the Winter Garden. *Swanee* brought down the house.

Jolson next introduced the song into his hit show *Sinbad*. Now *Swanee* caught on and swept the country like wildfire. Over two million records of the song and one million copies of sheet music were sold in that year. George Gershwin came into his own as one of the most gifted song writers this country had produced.

In the next five years the *George White Scandals* provided an ideal showcase for his songs. The *Scandals* were lavish spectacles that competed with the *Ziegfeld Follies* for the favor of the New York public. Of the many songs that he wrote for the *Scandals*, several—such as *Somebody Loves Me* (1924)—bear the true Gershwin stamp; that is, the melody is highly original, marked by a powerful rhythmic thrust, and wreathed in an atmosphere of devil-may-care gayety and charm.

During these years George found his ideal lyricist in his brother Ira. Ira's smooth, clever lyrics provided the perfect framework for the subtle type of song that George was trying to create. The two brothers worked together in perfect harmony. In the course of their long collaboration, the brotherly love they felt for one another was enriched by a deep respect for each other's talents.

Gershwin's career unfolded at a crucial moment in the history of American music. On the one hand our composers were strongly under the influence of the European tradition. On the other, they were trying to find their way to a musical language that would be specifically American. Yet most serious musicians in America looked down on jazz and the tunes of Tin Pan Alley. They built up a forbidding wall between "classical" and "jazz." Gershwin saw that jazz and classical were not necessarily opposed to one another. It was his great achievement to realize that, on the contrary, each might be used to enrich the other. As he put it, "Jazz is music. It uses the same notes as Bach used."

Even more important, he realized that jazz reflected the very soul of our country. Consequently, if American composers wanted to shake off the European influence and to portray the soul of our land, what better way than to base their serious works on jazz. "I regard jazz," he declared, "as an American folk music, a very powerful one which is probably in the blood of the American people more than any other style of folk music. Jazz is the result of the energy stored in America. I believe that it can be made the basis of serious symphonic works of lasting value." Thus Gershwin became the natural link between jazz and classical music. On the one hand he wrote popular songs that were more advanced, more sophisticated in melody, harmony, rhythm, and form than any that had gone before. On the other, he used the jazz idiom as the basis for serious symphonic works.

Naturally, he was not alone in believing as he did. Many jazz musicians were trying to give their art a greater dignity and importance than it had had up to that time. Among them was Paul Whiteman, whose orchestra was the leading jazz ensemble of the day. Whiteman, who was known as the "King of Jazz," and his orchestrator Ferde Grofé had brought popular music to a new high level by using orchestrations of a symphonic type that were carefully rehearsed and that were presented as artistically as possible. Despite his success in the popular field, Whiteman was painfully aware of the great distance that still separated Tin Pan Alley from the concert halls in New York where serious music was performed. He decided to invade the enemy's territory with a concert that would display to the world the possibilities of jazz as a serious art. He needed a major symphonic work for the end of the concert, and decided that George Gershwin was just the man who could provide him with such a work.

106

Gershwin was reluctant to accept the assignment, for he was busy at the time with preparing the scores for several musical shows. But the more he thought of it, the more challenging Whiteman's request seemed. Finally he composed a dazzling piece for piano and orchestra, in which he combined jazz, ragtime, and the blues with a brilliant piano style in the manner of Liszt's Hungarian Rhapsodies. He thought of naming the new piece *American Rhapsody*. It was his brother Ira who hit upon the title *Rhapsody in Blue*.

The work received its premiere at the history-making concert presented by Paul Whiteman in Aeolian Hall on Lincoln's Birthday, 1924. Gershwin himself played the piano part—and the audience went wild. The *Rhapsody in Blue* became one of the best-loved works of the twentieth century. During its first ten years it brought Gershwin, in royalties from the sale of sheet music and records, more than a quarter of a million dollars. And it carried his name around the world.

During the twenties and early thirties Gershwin produced many of the tunes that have become classics of our popular-song literature. The list includes *Somebody Loves Me* from the *Scandals of 1924*; *Oh, Lady Be Good*, *Fascinating Rhythm*, and *The Man I Love* from *Lady Be Good* (1924); *Looking for a Boy*, *That Certain Feeling*, and *Sweet and Low Down* from *Tip Toes* (1925); *Clap Yo' Hands, Do, Do, Do*, and *Someone to Watch Over Me* from *Oh Kay* (1926); *'S Wonderful* from *Funny Face* (1927); *Liza* from *Show Girl* (1929); *Embraceable You, I Got Rhythm*, and *Bidin' My Time* from *Girl Crazy* (1930); *I've Got a Crush on You, Soon*, and *A Typical Self-Made American* from *Strike Up the Band* (1930); *Love Is Sweeping the Country* and *Who Cares* from *Of Thee I Sing*, which was the first musical to win a Pulitzer Prize (1931); *Mine* from *Let 'Em Eat Cake* (1933); *Let's Call the Whole Thing Off* from the motion picture *Shall We Dance?*

(1937); *Love Is Here to Stay* and *Love Walked In* from the *Goldwyn Follies* (1938).

Many of these songs did not catch on with the public at once. Gershwin's subtle melodic line and tricky rhythms did not make for easy popularity. In some cases the melody did not reveal its true personality without the harmonies that formed its background, so that people did not enjoy humming or whistling the tune without an accompaniment. In others he varied the usual construction of four phrases with four measures in each. The form consequently was puzzling to the ear. As a matter of fact, Gershwin was trying to get away from the standardized structure of Tin Pan Alley. He was leading the Broadway show tune into new territory. He created a new type of sophisticated song that captured perfectly the spirit of the 1920s and 1930s. What is more, his songs retained their freshness and their popularity long after many of the song hits of those years had been forgotten.

On December 3, 1925, Gershwin appeared as soloist with the New York Symphony Orchestra under the baton of Walter Damrosch. At that point he successfully bridged the gap that lay between Broadway and Carnegie Hall. He introduced his Concerto in F. In this work he combined popular materials drawn from jazz, Charleston, and waltz rhythms with brilliant writing for the piano and the ample form of the classical concerto. Like the *Rhapsody in Blue*, the Concerto achieved immense popularity all over the world.

Gershwin was a handsome man who was endowed with a magnetic personality. He gave the impression of one who not only had enormous charm but who was gifted in the highest degree. He was the center of an adoring circle of friends. He enjoyed life, and threw himself into everything he did with the utmost enthusiasm. He fell in love frequently, but never married.

Gershwin's gifts were not limited to music. In his early thirties he became interested in painting, and he turned out a number of canvases that show genuine talent. Many of his friends remember him in exactly the same way as did Rouben Mamoulian, who directed *Porgy and Bess:* "George loved playing the piano for people and would do it at the slightest provocation. At any gathering of friends, if there was a piano in the room, George would play it. I am sure that most of his friends in thinking of George at his best, think of George at the piano. I've heard many pianists and composers play for informal gatherings, but I know of no one who did it with such genuine delight and verve. George at the piano was George happy."

Gershwin loved the music he wrote. That is to say, he knew that he had made a unique place for himself in the world of music, and he had a sense of his own achievement. At the same time he possessed the true humility of the artist and realized that there was very much about the technique of composition he did not know. He wished he had been given a broader musical training in his youth and often thought of studying with some European master in order to remedy his deficiencies. Accordingly, when he went abroad in 1928, he approached a number of celebrated musicians with the intention of studying with them. He wanted to take lessons from Maurice Ravel, but Ravel said to him: "Why do you want to become a second-rate Ravel when you already are a first-rate Gershwin?" He then asked Igor Stravinsky to teach him. When Stravinsky learned that Gershwin made over a hundred thousand dollars a year, he remarked, "In that case perhaps it is I who ought to take lessons from you." Both Ravel and Stravinsky realized that Gershwin needed no more formal training, for his best guide was his talent. Studying with a famous master might have strengthened his technique, but it might also have taken away something of his spontaneity and charm.

Throughout the years Gershwin was haunted by the idea of

writing an American opera. From the moment he read *Porgy*—
DuBose Heyward's novel of Negro life in Charleston—he knew
that he had found an ideal theme. But the project had to wait for
several years, as *Porgy* was being made into a play by Heyward
and his wife Dorothy.

In 1933, after the play had gone through a successful run in
New York, Gershwin began his adaptation. It was to become his
greatest work. "It's going to be a labor of love," he wrote to a
friend after signing the contract, "and I expect quite a few labor
pains with it."

Gershwin decided to visit Charleston in order to get the "feel"
of the city and its atmosphere. "I would like to see the town," he
wrote to Heyward, "and hear some spirituals, and perhaps go to
a colored café or two." He returned to Charleston in the summer
of 1934 and spent much time among the Gullah Negroes on James
Island. For Gershwin, as DuBose Heyward pointed out, this visit
was "more like a homecoming than an exploration." He now came
face to face with the creators of the jazz rhythms and the blues
that he had used so effectively in his songs. "The Gullah Negro,"
wrote Heyward, "prides himself on what he calls 'shouting.' This
is a complicated rhythmic pattern beaten out by feet and hands as
an accompaniment to the spirituals, and is undoubtedly of African
survival. I shall never forget the night when, at a Negro meeting
on a remote sea island, George started 'shouting' with them and
eventually, to their huge delight, stole the show from their champion 'shouter.' I think that he is probably the only white man in
America who could have done that."

We think of folk music as the product of countless anonymous
singers through the ages. But Gershwin believed that even a modern composer of sophisticated popular music could be a folk singer
at heart and could capture in his melodies the simplicity of folk
song. "When I first began work on the music," he wrote about

Porgy and Bess, "I decided against the use of original folk material because I wanted the music to be all of one piece. Therefore, I wrote my own spirituals and folk songs. But they are still folk music—and therefore, being in operatic form, *Porgy and Bess* becomes a folk opera. However, because *Porgy and Bess* deals with Negro life in America, it brings to the operatic form elements that have never before appeared in opera; and I have adapted my method to utilize the drama, the humor, the superstition, the religious fervor, the dancing and the irrepressible high spirits of the race. If, in doing this, I have created a new form which combines opera with the theater, this new form has come quite naturally out of the material."

Porgy and Bess opened at the Alvin Theater in New York on October 10, 1935, with Todd Duncan as Porgy and Anne Brown as Bess. Ira Gershwin had added some of his finest lyrics to DuBose Heyward's book. Despite the high level of the production, *Porgy and Bess* was just a little beyond what the Broadway theater at that time was prepared to accept. Gershwin's "folk opera" did not achieve success, and its first run lasted only four months.

However, little by little the principal songs—*Summertime, I Got Plenty o' Nuttin', It Ain't Necessarily So, A Woman Is a Sometime Thing,* and *Bess, You Is My Woman Now*—began to make their way around the country. After a few years the work was revived, first in the United States, then in Europe; and the public began to respond to the power, the beauty, the originality, and the dramatic fitness of Gershwin's score. Before long *Porgy and Bess* took its place in the eyes of the world as *the* American opera. Its ultimate triumph came in 1952 when our State Department sent a Negro company abroad so that Europe could see the work in its original form. The company returned to the United States for a long run, and was then sent by the State Department on a second tour that extended from Italy, Yugoslavia, Egypt, Greece,

Spain, and Israel to France, Switzerland, Belgium, Holland, South America, and the Soviet Union. In all these countries Gershwin's melodies, rising above the barriers of language and race, worked their magic and aroused audiences to scenes of indescribable enthusiasm. But neither Gershwin nor Heyward lived to see their work become an international favorite.

When the talking pictures became popular, Gershwin went to Hollywood and wrote two movies for Fred Astaire—*Shall We Dance?* and *A Damsel in Distress.* He began work on a third, the *Goldwyn Follies.* He was now at the pinnacle of his success. Then the fates caught up with him. One day, while he was playing the Concerto in F with the Los Angeles Philharmonic, his mind went blank for a moment. Soon thereafter he began to suffer from violent headaches. The doctors found that he had a brain tumor, and decided to operate. He did not survive the operation.

The *Rhapsody in Blue* and the songs from *Porgy and Bess* offer the best introduction to Gershwin's music. Next in popularity comes *An American in Paris.* Gershwin's aim in writing this symphonic poem was, as he explained it, "to portray the impressions of an American visitor in Paris as he strolls about the city, listens to the various street noises, and absorbs the French atmosphere." Although *An American in Paris* comes under the heading of program music—for it has a title and evokes a definite scene—the music does not attempt to tell a specific story. Rather, the piece is programmatic in a general way, so that, as the composer pointed out, "the individual listener can read into the music such episodes as his imagination pictures for him."

Gershwin's symphonic poem opens with a bright theme that suggests the excitement and gayety of the French capital. There is a vivid reference to Parisian taxis and the way they honk their horns. Then a saucy melody emerges such as one might hear at one of the French cafés. From there on the music—brash, saucy, gay—

hovers between jazz (with a slightly French accent) and the can-can (with a slightly American accent). Presently the mood of hectic animation gives way to a gentle nostalgia, as if the visitor suddenly faced a moment of homesickness. The music turns to a delicious "blues," one of those heart-warming, sweeping melodies of which Gershwin alone knew the secret. Even in Paris, it seems to say, one may find oneself longing for home. The moment passes. A jaunty Charleston rhythm sweeps through the orchestra. The finale, noisy and gay, brings back themes from the earlier part of the work. It is plain that our American is having a lot of fun in Paris.

The creator of this thoroughly attractive piece combined a great musical talent with the popular touch. George Gershwin was one of the most gifted composers of his generation, and he has remained the most widely loved among them. His death at the age of thirty-nine, just when he had found his mature style, was a tragic loss for American music.

10. AARON COPLAND

"I was born on a street in Brooklyn that can only be described as drab. Music was the last thing anyone would have connected with it." This is how Aaron Copland remembers the neighborhood where he was born on November 14, 1900. Like George Gershwin, Aaron was the son of a Russian-Jewish immigrant who had come to the United States in search of a better life. The elder Copland had done quite well in the New World. He owned a small department store in Brooklyn and made a comfortable living for his wife and five children. Aaron was the youngest.

When the boy was eight and a half years old he fell ill with a mild attack of typhoid fever. During his sickness his brother's wife was very kind and attentive. She sent him a bag of ripe red cherries—his favorite fruit. Aaron was eager to show his appreciation of her thoughtfulness. As soon as he recovered, he decided to write a song for her. It was his first attempt at composition.

The older children of the family had all studied music, but had not gone very far with it. Aaron's parents felt there was no point in wasting any more money on lessons for him. However, he was so eager to learn to play the piano that his sister Maurine began to teach him when he was around thirteen. His parents soon had good reason to be dissatisfied with his musical interests. Up to

114

that time Aaron's marks at school had been uniformly good. Now he became so absorbed in the piano that he neglected his school-work and fell behind in several subjects, notably mathematics.

Aaron entered Boys' High School when he was fourteen. He worked harder than ever at the piano and made rapid progress. His sister began to feel that she had taught him all she knew. Aaron begged his parents to allow him to go to a professional teacher. They were very much opposed to this at first, but in time they gave in to his pleading. At the age of fifteen he began to study with Leopold Wolfsohn, a very competent pianist whose studio was not far from Aaron's home.

By this time he had already made up his mind to be a composer. But a composer had to know harmony. Aaron tried to learn by taking a correspondence course. After a few trial lessons he realized that this was no way at all to learn harmony, and asked Mr. Wolfsohn to help him find a teacher. Wolfsohn sent him to Rubin Goldmark, who was one of the best-known harmony teachers in New York. Aaron presented himself at Goldmark's house and explained his ambition. Goldmark stared at him and asked him gruffly, "What do you want to become a composer for?" It was a very sensible question, considering the difficulties that attend a composer's career. But it would have taken much more than this to dissuade Aaron from pursuing his goal.

Goldmark was a thorough musician who gave his students a solid foundation in the rudiments of their art. At the same time, like most teachers of musical theory he was extremely conservative and warned his pupil against having anything to do with the "moderns." This of course only whetted the young man's appetite, and he eagerly studied the works of the new European composers who were beginning to be known in this country: the Russian Alexander Scriabin, the Frenchmen Claude Debussy and Maurice Ravel. Nor did Goldmark want him to write in the modern style.

115

Aaron soon found a solution that satisfied both his teacher and himself. He wrote one group of compositions that followed all the rules which Goldmark taught him. These he dutifully submitted to his teacher. But in his spare time he wrote other works like his early piano piece *The Cat and the Mouse,* in which he gave free rein to his imagination, rules or no rules. "By the time I was eighteen," he recalls, "I already had something of the reputation of a musical rebel—in Goldmark's eyes, at any rate."

Aaron was graduated from Boys' High School when he was eighteen. "It seems curious," he wrote years later, "that the school played so small a part in my musical training. I neither sang in the school chorus nor played in the school orchestra. Music classes were a kind of joke—we were not even taught to sight-read a single vocal line properly. Perhaps things have changed for the better in that respect. A young person with musical aptitude would probably find more scope in the regular school curriculum for his or her talents nowadays."

His parents wanted him to go to college. But he was now sure enough of his goal to realize that he must devote all his energies to music. More important, he was able to persuade his parents to go along with this. They were still hoping that he would prepare for a practical career like law or medicine. But they could not help being impressed by his seriousness and determination, and they were willing to give him a chance.

Much as he enjoyed studying with Goldmark, Aaron missed the atmosphere of a music school. It was a great disadvantage, he realized, not to be able to discuss music with other students. At this time he read that a new summer school for Americans, in music and art, was to be opened in the Palace of Fontainebleau in France. He sent in his application immediately and was the first student to be accepted. His parents promised that he could remain in Paris for a year in order to perfect himself in his chosen field.

Before the First World War young Americans had gone to Germany to study music (as Edward MacDowell did). Now, however, Paris had become the musical center of the world. So it was that young Copland, with high hopes, looked forward to spending a year in the lovely city on the Seine.

He set sail for Europe in June, 1921, with a group of students who were going to attend the new school. He was twenty-one years old. Fontainebleau, he found, was a quiet little town situated on the edge of a forest. The school was held in a palace that had originally been the hunting lodge of French kings. The most modern wing had been added by Napoleon and contained many objects associated with the Little Corporal's reign. Copland was disappointed in his composition teacher, who was just as conservative as Goldmark had been. But he soon began to hear about a wonderful harmony teacher called Nadia Boulanger. He was reluctant at first to attend her class. After all, he had finished his harmony course. But his curiosity soon got the better of him. And so he met the woman who more than any other musician influenced his career. "I had never before witnessed," he wrote later, "such enthusiasm and such clarity in teaching. I immediately suspected that I had found my teacher."

He had still to overcome a few prejudices in regard to Mlle. Boulanger. He had never before heard of anyone studying composition with a woman; and he knew that the idea would sound altogether strange to his parents. Nevertheless, when the summer session ended and he had to make plans for the winter, Copland visited Mlle. Boulanger and asked if he could work with her. He was her first full-time American student in composition. In later years so many others followed his example—among them Douglas Moore, Walter Piston, Virgil Thomson, and Roy Harris—that this remarkable woman had a tremendous influence on the course of modern American music. Two qualities, in Copland's estimate, made Mlle. Boulanger unique. One was her consuming love for music. The other was her ability to inspire a pupil with confidence in his own creative powers. Unlike many composition teachers, she did not seek to force her personality upon her students. On the contrary, she strove to guide each and every one of them to the fullest expression of his own individuality.

Copland benefited so much from his studies with Mlle. Boulanger that his parents allowed him to extend his stay in Paris. What was to have been one year abroad stretched out to two and then to three years. Through his teacher Copland met the leaders of the modern movement in music, such as the Russian composer Igor Stravinsky. He heard all the new music he could. And he began to find his own path as a composer. "The watchword in those days," he recollects, "was *originality*. The laws of rhythm, of harmony, of construction had all been torn down. Every composer set out to remake these laws according to his own conceptions. And I suppose that I was no exception despite my youth—or possibly because of it."

He returned to New York in 1924 with a number of compositions under his arm. A stroke of luck had come his way. Nadia Boulanger had been engaged to appear as organ soloist with the New York Symphony Orchestra and had asked him to write a piece for her. In order to earn a living Copland took a job with a trio in a summer hotel in Pennsylvania. He spent every spare moment in composing his Symphony for Organ and Orchestra, and finished the work in time. The following January the Symphony was presented in Carnegie Hall by Nadia Boulanger and the orchestra under the direction of Walter Damrosch. The famous conductor felt he should offer a word of comfort to the conservative listeners who had been shocked by so modern a work. After the piece was over he turned around to the audience and said, "Ladies and gentlemen, if a young man at the age of twenty-three can write a symphony like this, it seems evident that in five years he will be ready to commit murder." Everybody laughed, including the composer. Fortunately for all concerned, Dr. Damrosch's prophecy never came true.

In the next few years Copland wrote one work after the other. He still faced the problem of supporting himself, as it was impossible to earn a living by writing serious music. He found unexpected support in the critic Paul Rosenfeld, who believed in his talent and persuaded a wealthy music lover to help him. At this time, too, Senator Simon Guggenheim and his wife set up the Guggenheim Foundation in memory of their son John who had died in 1922. Their intention was to grant fellowships annually to deserving young artists. Copland was the first musician to receive one of these awards, which in subsequent years brought help to many of our composers. He found another supporter in Serge Koussevitzky, the Russian-born conductor of the Boston Symphony, who from the moment he arrived in this country firmly championed the cause of the American composer. In the summertime Copland went to the MacDowell Colony in New Hampshire where, along with other artists, he could devote himself to his work free from interruption and care.

In his early works Copland was, naturally, under the influence of French music. But he was most eager to develop an American style, and turned for inspiration to jazz. He used jazz in a different way than did George Gershwin. Whereas Gershwin belonged to the world of popular music, Copland employed the rhythms of jazz in serious, ultramodern works. The jazz influence is very strong in two important compositions of this period— *Music for the Theater*, which received its first performance at a concert of the Boston Symphony Orchestra under Koussevitzky in 1925, and the Concerto for Piano and Orchestra, which was presented by Koussevitzky two years later with the composer playing the solo part. In spite of their jazzy rhythms, these works did not have, and were not meant to have, the popular appeal of Gershwin's music. The Concerto contained complex rhythmic patterns and harsh dissonances that puzzled some listeners and made others furious. This music was still too advanced for the conservative public. After the Concerto, Copland realized that he had done all he could with the jazz idiom. He felt that jazz was limited, by and large, to two moods, the blues and the snappy number. He knew that he must look farther afield to find his true musical language. All the same, jazz rhythm became a permanent part of his thinking and feeling, and gave his music a special American tang.

In 1929 the RCA Victor Company offered a prize of twenty-five thousand dollars for a symphonic work. This was a huge sum of money to offer for a serious composition. Copland decided to enter the contest and began to work furiously on a symphony in one movement. He called it *Symphonic Ode*. Two weeks before the deadline he realized that he could not finish the *Ode* in time. He was in despair at not having a piece to submit for the prize. Suddenly he had an excellent idea. He brought out the manuscript of a ballet he had written in Paris. Selecting the three movements that he liked best, he named the piece *Dance Symphony* and sent it in on the final day. The judges decided that no one work deserved the full award, so they divided the prize among five contestants. Thus Copland's *Dance Symphony* brought him five thousand dollars. He later completed the *Symphonic Ode*, which was one of a series of modern works commissioned by the Boston Symphony to celebrate its fiftieth anniversary in 1930.

The pieces that Copland wrote in the early thirties, such as the *Piano Variations*, the *Short Symphony*, and *Statements for Orchestra*, aroused great interest among advanced musicians. But they were hard to play and very hard to understand as far as the average music lover was concerned. Copland felt more and more dissatisfied with what he was writing. He asked himself whom he was trying to reach with his music. It seemed to him that he and his fellow composers had lost touch with the big public. It was as if they were working in a vacuum; or writing just for each other and a few friends. He began to realize that an entirely new public had grown up around the radio and phonograph. "It made no sense to ignore them," he decided, "and to continue writing as if they did not exist. I felt that it was worth the effort to see if I couldn't say what I had to say in the simplest possible terms."

This period of self-questioning led to a vast change in Copland's manner of writing. He simplified his style so that the mass of music lovers could enjoy his music. He decided to create for the mass media of communication—radio, ballet, motion pictures; also to write music suitable for young people. He hoped in this way to reach out beyond the narrow circle that had appreciated his music up to this time. Once he had taken this decision he produced a succession of memorable works that spread his fame all over the world.

The new direction is apparent in three pieces he wrote in 1935: *What Do We Plant?*, a chorus for high-school students; and two children's pieces for piano, *Sunday Afternoon Music* and *The Young Pioneers*. A year later he completed one of his most widely played works, *El Salón México*, named after a popular dance hall in Mexico City. Based on songs and dances of Mexico, this piece evokes Copland's happy memories of a visit to the colorful land below the Rio Grande. Latin America gave him the inspiration for another work, *Danzón Cubano* (Cuban Dance), which is written for two pianos.

In 1936 Copland wrote *The Second Hurricane*, a "play-opera" specially designed for high-school students. The plot concerns six boys and girls and the exciting adventure that befalls them when an

121

aviator appears at their school to ask for help in bringing supplies to a region that has been hit by a hurricane. This operetta has been performed by high-school students all over the country. It shows that a modern composer can have something vital to say to young people when he puts his mind to it. In the same class is *An Outdoor Overture*, which Copland wrote for the orchestra of the High School of Music and Art in New York City. This piece has the bright, clear outdoor sound that is so characteristic of Copland's music.

Music for Radio, also known as *Saga of the Prairie*, was commissioned by the CBS Network and presented on a popular program called "Everybody's Music." Shortly afterward Copland wrote the music for *Billy the Kid*, which was presented by the Ballet Caravan in 1938. It soon became one of his most popular works. No less important are his two other ballets, *Rodeo* (1942) and *Appalachian Spring* (1944). *Rodeo* is a lighthearted cowboy ballet. The heroine is an energetic cowgirl who is determined to get her man—and does! Copland subsequently extracted four numbers from the score and arranged them into a breezy concert suite: *Buckaroo Holiday, Corral Nocturne, Saturday Night Waltz,* and *Hoe-down.* You may be sure that no listener has any difficulty in understanding this music. *Appalachian Spring* is a ballet about pioneer life in early Pennsylvania. It revolves around a young Quaker bride and her farmer husband, who celebrate the coming of spring and the building of their farmhouse. This work was made famous by the great American dancer Martha Graham, and brought Copland the Pulitzer Prize for 1945.

In the meantime he was invited to go to Hollywood to write music for motion pictures. He soon achieved a great reputation as a film composer. He wrote the score for five important pictures: John Steinbeck's *Of Mice and Men* (1939); Thornton Wilder's *Our Town* (1940); Lillian Hellman's *The North Star* (1943);

Steinbeck's *The Red Pony* (1948); and Henry James's *The Heiress* (1948). The score for *The Heiress* brought him an "Oscar."

During the years of the Second World War Copland was mindful of an artist's duty to his country. His music expressed the solemnity of the great ordeal through which our nation was passing. *A Lincoln Portrait*, for speaker and large orchestra (1942), was based on lines drawn from the speeches of the Great Emancipator, a tribute to the ideals of freedom and justice for which we were fighting. *Fanfare for the Common Man*, for brass and percussion (1942), is a stirring call to action. *Letter from Home* (1944) captured the loneliness and the longing that were felt by so many Americans far from home. To this period too belongs Copland's most important work for orchestra, the Third Symphony, which he completed in 1946. A few years later he wrote a Concerto for Clarinet and String Orchestra for Benny Goodman. He also composed *The Tender Land* (1954), an opera that is American to the core, and many other works which have brought pleasure to performers and listeners alike.

Copland realized at an early stage in his career that a composer today not only has the job of creating music but must also take a hand in educating the public to listen to it and appreciate it. He became active as a lecturer, writer, and teacher. He gave courses on modern music at the New School for Social Research in New York City. He wrote many magazine articles about his own music and the works of his friends and colleagues. Together with the composer Roger Sessions he organized the Copland-Sessions Concerts, which ran for four years and presented many new works. He was active in the League of Composers, an organization that promoted the performance of new music and that helped many young musicians to gain a hearing. He realized too that composers ought to band together in order to gain better economic conditions for themselves. To this end he helped to found the American Composers' Alliance, and served as its president for seven years. Amid all these activities he found time to produce two books, *What to Listen for in Music* and *Our New Music*. These are written in such a clear, simple style that the reader without musical background has no difficulty in understanding them. In 1951 Copland gave a series of lectures at Harvard University which were published in a third book, *Music and Imagination*. He has been associated with the Berkshire Music Center at Tanglewood, Massachusetts, ever since the founding of that remarkable summer school. Here he has been able to play an active part in training the young generation of American musicians, first as a member of the faculty and then as director of the school. Copland's interest in Mexico, originally that of a tourist, brought him a genuine appreciation of Latin-American culture. In 1941 he was asked by the Office of Inter-American Relations to undertake a good-will tour of nine Latin-American countries, and became the first American musician to be sent abroad in an official capacity. In 1947 our State Department sent him on a similar mission.

The best way to get to know Copland's music is to listen to a recording of *El Salón México*. You will be enchanted by the bright orchestral sound and the seductive Latin-American rhythms of this work. Or you can begin with *Billy the Kid*, which is so American in mood and atmosphere. The ballet revolves around the brief but eventful career of William Bonney, the desperado who became one of the legends of the Southwest. We first see Billy as a boy of twelve, when his mother is killed by a stray bullet in a street brawl. Billy stabs the man who caused her death. Later, during a card game with his cronies, ones of the players accuses him of cheating. Billy kills him. He is captured after a running gun battle and put in jail; but he murders the jailer and escapes. There is a romantic scene when he joins his Mexican sweetheart in the desert. Yet even as he holds her in his arms his pursuers close in on him. This time there is no escaping. At the end the girl laments the death of the dashing outlaw.

Copland selected five episodes from the music of the ballet and wove them into an exciting concert suite. First is the prologue, *The Open Prairie*, that conjures up the vast, lonely quiet of the open spaces. Then comes *Street Scene in a Frontier Town*, jaunty, gay, and brash, which quotes some famous cowboy songs—*The Old Chisholm Trail; Git Along, Little Dogies;* and *Good-bye, Old Paint. Card Game at Night* goes back to the wistful, quiet mood of the opening. We hear a beautiful setting of *The Dying Cowboy* (*Oh Bury Me Not on the Lone Prairie*). The next episode is *Fight,* which depicts the chase that leads to Billy's capture. The rat-tat-tat of the muted trumpets is so vivid that you can almost see the gun battle taking place before your eyes. The *Celebration* that follows Billy's capture is properly brassy and gay, with its lilting dance-hall tunes that evoke the spirit of the West. The epilogue brings back the *Open Prairie* music, as if to say that, though men may come and go, the prairie remains forever—remote and brooding and vast.

The composer of this eloquent music has had a distinguished career. Through ceaseless effort he perfected himself in his art. His unswerving dedication to his ideals has brought him fame and honor. In the eyes of the world he is the foremost American composer of our time.

11. SAMUEL BARBER

Samuel Barber was born on March 9, 1910, in West Chester, Pennsylvania, a quiet little town not far from Philadelphia. He grew up in a comfortable middle-class environment where music and art were very much appreciated. His father was a doctor, his mother played the piano. She was the sister of Louise Homer, one of the most famous opera singers of her time. Both Mme. Homer and her husband, the composer Sidney Homer, encouraged their nephew's first attempts to write music.

Sam showed his interest in music at an early age. By the time he was six he was playing the piano. Then, because his mother wished him to learn the cello, he studied that instrument for a year. But the piano was his first love, and he soon returned to it. "I began composing at seven," he reports, "and have never stopped."

His parents wanted him to share the interests of the average American boy and to participate in sports. But Sam knew his own mind even before he knew how to spell, as is evident from a note he wrote his mother when he was eight: "I was not meant to be an athelet I was meant to be a composer. and will be, I'm sure. Don't ask me to try to forget this and go and play foot-ball.—*Please*— Sometimes I've been worrying about this so much that it makes me mad! (not very)."

When he was ten Sam began to compose an opera on a libretto that was written for him by the family's cook, a Mrs. Noble. The action revolved around a famous operatic tenor who comes to a small town for his vacation and unexpectedly falls in love. Only the first act was written. After that Mrs. Noble ran out of ideas. The composer did not attempt an opera again until he had found a more inventive librettist.

When Sam was in high school he organized a small orchestra that gave concerts. He also played the piano at various club meetings. Despite these activities, he was a shy, withdrawn lad who was passionately fond of reading and of roaming by himself through the countryside. Within the intimate circle of his family and friends he was gay and confident. With strangers he was inclined to be reserved and distant.

His musical gift was so impressive that, when he was only fourteen, he was appointed organist at the Westminster Presbyterian Church and received $100 a month for his services. He did not keep the job long: he insisted on playing the hymns and responses as they were written, instead of stopping at the end of each phrase, as the congregation was accustomed to. But his brief career as a church organist had one good result: out of his earnings he bought a subscription to the concerts of the Philadelphia Orchestra, and this opened up for him a new world of music.

At just about this time Mary Curtis Bok, the daughter of the publisher Cyrus Curtis, founded the Curtis Institute in Philadelphia. Mrs. Bok's generosity made it possible for gifted students to study with such world-famous artists as the opera singer Marcella Sembrich, the pianist Josef Hofmann, and the conductor Leopold Stokowski. As a result, the new institution quickly established itself as one of America's most important conservatories. Sam was among the first group of students to be accepted at the Curtis Institute. Since his father, Dr. Barber, was head of the school board in West

Chester, a special rule was put through that permitted any high-school student in West Chester who was a composer to attend the Friday afternoon concerts of the Philadelphia Orchestra. As a result of this dispensation Sam was able to have his lessons at the Institute on Friday mornings, hear the orchestra later in the day, and at the same time continue with his high-school education. He was graduated from high school when he was sixteen. From then on he devoted himself exclusively to music.

He was soon known as one of the most gifted students at the Curtis Institute. Once again an exception was made in his case: he was allowed to major in three subjects—piano, singing, and composition. During his fourth year at Curtis he met a newcomer from Italy, a boy named Gian-Carlo Menotti, who was one year younger than he. Menotti was restless, talkative, full of temperament, the very opposite of the reserved American. They were soon inseparable, and formed a lasting friendship. West Chester became Menotti's second home. Years later the little Quaker town suggested the locale for Menotti's opera *The Old Maid and the Thief*.

When he was eighteen Sam read about the Bearns Prize of $1,200 offered by Columbia University for the best new work by a young American composer. He submitted a violin sonata and won the prize, which paid for a trip to Europe during his summer vacation. This was the first of several summers spent with Menotti's family in Cadegliano, a village on the Italian side of Lake Lugano. Cadegliano was the first spot in Europe where he felt completely at home.

"Hidden away in mountains of extreme natural beauty," he wrote to his parents, "almost unpastured, and overlooking a magnificent valley with parts of three lakes dividing new mountain-ranges which in turn form a background for the vistas of Switzerland—hidden away here, little known, not caring to be known, is this little settlement of quaint villas, of all styles, of diverse degrees of luxury, and most all of them owned and inhabited by relatives or members of Gian-Carlo's family. There are no hotels, hence there are no strangers but only guests."

Following his four years as an undergraduate, Sam served for two years as a student-teacher at the Curtis Institute. Upon his graduation, he could have joined the staff. But he had no desire to pursue a teaching career. Many of his composer friends taught music at various colleges and conservatories. Sam saw that their teaching seriously interfered with their composing. Indeed, most of them were able to compose only during week ends, holidays, or summer vacations. Sam was determined that no official position should keep him from doing the one thing he wanted to do. "Give me a place to live *in the country*," he wrote in a letter to his family, "and a peaceful room with a piano in which to work—and I ask for nothing more."

Instead of joining the faculty of the Curtis Institute, Barber went to Europe with Menotti. They spent the winter of 1933 in Vienna, where Barber studied conducting and gave a song recital. He also made his debut as a conductor. A touch of excitement was added to this event when Barber discovered (later) that underneath the platform on which he conducted were hidden guns and ammunition, placed there by a workers' group in preparation for a revolt against the government.

Fame came early to Samuel Barber. When he was only twenty-three the Philadelphia Orchestra performed his *Overture to "The School for Scandal"* at a summer concert in Robin Hood Dell. He had written the piece two years before. The Overture made a strong impression on all who heard it. Another important performance came the following year. The New York Philharmonic presented his *Music for a Scene from Shelley*, which he was inspired to write after reading Shelley's *Prometheus Unbound*. Shortly afterward, a program consisting entirely of his music was heard over the radio. These performances added considerably to Barber's growing reputation.

All the same, his financial situation was far from satisfactory. He settled in New York and tried to earn a living by singing on the radio, but without success. He applied for a Prix de Rome, one of the most valuable prizes open to young American composers, as it carries with it several years' residence at the American Academy in Rome; but his application was rejected.

However, things looked up for Barber when he was awarded a Pulitzer Traveling Scholarship of $1,500 for a year of study abroad. In the meantime his music was being presented in London with success. "Lady Astor," he informed his parents, "went behind the scenes during the concert and complimented my music by asking if I was dead yet!" Then the American Academy in Rome invited him to reapply for the prize. He sent in the same works that he had submitted the first time—his Cello Sonata and *Music for a Scene from Shelley*. Obviously the judges felt that they had made a mistake, for they gave him the prize.

Although he did not have to worry about finances during his stay in Rome, Barber did not relish the atmosphere of the Academy. "Do you know," he wrote to Menotti during his first month there, "that I have not yet unpacked my trunk, out of sheer perversity, because I do not wish to feel at home in this room? And I *shall not*. My half-full trunk stands open, in complete disorder. And I shall not unpack it. I will *never* call this room mine." He felt more kindly toward his studio, which, he stated, was "situated apart from the Academy, in the made-over stables of the old Villa Aurelia, which is full of charm, and I love the garden, the pines by moonlight, Rome in the distance, the yellow stone stairs." His parents wrote to ask whether he was happy. "Yes and no," he replied. "In fact no different from any place else. My great satisfaction and consolation is that I am not a bother to anyone for two years, and this means *a great deal:* and that I am able to do the work which interests me to my heart's content (or discontent)."

During his stay at the Academy Barber's *Symphony in One Movement* was performed in Rome, and was subsequently presented by Artur Rodzinski and the Cleveland Symphony Orchestra. In 1937 Arturo Toscanini, whom Barber and Menotti had visited at his summer home in Italy, began to take an active interest in Barber's career. The Maestro was not particularly fond of either contemporary or American music. All the same, he was deeply impressed by Barber's talent. In 1938 he conducted two works by Barber, the *Adagio for Strings* and the *Essay for Orchestra, No. 1.* The *Adagio* was the only work by an American composer that Toscanini put on his programs when he toured South America with the NBC Symphony Orchestra and was the first American work that he recorded. Toscanini's interest did very much to further Barber's reputation. His compositions were taken up by other conductors, and before long he was one of the most frequently performed of all contemporary American composers. He was not yet thirty, and he had realized his ambition to make a living as a composer. What with royalties, performance fees, and commissions for new works, he was free to devote all his time to composing.

At the outbreak of the Second World War in 1939 Barber, who was returning from Europe as the Nazi army marched into Poland, did not realize that a chapter in his life had come to an end and another was about to begin. For a time he continued in his accustomed way, immersed in his music and his books. But in 1943 he was inducted into the Army. Because of his defective vision he was assigned to Special Services and did clerical work. Some months later he was transferred to the Air Force. Barber's military career was summed up by Gian-Carlo Menotti, who remarked: "Sam is the only soldier in the United States Army who never learned how to take a gun apart and put it together again."

As a result of an unusually intelligent policy, Barber was allowed to serve in the best way he could—by composing. He wrote the *Commando March*, which received its first performance by the Army Air Forces Band. Next he was commissioned to write a symphony specially for the Air Force. Barber felt some misgivings when he had to play part of the work for the officer in charge of the assignment, a captain. He was afraid that a symphony written in the twentieth-century idiom would be above the captain's head. To his astonishment, the captain turned out to be a devotee of advanced modern music and criticized the piece for being too conservative. The *Symphony Dedicated to the Army Air Forces* was completed early in 1944 and received its first performance by the Boston Symphony Orchestra under Serge Koussevitzky. The event brought him the most memorable piece of fan mail he ever received. "Dear Corporal," the note ran, "I came to hear your symphony. I thought it was terrible, but I applauded vociferously because I think all corporals should be encouraged."

When he was discharged from the Army Barber settled at Mt. Kisco, New York, in a house that Menotti and he bought jointly. They called it Capricorn. Situated on a wooded hill, about an hour's drive from Manhattan, Capricorn is laid out in two separate wings with a studio at the end of each. Both composers are able to work without hearing each other. Here Barber finally found what he had long dreamed of, "a place to live in the country and a peaceful room with a piano in which to work."

Barber composes slowly. The themes for his compositions do not come easily. He discards many ideas until he has found exactly what he wants. While the search is going on he will be in a bad humor and quite absent-minded. The inner struggle is so intense at such moments that he is hardly conscious of anything around

132

him. Once he has found what he is looking for, his mood changes instantly. He becomes cheerful and is eager to set to work.

Barber retains the traits he showed as a boy. He is reserved and somewhat distant with people he does not know well, but relaxed and merry with his intimates. He still loves to take long walks in the country and to read. He has no patience with games of any sort. Although he plays the piano well, he never learned any other type of coordination. "He is constantly losing things," a friend once said of him, "and cannot fry an egg or operate a phonograph." However, in all that regards his work he is extremely punctual, well organized, and meticulous.

Barber is one of the few composers who was trained as a singer. (Most composers are instrumentalists.) This may help to explain the melodic quality of his music. He is at his best in works marked by poetic lyricism and romantic feeling. Although he is completely American in his background—he is a descendant of Robert Fulton —he does not share the folklore interests of composers like Douglas Moore, Roy Harris, or Aaron Copland. On the contrary, his many trips abroad and his long association with Gian-Carlo Menotti have made him highly responsive to the European tradition. Hence he is one of the internationally minded members of the contemporary American school. Both in his personal viewpoint and in his music he is a citizen of the world.

Barber's early works have remained extremely popular. Among them are the lighthearted *Overture to "The School for Scandal"* (1932); *Music for a Scene from Shelley* (1933), which evokes the flamelike imagery of that poet's *Prometheus Unbound;* the deeply expressive *Adagio for Strings* (1936), an arrangement for orchestra of the slow movement from the String Quartet, Opus 11; and the *Essay for Orchestra, No. 1* (1937). Barber uses the term *essay,* as did Lamb, Hazlitt, and other English writers, to indicate a form in which ideas are developed concisely within an intimate

133

framework. In his Symphony No. 1 (1936) Barber binds the four movements of the traditional symphony into a single movement with contrasting sections. (The piece is also known as the *Symphony in One Movement*.) To this period belong also *Dover Beach* (1931), a setting of Matthew Arnold's famous poem for solo voice and string quartet; *Three Songs Set to Poems from "Chamber Music"* by James Joyce (1936); the melodious Violin Concerto (1939); songs based on poems by Housman, James Stephens, Gerard Manley Hopkins, W. B. Yeats, and other poets; and the serenely beautiful setting of Emily Dickinson's *Let Down the Bars, O Death*, for four-part chorus (1936).

The second decade of Barber's career witnessed important changes in his style. The romanticism of the early years was enriched by his growing awareness of the techniques of contemporary music. His vocal line grew bolder and more expressive, his harmonies more dissonant, his rhythms more complex. The *Symphony Dedicated to the Army Air Forces* (1944) bears the mark of this turbulent period. This symphony, Barber's second, contains suggestions of whirring propellers, of the solitude of night flight, of hovering danger, and the suspense of waiting. The most important composition of this period is the Piano Sonata (1949), marked by an intensity and a bigness of conception that stamp it as a work of the artist's maturity. *A Stopwatch and an Ordnance Map* (1940), for chorus of men's voices and three kettledrums (four horns, three trombones, and tuba optional), is a moving work based on Stephen Spender's poem about the death of a soldier in the Spanish Civil War. It was followed by the *Second Essay for Orchestra* (1942); the *Capricorn Concerto* for flute, oboe, trumpet, and strings (1944), a witty piece named after the house at Mt. Kisco; and the Cello Concerto of 1945.

In 1946 Barber wrote a ballet for Martha Graham based on the legend of Medea and Jason. The climax of this work—which

Barber subsequently fashioned into an independent piece called *Medea's Meditation and Dance of Vengeance*—is marked by a dramatic intensity that his music had not shown up till that time. *Knoxville: Summer of 1915*, for soprano and orchestra (1947), is a setting of a prose poem by James Agee that first appeared in the magazine *Partisan Revue*. (This forms the first chapter of Agee's beautiful book *A Death in the Family*.) Barber's music captured the sensitive quality of Agee's memories of his childhood. Among the late works there stand out *Melodies passagères* (Transient Melodies, 1951) for voice and piano, a setting of five French poems by Rainer Maria Rilke; *Hermit Songs* for voice and piano, to poems translated from anonymous Irish texts of the eighth to thirteenth centuries; and *Prayers of Kierkegaard* for chorus, soprano solo, and orchestra, on texts drawn from the writings of the Danish philosopher-mystic. It is clear from this list that Barber is attracted to European more often than to American writers.

For many years Barber was eager to write an opera, but he could not find a suitable libretto. The problem was solved by his friend Menotti, who wrote for him the libretto of *Vanessa*, an opera with a European background. The work received its first performance at the Metropolitan Opera House in 1958. Barber had to overcome a number of problems in adapting his lyric style to the necessities of the opera house; for opera involves the unfolding of a plot, the development of characters through dramatic conflict, and a steady heightening of tension as the action proceeds. Naturally he did not fully solve all these problems at his first attempt. But he turned out an impressive score that shows his tasteful workmanship and his ability to create melody.

The *Overture to "The School for Scandal"* reveals the lighter side of Barber's gift. He did not try to represent specific incidents or characters of Sheridan's famous comedy. He wished rather to capture in his Overture the spirit of eighteenth-century comedy:

135

its classical elegance, its delightful artifice, its robust humor that forms an effective contrast to episodes of tender sentiment. Barber wrote the Overture as his graduation piece from the Curtis Institute. It has all the buoyancy and enthusiasm of youth. At the same time it displays the refined style that characterizes the works of Barber's maturity. The piece is marked *Allegro molto e vivace* (very fast and lively) and opens with a flourish. The first violins present a sprightly, strongly rhythmic theme that represents the comic element. This is worked up into a rousing orchestral crescendo. Then, at a somewhat slower tempo, a solo oboe sings a lovely melody that represents the romantic element. Tenderly expressive, it unfolds in a long lyric line. After an exciting development section, the two basic ideas are restated. However, this time the lyric theme is presented by the English horn (the alto of the oboe family). In the final section of the piece the comic spirit holds full sway.

Barber's works have established themselves firmly in the repertory. Most of them have been recorded and are heard frequently. He owes this eminence to the fact that his music issues from a genuine lyric impulse. Among the composers of his generation Samuel Barber stands out for his ability to communicate emotion with eloquence and charm.

12. WILLIAM SCHUMAN

William Schuman was born in New York City on August 4, 1910. His grandfather came to this country from Germany at the time of the Civil War, and was drafted into the Confederate Army. His father fought in the Spanish-American War. Bill was an active, fun-loving boy who excelled at sports. He was much keener on playing baseball than on practicing the violin. But practice he did, and by the time he was in high school he played the violin well enough to organize a jazz band, in which he also sang the vocal solos. In the summertime he worked as a counsellor in a camp in Maine. He began his career as a composer by writing songs for the camp shows. Together with his friend Frank Loesser he turned out about forty popular songs, of which one, *In Love with a Memory of You*, with lyrics by Loesser and music by Schuman, was published. This is the same Loesser who in subsequent years won fame on Broadway as the composer of *Guys and Dolls*, *Where's Charley?*, and other successful musicals.

When Bill was graduated from high school, he was not sure what he wanted to do. He registered at the School of Commerce of New York University, and earned some money on the side by working for an advertising agency. But he had not given up his dream of becoming a popular song writer.

His sister often asked him to go with her to concerts; but he refused, for he was convinced that he would be bored by an evening of "classical" music. One night she finally persuaded him to accompany her to Carnegie Hall, to a performance of the New York Philharmonic Orchestra. For the first time in his life he heard a great orchestra. An indescribable excitement took hold of him. It was as if a new world had opened up before him. That evening marked a turning point in his career.

The next morning, when he returned to the School of Commerce, he could not put the sound of the orchestra out of his mind. For the rest of the day he did not hear a word his teachers said. When he left the School of Commerce that afternoon, he knew with absolute certainty that he was not coming back. He had reached a major decision: he was going to become a musician.

On his way home he passed a building with a sign in front: the Malkin Conservatory of Music. He had heard somewhere that a composer had to begin his studies by learning harmony. Determined not to lose any more time, he entered the building and registered for a course in harmony.

His parents received the news with mixed feelings. "You're almost twenty," they told him, "and that's very late to begin studying music seriously." With his drive and intelligence, they said, he could achieve success in business or almost any other field. But music was in a class by itself. "Unless you have real talent," they argued, "you can never hope to get to the top." But Bill was not to be dissuaded. He had been searching for years for the thing he really wanted to do. At last he had found it! His parents gave in and hoped for the best.

In the next years Bill worked furiously to make up for lost time. He decided that, if he was going to be a composer of serious music, the best way to support himself would be by teaching music. So he entered Teachers College at Columbia University. He still had not given up his hopes of making a lot of money with a popular song hit, and he continued his efforts in that direction. But he soon realized that, in order to succeed on Tin Pan Alley, he would have to adapt himself to the formulas of a thoroughly commercial market. The more he listened to the works of the great composers, the less concerned he was with Tin Pan Alley. In the end he lost all interest in writing popular songs.

Even before his graduation from Teachers College, Schuman began to look for a position where he would be allowed to carry out his ideas of how music should be taught—ideas that did not in the least agree with the traditional methods. When he read the bulletin of Sarah Lawrence College, a progressive school for young women in Bronxville, New York, he knew he had found the institution he was looking for. He wrote to the college and was invited for an interview. He expressed his views to the president of Sarah Lawrence and several members of the faculty, and was so convincing that he was soon appointed to the staff.

At Sarah Lawrence Schuman soon established himself as an exciting teacher who was able to communicate to his students his own enthusiasm for music. He became conductor of the Sarah Lawrence chorus and persuaded it to commission new works from American composers. He performed compositions by students of the college. He arranged concerts where the chorus joined forces with choral groups from other schools. He took the chorus on tour. Under Schuman's energetic leadership the chorus contributed so much to the reputation of Sarah Lawrence that the college newspaper declared, "Our chorus is the football team of Sarah Lawrence. Notre Dame had Knute, but we have Bill!"

Several important things happened to Schuman during his first year at Sarah Lawrence. He completed his First Symphony (1935) —and also began to see its faults; in other words, he was growing rapidly as a composer. He began to study with Roy Harris at the summer session of the Juilliard School of Music, and found in Harris an inspiring teacher who gave him warm encouragement and helped him develop his talent. His music began to attract attention. And he married Frances Prince, the girl he had been in love with ever since he was twenty-one.

His Second Symphony, which he wrote in 1937, was performed in New York by the orchestra of the Federal Music Project. The work found an enthusiastic supporter in Aaron Copland. Before long Copland brought the score to Serge Koussevitzky, the conductor of the Boston Symphony Orchestra. Koussevitzky examined the score of the symphony and decided to play it. The New York performance—by a minor orchestra—was not a very good one, and left Schuman somewhat discouraged. Koussevitzky reassured him. "It is important that a composer should hear his music well played." Although the Boston Symphony Orchestra, one of the finest in the country, could be counted on to give a beautiful performance, Koussevitzky knew that his public was much too conservative to appreciate the work of a new American composer. "To be sure," he told Schuman, "your symphony will probably have no success with my public. But with me it has a success."

Schuman finished his Third Symphony in 1941. The piece was presented by Koussevitzky and the Boston Symphony Orchestra, and made an extraordinary impression on all who heard it. The critics who had torn down Schuman's earlier works hailed the new symphony with enthusiasm. They said that he had changed. "It was *they* who had changed," Schuman commented wryly, and he was right. They were now more familiar with contemporary music and were ready to praise a piece which, only a few years earlier, they would have been eager to attack.

Schuman now found a powerful ally in the publishing house of G. Schirmer. The first manuscript that he submitted to Schirmer had been turned down; but he tried again, this time with success.

Soon Schirmer was publishing everything he wrote, and agreed to pay him a monthly retainer so that he might teach less and compose more.

By the early 1940s Schuman had firmly established his reputation as one of the foremost composers of his generation. His music was performed by major orchestras both in this country and Europe. He had received a number of important prizes and honors, among them two Guggenheim fellowships, the Composition Award of the National Institute of Arts and Letters, and the first Pulitzer Prize ever awarded in music—for his choral piece *A Free Song* (1942).

In 1945 Schuman was appointed director of publication of G. Schirmer. This was the first time that a major music publishing house had invited a composer to head its publication department. Up to this time the decision to accept or reject a new work was often made by someone totally out of sympathy with modern music (as was the case during the careers of Charles Ives and Charles T. Griffes). Now times had changed. It was a composer himself— and one most actively identified with the cause of contemporary American music—who was going to decide which new compositions were fit to print.

During his years at Sarah Lawrence College, Schuman often talked with his friends about his theories of music education. He outlined the things he would do if he were ever to become the head of a great music school. Among those with whom he discussed his ideas were two directors of the Juilliard School of Music. When the famous pianist Ernest Hutcheson retired as head of the school, the directors asked Schuman to succeed him. But Schuman's answer, when he was asked if he wished to become head of the Juilliard School, was that he was not interested in accepting the job if he was expected to continue in the traditional paths. He wanted a free hand in instituting the reforms that he felt were necessary. The board of directors assured him that they were seeking a progressive educator, not a traditional one. And so, in 1945, William Schuman's dream came true. At the age of thirty-five he found himself at the head of one of the most important conservatories in the world, free to carry out his exciting ideas.

Like Howard Hanson at the Eastman School twenty years before, Schuman approached his task from the standpoint of the American composer. He brought young composers into the faculty. He made the students aware of the modern movement in music and of what contemporary composers were doing. He saw to it that the Juilliard Orchestra performed twentieth-century works and that the opera department presented new operas. In short, under Schuman's dynamic leadership the Juilliard School took on a twentieth-century point of view.

He was especially interested in broadening the students' horizons, so that they would see the whole field of music instead of concentrating exclusively on a particular instrument. He argued that the different branches of music—whether theory, harmony, counterpoint, ear-training, sight-singing, orchestration, composition, or history—must be taught not as separate subjects but in relationship to each other, so that the student would achieve a comprehensive view of the art as a whole. He insisted that students play and listen to all kinds of music, and grow familiar with the great works of every century. In this way they would begin to understand the music of the different historical periods; they would not apply the standards of the nineteenth century to the music of the twentieth, but would learn to judge every kind of music on its own merits.

Up to this time the students at Juilliard had been, for the most part, pianists, violinists, and singers who dreamed of giving a concert in Carnegie Hall that would launch them on an international career. Needless to say, this dream was seldom fulfilled

Now the school turned to the more practical—and more important —objective of training well-rounded musicians equipped to play a constructive part in their community as teachers, leaders of choruses and bands, directors of schools, and organizers of a vigorous musical life throughout the country.

The world thinks of the composer as an impractical dreamer shut away in his attic, removed from the concerns of his fellow men. William Schuman is no such dreamer. He is a man of action, thoroughly at home in the world, and with a talent for getting things done. He had to call on all his great reserves of energy to continue with his composing in spite of his arduous duties as president of the Juilliard School. By dint of carefully organizing his time, he was able to carry on his work as a creative artist along with his duties as an administrator.

He settled in New Rochelle, a residential community within commuting distance of New York. There he found a congenial home for his wife and their two children, Anthony and Andrea. He composed every morning for two hours before going to his office at the school. Often he returned to his writing table when he came home at night. Then there were the week ends, holidays, and summer vacations when he could devote himself entirely to creative work.

Schuman's music reflects the man. It is the music of an active personality—optimistic, vigorous, assertive. It is planned on a large scale. This bigness of gesture is characteristic of Schuman. "If my music should eventually prove a failure," he has said in typical fashion, "I want it to be a great big failure, not a little piddling failure." His tunes are bold and sweeping. "My music," he says, "is completely melodic. I write by singing, not by sitting at the piano." His rhythms are thoroughly American, as might be expected of one who found his way to music through jazz. When he was asked if one of his ballets did not show the influence of jazz, he retorted, "That's no influence—that *is* jazz." The jazz element

143

is especially apparent in the way he has of setting up a steady pulse in the bass while above it unfold all kinds of syncopations. (The accent in music generally falls on the strong beat, the *one*. In *syncopation*, which is the basis of jazz, the accent is shifted to the off-beat.)

Schuman has a natural flair for the large forms of instrumental music—symphony, concerto, string quartet. This tendency places him among the classicists. The large forms are based on the development of musical ideas in a continuous line, so that each detail will spring out of what came before and will lead as inevitably to what follows. Such a structure appeals to Schuman's logical, orderly mind. His orchestral sound is bright and vigorous. He achieves unusual effects by pushing the instruments to the limits of what they can do. He is fond of vivid contrasts between soft and loud, between high and low register, between the string instruments and the brass. Such contrasts emphasize the vitality and vigor of his music.

Schuman's music is thoroughly American even though he does not make direct use of folk tunes. Neither the song of the cowboy nor the poetry of the prairie fires his imagination. Having grown up in New York, Schuman has retained the mentality of the big-city boy. His music is American in the impression it gives of physical activity and enthusiasm, in its freshness and bounce. These traits are to the fore in his seven symphonies, of which the best known is the Third. Among his full-scale works are the Concerto for Piano and Small Orchestra (1942), the Violin Concerto of 1947, and the Fourth String Quartet (1950). The *American Festival Overture* (1939) is a bright, festive piece in Schuman's earlier manner. The first three notes, the composer explains, "will be recognized by some listeners as the 'call to play' of childhood days. In New York City it is yelled on the syllables 'Wee-Awk-EE' to get the gang together for a game or a festive occasion of some sort." Schuman naturally was not interested in duplicating the 'call to play' of his boyhood days. His aim rather was to capture the mood of adventure and expectancy with which a boy on a city street will summon his comrades. The Overture shows the breezy Americanism of Schuman's music at its best. While Schuman has retained the buoyancy that characterized his early works, in later years he has turned increasingly to more serious moods and a more personal type of expression.

He is fond of writing choral music, in which he became interested while he was conducting the chorus at Sarah Lawrence College. His choral pieces have a full, sturdy sound. He feels especially close to poetry such as Walt Whitman's, which enables him to communicate emotion of a vigorous, manly kind. Whitman's lines inspired *Pioneers*, for unaccompanied chorus (1937), as well as Schuman's most successful choral work, *A Free Song* (1942). Another favorite poet is Genevieve Taggard, whose verses he set in *Prologue for Chorus* (1939), *This Is Our Time* (1940), and *Holiday Song* (1942). In these pieces Schuman has provided a useful repertory suitable for school and community groups. "Music which the layman can perform," he believes, "is essential if we hope to reach a wide audience. Only in this manner can we communicate to our countrymen in intimate fashion the unique feelings of the contemporary composer."

Schuman's vivid sense of rhythm enables him to write effective ballet music. *Undertow*, which he composed for the Ballet Theater, was presented at the Metropolitan Opera House in 1945, with choreography by Anthony Tudor. Schuman produced a powerful score, rich in mood and color, that evoked the big-city atmosphere so dear to his imagination. He also wrote two ballet scores for the distinguished American dancer Martha Graham—*Night Journey* (1947) and the intensely dramatic *Judith* (1949), based on the Biblical story of Judith and Holofernes.

Schuman shares the recent upsurge of interest in American opera. He conceived the idea of writing a one-act opera about his once favorite pastime, baseball. Thus came into being *The Mighty Casey* (1953), a dramatization of Ernest L. Thayer's immortal poem *Casey at the Bat*. The work is as American as an opera could possibly be.

Credendum: Article of Faith, for orchestra, was written in 1955 at the request of the United States National Commission for UNESCO through the Department of State; it was the first symphonic composition to be commissioned directly by an agency of our government. In 1943 Schuman wrote his *William Billings Overture,* in which he turned for inspiration to William Billings, the eighteenth-century American composer whom we discussed in our Introduction. He subsequently refashioned the material into a longer work called *New England Triptych.* (A triptych is a composition in three parts.) This orchestral piece, which he completed in 1956, is based on three hymns by Billings—*Be Glad Then America, When Jesus Wept,* and *Chester.* He also wrote an overture for brass band on *Chester.* This thoroughly attractive work offers a fine introduction to William Schuman's music.

Chester was one of the most popular of Billings' hymns. During the American Revolution it became a marching song for the Continental Army, as both the words and the tune expressed the faith of Washington's soldiers in the justice of their cause:

> Let tyrants shake their iron rod
> And slav'ry clank her galling chains,
> We'll fear them not, we trust in God,
> New England's God forever reigns!

> What grateful off'ring shall we bring,
> What shall we render to the Lord?
> Loud Hallelujahs let us sing,
> And praise His name on every chord!

Schuman's Overture is in the form of a theme and variations. This has always been a favorite form with composers, for it enables them to exercise their imagination in transforming a melody, whether their own or someone else's. In varying a theme the composer may change the melody, the harmony, or the rhythm; he may shift the tune up or down to a higher or lower register; he may change the tempo, that is, the speed of the music; or he may alter the dynamics from soft to loud or the other way around. He may change the color by assigning the tune to different instruments, or he may combine the theme with other themes. As a result, we glimpse the theme in ever new transformations, just as we may see a character in a play appear in each scene in a new costume, or come out in disguise. In recognizing the familiar features of the original melody we are aware at the same time that they have been altered in a number of ways.

Chester opens with two statements of the hymn tune, first in a mood of quiet faith, the second in a majestic *fortissimo* (very loud) that suggests the "loud Hallelujahs" mentioned in the second stanza of the poem. The composer here reveals this historic American tune in all its simplicity, dignity, and strength. From then on Schuman uses all the resources of his craftsmanship and his fantasy to play around with the melody, presenting it in ever varied garb. Now it appears as a lively marching song that suggests a fife and drum, conjuring up the indomitable Spirit of '76—the spirit of the ragged soldiers who, throughout all the hardships that confronted them, never lost faith in their ultimate victory. Now the melody appears with new harmonies, and now it is brightly arrayed in jazz rhythms. One part of the tune hurries by in shorter notes; another holds back in longer ones. Presently we hear the melody sung in stately fashion by the trumpets. Throughout all these transformations the hymn tune retains its sturdy contours, its optimistic spirit, its hope and faith, until the rousing climax in

147

which Schuman exploits to the full the powerful effects of which the massed brass is capable.

A new honor came to William Schuman in 1961: he was appointed president of Lincoln Center of the Performing Arts in New York City, a bold new project for the performing arts—opera, symphony, ballet, and drama—designed on a vast scale such as has never before been approached in this country. At Lincoln Center Schuman will not only have a greater outlet than ever before for his abilities as an administrator; he will also be able to exercise a significant influence upon the artistic life of the United States.

William Schuman won success without any compromise on his part. It is precisely because he remained faithful to his ideals that he has been able to impress his personality, both as a composer and educator, upon the American scene. In both capacities he has made a vital contribution to our musical life.

13. GIAN-CARLO MENOTTI

Gian-Carlo Menotti does not belong, strictly speaking, in a book about American composers. Out of loyalty to his native land he has never renounced his Italian citizenship. Nevertheless there are good reasons for regarding him as one of us. In the first place, he received his musical training in this country and has spent most of his life here. In the second, he writes his librettos in English. Most important of all, it is in the United States that he has won his great success.

He was born on July 7, 1911, in a little town in northern Italy named Cadegliano, in a pink villa that stood high on a hill over-looking Lake Lugano. He never lacked for company, for there were ten children in the family; Gian-Carlo was the ninth. His grandfather had been the mayor of the town and his family was not only important but also wealthy; his father ran a successful import-export business with South America.

Gian-Carlo cannot remember a time in his life when he was not surrounded by music. His brothers and sisters sang and played, and the family spent its evenings making chamber music. His mother gave him his first music lessons. He wrote a song when he was four and at the age of six decided to become a composer. Three years later he received a fascinating gift: an elaborate puppet theater. The boy's career as a puppeteer centered about his vivid presentation of the Devil, whom he wreathed in clouds of suffocating smoke by burning sulphur behind the scenes. Once his interest in the theater was aroused, the next step was an opera, which Gian-Carlo wrote when he was eleven years old. He called it *La Morte di Pierrot* (*The Death of Pierrot*). In this work, as he describes it, "everyone sings and plays all the time and dies in the last act."

The Menotti family moved to Milan, where Gian-Carlo entered the Conservatory. Having started out as a child prodigy, he did not think it necessary to pay much attention to his studies. Why bother to work when composing came to him so easily? He was a good-looking boy with a charming personality; he played the piano well; and so he was invited to all the aristocratic homes of Milan. Since he loved people and parties, he was soon frittering away his time in society instead of buckling down to his studies.

His mother watched all this with dismay. She was afraid that if he continued in this manner he would squander his musical gifts. Then Gian-Carlo's father died, leaving the family business in difficulties. Signora Menotti decided to go to South America in order to restore the family fortunes. She was convinced that Gian-Carlo would study much better if he were left alone, with no one to distract him, in a foreign land. So she took him with her on the trip to South America, and left him in the United States.

Accordingly, at the age of seventeen Gian-Carlo found himself enrolled at the Curtis Institute of Music in Philadelphia. He spoke no English. He wore a foreign-looking pair of knickers that made people stare. And he knew no one save his countryman Rosario Scalero, the professor of composition at the Curtis Institute. It had been the custom for American musicians to go to Europe to complete their studies. Now Gian-Carlo reversed the process.

His first concern was to buy American clothes. His second, to learn English; in order to do so he would go to the movies four times a week. His mother had been right in supposing that he would work more diligently once he was removed from the social life of Milan. Shy and lonely in his new surroundings, Gian-Carlo applied himself to his studies with zeal. He realized how much time he had wasted in Milan and worked hard to make up for it. He was helped by the fact that his new teachers did not in the slightest treat him as if he were a genius. On the contrary, they were extremely strict with him and gave him a thorough grounding in the technique of his art.

Before long Gian-Carlo found a friend in his schoolmate Samuel Barber. The two young musicians became inseparable. Gian-Carlo enjoyed his visits to Sam's home in West Chester, Pennsylvania, where he had his first glimpse of life in a small American town. His friendship with the Barber family did much to make him feel at home in the new world. Some time later he was able to reciprocate by inviting Sam to the Menotti home in Cadegliano.

When he was twenty-two Gian-Carlo began to compose his first successful opera, *Amelia Goes to the Ball,* a lighthearted comedy in one act for which he wrote his own libretto. He did not trust his English, so he first wrote the text in Italian and then translated it into English. In *Amelia* Gian-Carlo gently poked fun at the aristocratic salons that he remembered so vividly from his years in Milan. By this time Mrs. Curtis Bok, who had endowed the Curtis Institute, was taking an active interest in Gian-Carlo's career. She saw to it that *Amelia Goes to the Ball* was produced at the Curtis Institute in the spring of 1937. Gian-Carlo's opera delighted everyone who saw it.

He returned to Italy at the end of the school year in order to spend the summer with his family in Cadegliano. The townspeople were proud of his success and welcomed him warmly. They were doubly proud one day toward the end of the summer when the postmistress, an excitable little woman, came bicycling down the main street as fast as she could, waving a telegram in her hand and shouting its contents to everyone she encountered. Finally she reached the Menotti home and cried, "*Il Metropolitano! Il Metropolitano!*" It was true: the Metropolitan Opera House had decided to present *Amelia Goes to the Ball* during its next season.

The production of *Amelia* at the Metropolitan established Gian-Carlo's reputation as one of the most promising among the younger composers. The work was so successful that he received a communication from the Italian Embassy in Washington, informing him that Mussolini's Minister of Culture wanted to make him an honorary member of the Fascist party. Gian-Carlo declined the honor even though he knew that by doing so he endangered the success of his opera in Italy. The work was presented in his homeland the following year, not in Rome but at a small provincial theater. When Gian-Carlo asked the director of the Rome Opera why his work had not been given there, that gentleman pointed to Gian-Carlo's empty lapel, indicating that it was because the composer lacked a Fascist party button.

In 1939 the National Broadcasting Company commissioned Menotti to compose an opera. He wrote *The Old Maid and the Thief*, a lyric comedy that was even more successful than *Amelia Goes to the Ball*. This time Menotti wrote the libretto directly in English, and has done so ever since. In writing *The Old Maid and the Thief* Menotti remembered his visits to Sam Barber's family in West Chester, and evoked the atmosphere of that quiet Quaker town.

After the war Menotti settled at Mount Kisco, New York, where he and Sam Barber bought the house that they named Capricorn. Here Menotti was able to pace up and down, shout, sing, and bang the piano as he created the scenes of his operas. Here too, in congenial surroundings, he was able to relax with his many friends and to enjoy his favorite sport, tennis. At Capricorn Menotti produced the works that carried his name around the world.

For many years he dreamed of bringing his native land closer to his adopted country. He realized this ambition by organizing the "Festival of Two Worlds" that takes place every summer in Spoleto, a little town not far from Rome. Spoleto, set on a hillside, has retained all the charm of the past. Here American and Italian works are produced and performed by American and Italian artists, thereby fulfilling Menotti's desire, as he put it, "to bring young artists from the New World into contact with those of the old." Many American tourists as well as Italians come to Spoleto for the Festival, which presents opera, ballet, drama, and chamber music. A number of scholarships are granted to young American musicians and students of the theater, so that they may become acquainted with Italy and her culture. Although Menotti has put much time and effort into the Spoleto Festival, he feels that the artistic results are well worth it.

As a composer Menotti finds his natural outlet in the opera house. He has the theater in his blood. "As far back as I can remember," he writes, "I wanted to be on the stage. Apparently I was so desperate that no one would let me. The only chance I got was in a school show, and I must have hammed it up so badly they never gave me another. And now, of course, I can't sing well enough to appear in my own pieces. All that's left for me is to write them." Endowed with a vivid imagination, Menotti sees life in terms of dramatic conflict, suspense, shock, surprise—in short, in terms of the theater. Hence his operas are extraordinarily effective from the dramatic point of view.

The human appeal of his stage works derives from his ability to arouse emotion. "First, last, and always," he maintains, "the appeal of any stage piece must be to the heart." He selects themes that are rich in feeling, in compassion, in sympathy for the under-

153

dog. He shows extraordinary sensitivity in his portrayal of children. He has no interest in sophisticated subjects; his art springs out of the Italian theater, which is based on strong, simple emotions. (You become aware of this when you see any of the great Italian films.) "Music," he believes, "can express only fundamental immediate emotion. In the theater the medium is usually prose. But when prose cannot say a thing, you must turn to poetry. And when poetry can no longer say what you have to say, you must turn to music. You must sing it out. In each case you must move to another area of expression to get more truly at the human heart." This desire to move the heart is the mainspring of Menotti's dramas.

The opera composer is strongly dependent on the dramatist or poet who writes his libretto. He has to work as closely as possible with the librettist so as to shape each act in such a way that the arias, duets, trios, quartets, choruses, and ballet numbers will come at the most effective spots in the dramatic action. Both the composer and his librettist have to revise their work many times in order to coordinate the drama and the music in the most harmonious manner. It is therefore a great advantage for a composer to be able to write his own librettos. He is then able to create the drama and the music simultaneously, and to make them fit one another from the very start. Very few composers have written their own librettos, for it happens only rarely that a man who has the talent to write music will also have the talent to write dramas. The outstanding example in the nineteenth century was Richard Wagner. The most successful composer-dramatist of our time is unquestionably Gian-Carlo Menotti. By writing his own librettos Menotti is sure to have the kind of story that will release the music within him. In his operas, music and text are so closely interwoven that the one hardly exists apart from the other. For this reason he regards his operas as "plays with music" or "musical dramas."

Menotti handles the English language in a most personal way. The fact that he learned it when he was grown made him sensitive to all sorts of expressions that the rest of us take for granted. "To me English is an exotic language. An American in Italy may hear the word *andiamo,* and it sounds fresh and strange and rich to him. To an Italian it is just another word and has as much impact on him as the words 'Let's go' (which it means) on an American. But ordinary English words sound different and good to me. The phrase 'A pane of glass' which I use in *The Consul* has a special tang to me. The word *paper* is somehow different to me. These words set me to thinking in terms of music." There are people who consider English a difficult language to sing. Menotti is most certainly not one of them. In his estimation, English is the ideal language for opera.

The dialogue that carries the action and the plot of an opera is known as *recitative* (reh-tchee-tah-teev'). At the emotional moments lyric melody takes over; here we find the arias. It has always been difficult to make recitative sound natural in English. For this reason, in a popular Broadway musical only the arias—that is to say, the songs—are sung; the dialogue relating to plot and action is spoken. In traditional opera, on the other hand, the recitative is sung. Menotti has been extremely successful in developing a recitative in English that sounds natural and convincing. The plot and the action of his operas are revealed in a suave musical declamation that is molded to the rise and fall of everyday English speech. This recitative is so distinctive that an opera can immediately be recognized as his from the dialogue alone.

Menotti comes out of the great tradition of Italian opera, which is based on the beauty of vocal melody. He is a master of melody. "I am convinced," he states, "that every great melody is buried somehow deep in the memory of man, and when a composer brings it forth we all recognize it and respond to it at once, as though we

155

had known it all our lives." Menotti's operas abound in melody —a flowing, poetic melody that is molded to the curve of the human voice.

One of Menotti's strongest works is *The Medium*, which was first presented by the opera theater of Columbia University in 1946. The eerie plot concerns Madame Flora (Baba), a fake spiritualist, her daughter Monica, and Toby, a mute Gipsy boy whom Baba has adopted. Monica loves Toby. Baba tolerates him, and mistreats him when she is drunk. Baba tricks her clients into believing that they are speaking with their dear departed ones. One night, at a seance, the unexpected happens; something touches her in the dark, and she cannot explain it. She begins to fall victim to the very delusions that she had been foisting upon others. Finally, half crazed with fear, she shoots at the ghost that seems to threaten her—and inadvertently kills the mute Gipsy boy. *The Medium* generally is presented on a double bill with *The Telephone* (1947), a comic opera in one act about a young man who is unable to propose to his girl because her telephone is constantly ringing. He finally conceives the bright idea of going out and telephoning her himself. Needless to say, he wins the girl.

The Consul brought Menotti a Pulitzer Prize for 1950. In this deeply compassionate opera the composer concerned himself with the plight of those who were trapped by history in our troubled time; who had to flee their country when tyranny took over but found themselves unable, because of red tape and bureaucracy, to obtain the precious visa that alone would admit them to another land. Magda Sorel's great aria in the second act, "To this we've come—that men withhold the world from men!"; the scene in the Consul's office when the Magician is able to conjure everything out of his sleeve except the precious visa; and the duet between the sad little woman who sings of her woes in Italian and the sad little man who translates her words into English are among the high points of this profoundly moving lyric drama.

Among Menotti's other operas are *Amahl and the Night Visitors* (1951); *The Saint of Bleecker Street* (1954), which brought him another Pulitzer Prize; and *Maria Golovin*, which received its premiere at the Brussels World Fair in the summer of 1958. Menotti's theater pieces, standing approximately midway between traditional opera and the popular musical theater of Broadway, succeeded in bridging the gulf that had separated the two types of entertainment. His career opened at a time when Broadway still regarded opera as being "long-hair" and forbidding. *The Medium* was first produced on Broadway in 1947 and received enthusiastic notices; yet the public stayed away. The production was about to close. But word had got around that here was a serious musical play that made exciting theater. There was a sudden upsurge of interest, and *The Medium* ended by running on Broadway for seven months. Since then this opera has been performed more than two thousand times all over the world.

With *The Medium* and *The Consul*, which also had an impressive run on Broadway, Menotti created a new public for modern opera, a much broader public than that which attends the Metropolitan Opera House. This new audience, he points out, "is anybody and everybody, not an audience of specialists or subscribers. These are people who come without fixed views. They want to be entertained and moved. It is an audience that represents every phase of American life, and if this audience approves, any audience in the world will approve. Frankly, I want to write for no other audience."

Amahl and the Night Visitors offers an enchanting introduction to Menotti's style. "This is an opera for children," he writes in his introduction to the recording of *Amahl*, "because it tries to recapture my own childhood. You see, when I was a child I lived in Italy, and in Italy we have no Santa Claus. I suppose that Santa Claus is much too busy with American children to be able to handle Italian children as well. Our gifts were brought to us by the Three

Kings, instead. I actually never met the Three Kings—it didn't matter how hard my little brother and I tried to keep awake at night to catch a glimpse of the Three Royal Visitors, we would always fall asleep just before they arrived. But I do remember hearing them. I remember the weird cadence of their song in the dark distance; I remember the brittle sound of the camel's hooves crushing the frozen snow; and I remember the mysterious tinkling of their silver bridles.

"To these Three Kings I mainly owe the happy Christmas seasons of my childhood and I should have remained very grateful to them. Instead, I came to America and soon forgot all about them, for here at Christmas time one sees so many Santa Clauses scattered all over town. They made me forget the three dear old Kings of my own childhood. But in 1951 I found myself in serious difficulty. I had been commissioned by the National Broadcasting Company to write an opera for television, with Christmas as a deadline, and I simply didn't have one idea in my head. One November afternoon as I was walking rather gloomily through the rooms of the Metropolitan Museum, I chanced to stop in front of the *Adoration of the Magi* by Hieronymus Bosch, and as I was looking at it, suddenly I heard again, coming from the distant blue hills, the weird song of the Three Kings. I then realized that they had come back to me and had brought me a gift." The gift was one of the most enchanting operas ever written. *Amahl and the Night Visitors* was presented by the NBC Television Theater on Christmas Eve, 1951, and speedily established itself as a classic.

The action centers about a crippled shepherd boy called Amahl and his mother, an impoverished widow. One night, as he sits playing on his pipe, he sees a large star flaming in the sky. When his mother calls him he hobbles into the cottage on his crudely made crutch and tells her about it. But she doesn't believe him, for Amahl has the imagination of an artist and is always telling tall tales. She is the realist; and reality for her is an empty cupboard and an empty pocket. "Unless we go begging," she tells her son, "how shall we live through tomorrow?" Amahl tries to console her. "Don't cry, Mother dear, don't worry for me. If we must go begging, a good beggar I'll be. I know sweet tunes to set people dancing. We'll walk and walk from village to town, you dressed as a gipsy and I as a clown." He paints a bright picture of their future. Then mother and son bid each other a tender good night.

On this night the Three Kings and the Page, guided by the star, go forth to bring gifts of gold and silver, frankincense and myrrh to the newborn Child. The night is cold; they seek shelter in the widow's humble abode. Amahl and his mother can scarcely believe their eyes as their royal visitors, clad in splendid robes, enter the wretched cottage. King Kaspar, who is quite deaf, sings a lovely aria telling Amahl about the contents of his magic box. In the top drawer he keeps his magic stones, in the second drawer his beads. "In the third drawer . . . Oh, little boy! oh, little boy! . . . In the third drawer I keep—licorice . . . black, sweet licorice. Have some." The scene reaches its climax in the duet between King Melchior and Amahl's mother. Melchior sings of the Child to whom they are bringing their gifts: "Have you seen a child the color of wheat, the color of dawn? His eyes are mild, His hands are those of a King, as King He was born." The Mother sings, as if to herself: "Yes, I know a child the color of wheat, the color of dawn. His eyes are mild, his hands are those of a King, as King he was born. But no one will bring him incense or gold, though sick and poor and hungry and cold. He's my child, my son, my darling, my own . . ."

In the meantime Amahl has been sent by his mother to summon the shepherds from the neighboring huts, since she has nothing to offer her royal guests. The shepherds and shepherdesses arrive, bearing baskets of fruits and vegetables. They dance in honor of the Kings. Their dance, as Menotti conceived it, "should combine the qualities of primitive folk dancing and folk ritual. It is both an entertainment and a ceremony of welcome and hospitality. The dancers are at first shy and fearful at the realization that they are in the presence of three great Kings, and their movements are at times faltering and hesitant. But later, the dance assumes the character of a tarantella, gaining in pace and sureness and ending in a joyous frenzy." The shepherds leave. The three Kings and the Page lie down to sleep.

But Amahl's mother cannot sleep. She is wrung by anxiety for the future. She cannot take her eyes from the treasure guarded by the Page. "All that gold! All that gold! I wonder if rich people know what to do with their gold! Do they know how a child could be fed? Do rich people know? Do they know that a house can be kept warm all day with burning logs? Do rich people know? . . . Oh, what I could do for my child with that gold! Why should it all go to a child they don't even know? They are asleep. Do I dare? If I take some they'll never miss it. For my child . . . for my child . . ."

She reaches out her arm for the gold. The Page awakes, seizes her arm. Crying "Thief! Thief!" he arouses his masters. The Kings awake. Amahl, choking with tears of shame, staggers toward his mother and, letting his crutch fall, collapses, sobbing, into her arms. Finally King Melchior speaks, saying with great dignity: "Oh, woman, you may keep the gold. The Child we seek doesn't need our gold. On love, on love alone He will build His kingdom. And the keys to His city belong to the poor." He tells his companions to make ready to leave. Amahl's mother throws herself on her knees before the Kings, spilling the gold onto the floor. "Oh no, wait . . . take back your gold! For such a King I've waited all my life. And if I weren't so poor I would send a gift of my own to such a child."

Amahl has a happy thought. Why not send his crutch as a gift? As he turns to offer it to the Kings, a miracle occurs. He takes a step forward, then another, without the crutch. Incredulous, he whispers, "I walk, Mother . . ." And the others, overcome with wonder, echo, "He walks." The Kings accept the miracle as a sign from God. Amahl, like a bird released, cries in joy, "Look, Mother, I can dance, I can jump, I can run!" He asks his mother if he may take the crutch to the Child himself. The Kings promise to take care of him on the way, and she consents. "Yes. I think you should go and bring thanks to the Child yourself."

Here is how Menotti describes the end of the opera: "Amahl rushes into his mother's arms, bidding her goodbye, then hurries to catch up with the departing Kings. Having taken his place at the end of the procession, Amahl begins to play his pipe as he goes. Outside, the soft colors of dawn are brightening the sky, and a few great flakes of snow have begun to fall upon the road. The Mother stands alone in the doorway of the cottage. Then she goes outside to wave once more to Amahl, as he turns to her, just before he disappears at the bend in the road. The curtain falls very slowly."

The creator of this beautiful fantasy is one of the most widely loved figures in the music of our time. Gian-Carlo Menotti occupies a special place in the musical world. He has created a popular operatic theater all his own.

14. NORMAN DELLO JOIO

Norman Dello Joio's musical development reflects the influences he absorbed in his early years. He is a first-generation American whose outlook on art unites the heritage of his forefathers with the thought and feeling of the land of his birth.

He came from a line of Italian musicians who had been organists in a little town near Naples. His father followed the family tradition by becoming a church organist, choirmaster, and composer; and he continued in his profession after he came to the United States. Norman was born in New York City on January 24, 1913. He grew up in a home that was always filled with music and musicians, especially opera singers. He took to music as naturally as a child takes to walking and speaking.

His father encouraged his love of music, but under strict, old-world discipline. He gave Norman thorough training in the fundamentals of piano, organ, and harmony, and saw to it that the boy practiced conscientiously every day. He would play with Norman four-hand piano arrangements not only of the classical symphonies but also of such twentieth-century masterpieces as Stravinsky's *Petrushka*. This broad interest in all kinds of new music was most unusual, at that time, in musicians of the older generation. As a result of his father's excellent teaching, Norman was a thoroughly

professional musician at an age when others are beginning to master the technique of music. When he was fifteen he was able, in
his own words, "to read anything at sight."

By this time Norman was studying the organ with his godfather,
Pietro Yon, the organist of St. Patrick's Cathedral. On occasion
he was permitted to try the magnificent organ in the cathedral.
His heart leaped with excitement the first time he pressed the keys
and released the rich harmonies that soared aloft through the great
open space of the church. Although he knew that he was going
to be a musician, he did not yet know precisely which branch of
the art he would pursue. He simply assumed that he would follow in his father's footsteps as a church organist. He became quite
sure of this when he obtained his first job: he was engaged to play
the organ at a church on City Island called The Star of the Sea.
He had to rise at dawn in order to get to the church in time for
early Mass. The first Sunday he lost his way, and almost came
late. Yet the inconvenience of the long trip was more than com-
pensated for by the glow of satisfaction he felt at taking part, in
such an important way, in the religious ceremony.

Norman's interest in the music of the Roman Catholic Church
represented only one aspect of his life. His other interests were
those of a typical New York boy responding to the exciting city
about him. From his earliest years he loved the crowded streets
that teemed with life and movement. He joined the boys on his
street in their games and developed a passion for baseball. Indeed,
he became such a fine player that he was offered a job on a professional team. His interest in jazz represented another important
facet of his life. At the age of sixteen he was playing in dance
bands, and for a number of years thereafter he led his own band.
There was a violent contrast between the cloistered world of the
Church and the hectic life of the city, as great as the contrast between the ancient Catholic chants that he played on Sunday morn-

ings and the pulsating jazz rhythms to which he surrendered on Saturday nights. He seemed to be torn between two irreconcilable worlds. His religious upbringing urged him toward the one, even as his hunger for life impelled him toward the other.

This inner conflict made it difficult for Norman to decide on a career. On the one hand he toyed with the possibility of becoming a professional ballplayer. On the other, he came under the influence of a Monsignor who took a personal interest in his spiritual development. As a result, Norman for a time thought of becoming a priest. Between these opposing goals was a third: his love of music. The musician finally won out. After graduating from All Hallows School he entered the Juilliard School of Music, where he studied the piano and organ. More important, he made his first attempts at composition. He also attended the College of the City of New York. But he left after a year in order to devote himself entirely to music.

Every composer goes through an arduous preliminary training during which he follows the rules laid down by his teachers. Then comes the exhilarating period when he begins to discover what he wants to say, and how to say it. He now has to make the rules obey him instead of blindly obeying them himself. There is no one any more to tell him "This is right" or "That is wrong." He must look within himself, and bring out what lies hidden there according to his own taste and judgment. In short, he must find his own voice. Norman Dello Joio remembers his last year at the Juilliard School as having been "terrific," for he was embarking upon an exciting journey of self-discovery. Nor did he have to wait long for recognition. When he completed his Trio for piano, violin, and cello, the piece was submitted for the Elizabeth Sprague Coolidge Award in chamber music and won the thousand-dollar prize.

Dello Joio went on a trip to Europe shortly before the outbreak of the Second World War. At that time most American composers were fascinated by Paris, for the French capital was the center of the modern movement in art and music. But for Dello Joio it was Italy that proved to be the most significant experience of his journey. When he reached the land of his forefathers, he felt almost as if he were returning home. Rome, Venice, Milan—each fascinated him in turn. But it was the region around Naples, where his ancestors had lived for generations, that moved him most deeply. The people, the language, the music—all seemed wonderfully close to his heart. He realized for the first time how much this lovely land had contributed to his heritage.

An equally significant experience awaited him upon his return. That summer he attended the Berkshire Music Center at Tanglewood, Massachusetts, where he studied with the famous German composer Paul Hindemith. Until that time Dello Joio had not thought very deeply about the problems of contemporary music. Hindemith opened up a new world to him, the world of twentieth-century musical thought. Even more, the German master held up to him the high ideals of perfect craftsmanship, of clarity of thought and logical design. Hindemith's powerful intellect and his grasp of all aspects of musical art made a profound impression upon young Dello Joio. When the summer was over Hindemith returned to New Haven, as he was then teaching at Yale University. Dello Joio followed him there and continued his lessons.

Like all the musicians who came under Hindemith's influence, Dello Joio received from his teacher a deep sense of the ethical power of art. Hindemith maintained that music is not only an entertainment or a beguiling of the senses, but a high moral force; and that he who truly lays himself open to its ennobling power must lead a good life. The religious side of Dello Joio's nature responded happily to this philosophy. He believes that "Music is an expression of something real in human life. It is not a retreat from life." So too he writes: "To know music is to become greater in knowledge and insight and to know many other things than music. It is to develop a sense of values about art and to learn about another dimension of reality previously hidden."

Dello Joio felt that he should have made up his mind much sooner to become a composer. He now worked furiously to make up for the time he had lost, with the result that he soon became one of the best known among his generation of composers. His *Magnificat* for orchestra won the Town Hall Composition Award for 1943. He received Guggenheim Fellowships in 1944 and 1945, and a thousand-dollar grant from the American Academy of Arts and Letters in 1946. His *Variations, Chaconne and Finale* for orchestra won the New York Music Critics' Circle Award in 1949. In 1957 his *Meditations on Ecclesiastes* brought him a Pulitzer Prize.

Dello Joio taught composition for six years at Sarah Lawrence College. Although he enjoyed teaching, he felt that it interfered with his creative work and ultimately resigned from his post. In 1947 he was invited by the Polish government to appear in a series of concerts in that country. He served for several seasons as commentator on the Saturday afternoon broadcasts from the Metropolitan Opera House. But these have been no more than passing distractions; his main activity has been the writing of music. He lives in New York City with his wife Grayce, a former ballet dancer who gave up her own career in order to devote herself to his. They have three children, Victoria, Justin, and Norman, Jr.

An important element in Dello Joio's style springs from his early immersion in church music, especially the Gregorian chants, which he came to know through his father. These chants, which sound wonderfully ancient and remote, date from the first centuries of Christianity. They take their name from Pope Gregory the Great, who reigned from the year 590 to 604 and helped to as-

166

semble the chants into a fixed religious service. Gregorian melodies figure in a number of Dello Joio's works, imparting to them an archaic charm.

Italian opera is another important element of Dello Joio's style. Some of his earliest memories of music center around the arias sung by the opera singers who used to visit his father. As he himself points out, "If my father had remained in Italy, I should probably have been an Italian opera composer, following faithfully in the footsteps of Bellini, Donizetti, and Verdi." He admires intensely the freely flowing melody of the Italian masters. "What I strive for most of all," he has stated, "is the complete confidence, the lyric quality, the feeling for line we find in Verdi." Dello Joio is a lyricist by nature; the focal point of his music is the melody. His melodies are supple and expressive. They range in mood from gentle longing to a robust joviality, but they are all unmistakably his.

An equally important ingredient in Dello Joio's style stems from his interest in jazz. Lively jazz rhythms give his music its lightness and forward thrust. He will subdivide the measure into all kinds of intricate patterns. Yet these unfold above the regular beat of the meter, as is characteristic of American jazz. Despite the strong European influences in Dello Joio's style, his rhythm is unmistakably American.

His flair for rhythm has made Dello Joio a successful composer of ballet music. From 1941 to 1943 he was the musical director for Eugene Loring's Dance Players, and he composed the score for two ballets that were produced by Loring in 1942—*The Duke of Sacramento* and *Prairie*. In 1945 he composed the score for Michael Kidd's ballet *On Stage!*, which became one of the hits of the Ballet Theater. He wrote a ballet for Martha Graham, first called *Wilderness Stair* but later renamed *Diversion of Angels*. The gentle lyricism of this score influenced Miss Graham to pro-

167

duce a ballet of serenely lyrical movement, with none of the brooding intensity that generally marks her choreography.

The types of music that have most strongly influenced Dello Joio—Gregorian chant, Italian opera, American jazz, and modern ballet—are very different in character. But they have one feature in common: they all communicate to a mass audience. Dello Joio stands among those contemporary composers who have sought to lead music back to the public. He feels that art should be emotional rather than intellectual so as to reach a broad mass of listeners and to move them in the most direct way possible. Hence his preoccupation with melody and rhythm, the two elements of music that most directly convey feeling. Dello Joio's art is rooted in the past. As he says, "I was never consciously a modernist." He has been intensely aware of the currents of change within our time, and is thoroughly contemporary in his use of dissonant harmony and driving rhythms. At the same time he has tried to remain tender and simple in his music, a not altogether easy task for a composer of the twentieth century. He feels that the composer of today should not abandon tradition. Instead, he should adapt the great traditions of the past to the needs of the present.

Dello Joio is the kind of natural musician who would rather write music than sit back and theorize about it. He does not approve of the composer who writes one piece a year and carefully analyzes every measure of it. A composer, he feels, should compose all the time. True, not all his works are apt to be on a high level. But those that are less good will prepare the way for his better ones—as in the case of the old masters, who finished one work and immediately began the next.

Dello Joio has turned out a variety of works for orchestra. The *Sinfonietta* of 1941 and *Magnificat* of 1942 are two early works in which the composer is moving toward his fully formed style. *To a Lone Sentry* (1943) is a mood piece dating from the war years; it shows the composer's fondness for a quiet, meditative lyricism. *Concert Music* (1944) is full of color and movement; the middle part contains effective writing for the brass. Dello Joio's ability to make the orchestra sing is illustrated by the *Serenade* (1948), *Epigraph* (1951), and *Meditations on Ecclesiastes* (1957). In *New York Profiles* (1949) he evokes four scenes dear to every New Yorker: *The Cloisters*, *The Park*, *Grant's Tomb*, and *Little Italy*. *The Cloisters* is based on a Gregorian melody that suggests the medieval atmosphere of the monastery-like museum overlooking the Hudson. The theme is then ingeniously varied in order to create the mood and atmosphere of the other three movements. His most ambitious orchestral piece is the *Variations, Chaconne and Finale* (1947), which has been performed by leading orchestras throughout the country. (A *chaconne* is a type of composition in which a succession of chords is repeated over and over as the basis for variations.)

Dello Joio has written a number of concertos, the most important of which is the brilliant piano concerto, in the form of a *Fantasy and Variations*, that was introduced by Loren Hollander and the Cincinnati Orchestra in 1962. Of his chamber music we should mention his Trio for flute, cello, and piano (1943), and the *Variations and Capriccio* for violin and piano (1948). He has written several large works for the piano, such as the Second Piano Sonata (1943) and the Third (1947), as well as a number of short pieces.

Dello Joio's gift for heartfelt lyricism has found expression in a number of songs. *The Assassination* is a powerful song that shows his ability to create dramatic tension. One of his most important vocal works is *The Lamentation of Saul* (1954), a "dramatic cantata" for solo baritone accompanied by orchestra. (There is also a version of this piece that uses flute, oboe, clarinet, viola, cello, and piano to accompany the voice.) Dello Joio is among the many American composers who have found inspiration in Walt

169

Whitman. Three of his choral works are based on poems by Whitman: *Vigil Strange*, *The Mystic Trumpeter*, and *A Jubilant Song*. Stephen Vincent Benét's *Western Star* furnished the text for a "symphony for voices"—for soloists, chorus, and orchestra (1944) —that celebrates the American pioneering spirit. An altogether different type of piece is *A Psalm of David* (1950), which gives expression to Dello Joio's fondness for lyricism of a somberly meditative cast.

Given his love of vocal melody and his dramatic temperament, it was to be expected that Dello Joio would be among the large group of American composers who in recent years have turned to opera. His first attempt in this field was a full-length opera on the life of Joan of Arc, called *The Triumph of St. Joan* (1950). He subsequently reworked this into a shorter opera centering about Joan's final days, *The Trial at Rouen* (1950). Next came *The Ruby* (1955), a one-act opera based on Lord Dunsany's famous play *A Night at an Inn*. The action revolves around three thieves who steal the precious stone that serves as a Hindu idol's eye, whereupon the idol himself comes to reclaim it. In *Blood-Moon* (1961) Dello Joio wrote a three-act opera on a romantic theme based on the life of a famous actress of the Civil War period, Adah Menken, who was half Negro. She guards the secret of her birth from the Southern aristocrat who loves her, but in the end realizes that she can never marry him.

In November, 1958, the Columbia Broadcasting System presented a series of documentary films on television, tracing the development of air power from its earliest beginnings to the age of the jet. Dello Joio was asked to compose the music for this ambitious project. He subsequently arranged the material into an exciting suite for orchestra called *Air Power*. (By a suite we mean a musical work consisting of several movements based on a central idea. The suite may present a group of numbers extracted from a longer work such as an opera, ballet, film score, or music for a play. Or the suite may be an independent work.) Dello Joio's *Air Power* Suite is typical of his musical style.

The first half of *Air Power* contains three movements: 1. *Introduction.* An eloquent melody sings of vast open spaces, of mountaintops and the endless sea, of brave men poised for adventure. 2. *Frolics of the Early Days.* This movement is in three parts. *Parade of the Daredevils* is a breezy number that evokes the early years of our century. *Skylarking* is a lively little piece in three-four time. Light and gay, it creates the proper devil-may-care mood. *Sports Meet*, with its energetic rhythm, continues the suggestion of physical well-being and carefree gayety. The music conjures up the exciting scenes in the early days of aviation when daredevil flyers came together and performed all sorts of hair-raising stunts, such as standing on the wings of their planes or flying upside down. 3. *Mission in the Sky.* This movement too is divided into three numbers. *Alert and Take-off* again suggests the open air, and vistas of distant horizons. The music conveys an image of purposeful men aware of impending danger. *Air Battle.* The composer's imagination transforms the rat-tat-tat of guns into a musical rhythm. This is music of action and suspense as the planes engage each other high in the sky. *Safe Return.* The planes swoop down toward their base, their mission accomplished. The music rises to a triumphal climax, then subsides to a serenely lyrical ending.

The second half of *Air Power* is given over to a series of war scenes. 1. *March of the German Legions.* Trumpets and drums envelop this military piece in an atmosphere of grim determination. The music conjures up a vision of goose-stepping battalions. 2. *Lonely Pilot's Letter Home.* A poetic meditation filled with longing and tenderness. There is deep feeling in this piece, and an introspective lyricism. 3. *Russian Soldier Dance.* A vigorous dance tune in the style of Russian folk music. You can almost see the manly figures bobbing up and down, arms crossed in traditional fashion across their chests, heels flying. 4. *Japanese Prayer for Victory*. This piece accompanied scenes in the film showing Japanese pilots going through religious ceremonies before taking off on their missions. The music takes on the character of the ancient Japanese ritual chants, evoking the atmosphere of an Oriental shrine amid whose shadows lurk impassive faces and prostrate figures. 5. *Convoy and Wolf Pack Attack*. Vistas of sky and sea; the suspense of the chase; the atmosphere of danger. A bell tolls. The orchestra takes on a dark menacing sound. 6. *The Liberators and War's End*. The day everyone longed for has finally arrived. The music leaps with excitement, thrusting forward in energetic rhythms. Melodies heard earlier in the suite now reappear in a mood of triumph. This return to themes from earlier movements not only has all the charm of remembrance, but also serves to unify the form as the suite comes to a happy ending.

This music, with its singing melodies and spirited rhythms, makes an immediate appeal. It is not to be wondered at that Norman Dello Joio has become one of the most widely performed American composers of his generation. He is a leading representative of the new romanticism.

15. LEONARD BERNSTEIN

Leonard Bernstein is known to millions of Americans as one of the most dynamic personalities in the musical world. His rise to fame and his subsequent career have been nothing short of spectacular.

Leonard—or Lenny, as he is known to an adoring circle of friends—was born in Lawrence, Massachusetts, on August 25, 1918. His father was a Russian-Jewish immigrant who, after years of poverty and hard work, built up a successful business supplying equipment to beauty parlors and barber shops. "I was a scared, sickly, skinny kid." Thus Bernstein remembers his early years. He suffered from frequent attacks of asthma; and he was lonely, because he was unable to stand up to the neighborhood boys who bullied him whenever they felt like it.

One day when he came home from school he found a piano in the living room. His aunt had sent it to the Bernstein home for storage. It was an old, shabby instrument. But to Lenny, who was eleven at the time, it seemed the most beautiful object he had ever seen. "I made love to it right away," he remembers; he sat down and tried to pick out on the keyboard Irving Berlin's *Blue Skies*. A new chapter opened in his life. The piano became his friend, his refuge from all the difficulties presented by the outside world.

Here he could sit for hours on end, losing all sense of time as he made up melodies of his own. He often continued to play into the night. One night his parents were awakened by the sounds of the piano. His father rushed into the living room.

"Lenny, it's two o'clock in the morning! Why are you playing?"

The boy looked up, unruffled. "I have to. The sounds are in my head and I have to get them out."

Lenny begged his parents for piano lessons. They opposed the idea. Mr. Bernstein remembered the half-starved musicians of his native town in Russia, and was determined that no son of his should embark upon so uncertain a career. He wanted Lenny to receive a thorough education and then take over his thriving business. Piano lessons, he felt, would only distract Lenny from his schoolwork. But the boy was so insistent that his father finally gave in. After several years with neighborhood teachers, Lenny came to Helen Coates, a fine musician who opened up to him the world of the great masters. Miss Coates guided and encouraged her pupil in his insatiable quest for musical knowledge. "He was frighteningly gifted," she said in later years. "He could read, sing, and memorize anything. He absorbed in one lesson what took most of my pupils five or six lessons to learn." As for Lenny, he had already made up his mind about his future. "I knew with finality that I would be a musician!"

His musical studies, far from interfering with his schoolwork, seemed actually to stimulate him. At the Boston Latin School, which had exceptionally high standards, he became an outstanding student. He was equally conscientious in his religious studies at the school attached to his father's temple. When he had to deliver the customary speech at his confirmation, he wrote it himself in Hebrew. And the "skinny, sickly kid" was also becoming an all-around athlete. "One day," he recalls, "I was a scrawny little thing that everybody could beat up, and the next time I looked around I was the biggest boy in class. I could run faster, jump higher, dive better than anybody." He no longer held back from meeting boys and girls of his own age. On the contrary, he kept his friends spellbound with his lively performance of popular songs and jazz. At social gatherings Lenny was the life of the party. As he himself recalls, "I just ran for the piano as soon as I got in the door and stayed there until they threw me out. It was as though I didn't exist without music."

Lenny now began to attend concerts. He listened to records and radio broadcasts; he borrowed musical scores from the public library, which he read as avidly as other boys read books. "I can hear it in my head as I read it," he told a friend. These experiences gave him the feeling of being on a wonderful adventure, a journey of exploration through an enchanted land. One night, after a concert of the Boston Symphony, Lenny sat brooding while the conductor, Serge Koussevitzky, was given an ovation by the audience. The girl who was with him noticed the grim look on his face. "What's the matter?" she asked. "Didn't you like what Koussevitzky did?" "Not like it?" he answered. "I *loved* it. That's the trouble. I'm just jealous of any man who can make that kind of music."

Lenny's father watched these activities with consternation. What kind of future awaited his son? "Are you going to be a piano teacher and spend your life teaching children to play scales at three dollars a lesson? Or will you play jazz in some hotel and be unemployed six months a year? Or are you going to compose that crazy modern music which nobody ever plays and nobody ever listens to?" Finally, to placate his father, Lenny spent one summer as a shipping clerk in the Samuel Bernstein Hair Supplies Company. Mr. Bernstein wanted him to learn every aspect of the business; but Lenny suffered untold misery in his father's stock room, and came out of the experience determined more than ever to become a musician.

The arguments between father and son mounted in bitterness.

Mr. Bernstein even appealed to Helen Coates to persuade Lenny not to be a musician; but she would do no such thing. Finally, when Lenny was about to enter Harvard, a compromise was reached. Mr. Bernstein agreed not to oppose Lenny's musical activities as long as they did not interfere with his schoolwork. As for Lenny's future, that decision could wait until he had finished college. In the meantime Mr. Bernstein refused to pay for any more piano lessons. Lenny solved that problem by teaching the piano at a dollar an hour, and continued his own lessons alongside his studies at Harvard.

He threw himself enthusiastically into the musical life of Harvard. He appeared as soloist with the college orchestra, accompanied the glee club, played the piano when a student film club presented silent movies. He was a leading spirit in the concerts organized by the Harvard Music Club, and wrote music criticism for the college literary magazine. In his last year at Harvard he conducted the orchestra in a production of Aristophanes' comedy *The Birds*. And he composed a number of piano pieces. In the summertime he continued his musical activities as a counsellor at Camp Onota in Massachusetts, where he put on a production of *The Pirates of Penzance*.

The most important event of his career at Harvard was a chance meeting with Dimitri Mitropoulos. The famous Greek conductor was making some guest appearances with the Boston Symphony Orchestra, and the Hellenic Society of Harvard gave a tea in his honor. Lenny heard about the tea quite by accident. He had intended to spend the day studying for his examinations, but decided at the last minute to drop in at the reception. Mitropoulos was immediately impressed by the young man's knowledge of music, and asked Lenny to play for him. Lenny was nervous, and felt that he played horribly; but Mitropoulos evidently did not think so, for he invited Lenny to attend his rehearsals with the Boston

Symphony. That week Lenny for the first time in his life watched a conductor leading a great orchestra through a rehearsal. It was an unforgettable experience. Before the week was out, Mitropoulos was calling Lenny a "genius boy" and was asking him why he did not consider becoming a conductor. Although neither knew it at the time, this was a fateful encounter for Lenny: Mitropoulos was destined to play a crucial part in his career.

In June, 1939, Lenny was graduated from Harvard, with honors. The vexing question was: what next? Mr. Bernstein offered to pay his son a hundred dollars a week if he would enter the family business. But Lenny remembered the summer of agony he had spent in his father's stock room, and declared that he wouldn't take the job for a thousand a week. There was a violent scene between Mr. Bernstein and his headstrong son, at the end of which the father announced that he was cutting off all further financial support. If Lenny insisted on becoming a musician, he would have to do so on his own.

On a sunny day in the summer of 1939 Lenny arrived in New York, determined to make a place for himself in the world of music. He had just enough money to see him through a few weeks. He looked up Adolph Green, a young actor-writer who had played a part in Lenny's production of *The Pirates of Penzance* at Camp Onota. Green was a member of a group called The Revuers, which presented sophisticated songs at The Vanguard, a night club in Greenwich Village. (One of the Revuers was Judy Holliday, who later won fame as a stage and screen star. Another was Betty Comden, who collaborated with Green in writing songs and humorous material for their act.) Green welcomed Lenny and let him move into his apartment. He and Betty Comden took Lenny to parties where he made many new friends among writers and artists, and enchanted everyone with his piano playing and his wit. Yet as the weeks passed, his efforts to find a job in the music world

177

came to naught. "There was just no place for me," he recollects. His money was dwindling; he became more and more depressed. Finally he had just enough left to take him back to Boston. For the first time he was ready to admit that his father had been right, and that there was no point in trying to pursue a musical career. "I went home with my tail between my knees."

No sooner had he reached Boston than he heard from a friend that Dimitri Mitropoulos was stopping at the Biltmore Hotel in New York, on his way to Europe. Hope suddenly reawakened in Lenny's heart. Mitropoulos had encouraged him. Perhaps the great man would now find a way out for him. It was a wild gamble, but it seemed to Lenny that this was his last chance before accepting defeat. He borrowed some money, took the first train back to New York, and poured out his unhappy story to Mitropoulos.

The conductor listened most sympathetically. He felt that it was out of the question for Lenny to give up music. "I have great faith in you," he told the young man, "and I feel that you have in you the makings of a fine conductor. But you do need some specialized training." He promised Lenny to obtain an audition for him at the Curtis Institute of Music in Philadelphia. There Lenny would be able to study with Fritz Reiner, who was not only a great conductor himself but was also particularly skillful in teaching his pupils how to conduct. "How will I pay for all this?" Lenny asked. "Don't worry," Mitropoulos reassured him. "I am quite sure that I can get you a scholarship." And he promised besides to give his protégé a small allowance for living expenses.

Reiner asked Lenny to read an orchestral score at sight. Lenny did this with such ease that Reiner gave him a scholarship without further ado. Thus Lenny entered the Curtis Institute, where he studied for the next two years. He had to count his pennies, and could afford nothing but the barest necessities. But he thoroughly enjoyed his classes in conducting, orchestration, and piano. His fellow students stood in awe of his extraordinary ability to read at sight any music that was placed before him. Fritz Reiner was greatly impressed. Lenny, he later stated, "was the most talented all-around student I ever had." Before long the young man was given an opportunity to conduct the Curtis Institute Orchestra. "I was scared, tremendously scared," he remembers; but this was only beforehand. The instant he mounted the podium his nervousness disappeared. "It then seemed the most natural thing in the world for me to be conducting."

Now a third great conductor entered Lenny's life: the redoubtable Serge Koussevitzky. The Russian conductor, whom Lenny had envied long ago when he heard him conduct the Boston Symphony Orchestra, had organized the Berkshire Music Festival that took place every summer at Tanglewood, Massachusetts (the scene of Nathaniel Hawthorne's *Tanglewood Tales*). In 1940 he added the Berkshire Music Center, a unique summer school, where gifted students could receive the best possible instruction in conducting and composition, as well as vocal and instrumental training. Koussevitzky himself taught conducting, and offered several scholarships in this course. Upon Fritz Reiner's recommendation, one of these went to Lenny.

The next two summers at Tanglewood were like the realization of a wonderful dream. He could live, breathe, think music all day long. Most important of all, he quickly became Koussevitzky's favorite pupil. The great conductor had no children of his own and came to love Lenny like a son. He enjoyed the young man's enthusiasm and self-confidence, his boundlessly curious mind, the zest with which he attacked books, music, sports—every aspect of living. Koussevitzky never tired of listening to Lenny. He was something of an autocrat and insisted on being obeyed; Lenny was the only one whom he allowed to contradict and argue with him. On one occasion Koussevitzky became convinced that Lenny ought

179

to change his name. Whoever heard of anyone conducting a great orchestra with a name like Leonard Bernstein? But Lenny stood his ground. If he was going to achieve fame, he insisted, it would have to be under the name with which he was born. For once Koussevitzky gave in.

The summer of 1941 marked the end of Bernstein's studies. This was hardly anything to be happy about. "In a way I was worse off than before. I was a trained conductor. But who hired kid conductors? And if I could not earn a living conducting, then how? I was twenty-three. And I had nowhere to go." When the autumn came Koussevitzky advised him to go back to Boston, and was going to have him play a piano concerto with the Boston Symphony. At that time, however, the orchestra was involved in a dispute with the Musicians' Union. Lenny, as a member of the union, was not permitted to play. In despair he rented a small piano studio and waited for students to turn up. "I did the usual things. I sent out announcements, and waited for results. Nobody came. *Nobody!*" There was a reason. That very week Japanese planes had bombed Pearl Harbor. People were thinking of other things than piano lessons.

Lenny tried to enlist in the Army, but he was turned down because of his asthma. He spent the winter in Boston, composed a sonata for clarinet and piano, took part in musical events. He was frequently at Koussevitzky's home in Brookline. In the summer he returned to Tanglewood. This time he was no longer a student, but Koussevitzky's assistant in conducting the Boston Symphony. Yet when autumn came he did not feel that he could face another winter in Boston. Armed with two enthusiastic letters of recommendation from Koussevitzky and Reiner, he again tried his fortunes in New York. He rented a furnished room for eight dollars a week and tried to make a living teaching the piano and accompanying dancers. But he could not make ends meet. That winter he refers to as "my Valley Forge." "Bad though the year before had been in Boston—and it had been awful—I used to walk up and down Broadway and look back upon it as heaven. God, how I was miserable in New York." On one occasion he was forced to send his father a telegram asking for twenty-five dollars because he had not paid his rent for four weeks and was about to be dispossessed.

Once again he lost heart. Once again he began to feel that his father had perhaps been right after all. Why didn't he give up the hopeless struggle and find a safe haven in supplying beauty parlors? Then, on Broadway, he ran into Irving Caesar, a successful lyric writer who had written the words for Gershwin's *Swanee* and other song hits. Caesar had heard Lenny play the piano at a party and had been impressed. When he heard that Lenny couldn't find any work he cried, "What! You, a genius—starving?" He immediately brought Lenny to one of his friends in the song-publishing business, and Lenny was hired by Harms-Remick at a salary of twenty-five dollars a week. He had a variety of odd jobs to do, the most important of which was to arrange popular songs for the piano; as he later described it, "for four hands on two pianos, eight hands on two pianos, two hands on eight pianos."

Now that he knew where his next meal was coming from, Lenny took a studio in Carnegie Hall and threw himself into the musical life of New York. He helped to organize and appeared in several concerts of modern music. These engagements paid him nothing, for modern music did not attract much of an audience in those days. But they enabled him to play the kind of music he loved, and brought him into contact with such musicians as Aaron Copland and Virgil Thomson. He was so stimulated by his new activities that he began to compose again. He wrote a song cycle, *I Hate Music: Five Kid Songs,* which was published by the firm of Wit-

181

mark. Then he learned that the New England Conservatory in Boston was running a contest for a symphony by an American composer. Lenny decided to enter it, and wrote a symphony based on the Lamentations of the prophet Jeremiah. He worked at white heat, barely making the deadline.

The symphony failed to win the prize. Worse still, it failed to impress his mentor Koussevitzky. Another blow came when Tanglewood failed to open that summer, because of the war. He went to Lenox, Massachusetts, to assist Koussevitzky in a series of lectures for the benefit of the Red Cross. But first he went to Boston to try once more to get into the Army; he was again rejected. The result of all these disappointments was that he reached Lenox in a dark mood. It was his twenty-fifth birthday, and he was still nowhere.

A message was waiting for him at Lenox. Artur Rodzinski was staying at nearby Stockbridge, and wanted to see him the next morning. Rodzinski was one of the foremost conductors in the country, and had just been appointed musical director of the New York Philharmonic. When Lenny went over to Stockbridge the following morning, Rodzinski took him for a walk. They finally sat down "on a kind of haystack." Rodzinski told Lenny that he had heard him conduct the student orchestra at Tanglewood the previous summer and had been impressed. After a bit of conversation Rodzinski turned to Lenny and said: "How would you like to be assistant conductor of the New York Philharmonic next season?" Thus, out of the blue, came the opportunity for which he had been hoping. A few days later *The New York Times* carried the announcement of Lenny's appointment. He tore the clipping out of the paper and sent it to his old teacher Helen Coates. Above the announcement he wrote in red ink: "Here we go!"

His duties, for which he received a hundred dollars a week (the same salary that his father had offered him for going into business) consisted mainly of assisting Rodzinski in rehearsing the orchestra. Lenny dreamed of a chance to conduct a real performance, yet this seemed a remote possibility. But his chance came sooner than he expected. One Saturday night shortly after the beginning of the season, the singer Jennie Tourel performed his song cycle *I Hate Music* at Town Hall. Lenny was especially pleased because his parents had come down from Boston to hear his songs. After the concert they all went to a party at Miss Tourel's. Suddenly the telephone rang; the manager of the Philharmonic was calling to say that the guest conductor, Bruno Walter, was sick in bed and might not be able to conduct the Sunday afternoon concert. They were trying to reach Rodzinski at Stockbridge. Lenny was sure that Rodzinski would get back in time for the concert. Nevertheless he left the party and went back to his studio in order to look through the scores of the works on Sunday's program, "just in case."

"I stayed up until about 4:30 A.M. alternately dozing, sipping coffee, and studying the scores. I fell into a sound sleep about 5:30 A.M. and awakened at 9. An hour later Mr. Zirato telephoned and said, 'You're going to conduct.' My first reaction was one of shock. I then became very excited over my unexpected debut and, I may add, not a little frightened. Knowing it would be impossible to assemble the orchestra for a rehearsal on a Sunday, I went over to Mr. Walter's home and went over the scores with him." He returned to his studio for a few more hours of study. Then he called his parents, who were planning to return to Boston that afternoon, and told them, "You're going to see me conduct the Philharmonic." At half-past one in the afternoon he began to dress. Since he did not own the formal outfit that conductors wear at an afternoon concert, he put on a gray sack suit, the best he had. He had slept very little, he was keyed up; but there was no trace of nervousness about him as, at three o'clock, he stepped out on the stage. The manager of the orchestra announced to the audience that Bruno Walter was ill and Leonard Bernstein was going to substitute in his stead. "You are now going to witness," he added, "the debut of a full-fledged conductor born, educated, and trained in this country."

From the moment that the opening chords of Schumann's *Manfred* Overture rang through the hall, Lenny forgot the audience sitting behind him, forgot the audience of millions listening to the concert over the radio. He lost himself in the music, molding each phrase as he felt it in his heart, leading the orchestra with a sure hand. At the end of the program the audience gave him an ovation. As he stood there, exhausted, wet with perspiration, bowing first to the cheering public and then to his parents, he knew that his struggles were over—and that they had been worth it. The next morning, newspapers all over the country carried the story of this spectacular debut. Leonard Bernstein was famous.

In the next few years Bernstein came to be regarded as the most glamorous musician of his generation. He conducted orchestras all over the world. He composed serious music as well as the scores for successful Broadway shows. He appeared as a pianist in concertos, conducting the orchestra as he played. And his warm, vibrant personality became known to millions throughout the United States because of his memorable programs on television. Few musicians have been so adored by the public. Certainly none other has ever earned such huge sums from a career in serious music. It has required a tremendous amount of energy for him to be able to carry on at the same time as composer, conductor, pianist, television personality, organizer of musical events, and educator. He has been helped by his extraordinary memory and the speed with which he learns a piece of music, by his unflagging enthusiasm for every aspect of his art, and by his seemingly inexhaustible capacity for work. "An artist," he maintains, "has the compulsion to work. He'd go crazy if he didn't. I love my work—all of it!"

He rests by going from one branch of musical activity to the other. As he puts it, "Shifting from one thing to another is my vacation."

In 1951 Bernstein married Felicia Montealegre, a beautiful actress from Chile. The Bernsteins have three children: a daughter named Jamie, born in 1952; Alexander Serge, who was born in 1955 and was named after Bernstein's benefactor, Koussevitzky; and Nina, born in 1962. In 1957 Bernstein was appointed co-director of the New York Philharmonic along with his old friend Dimitri Mitropoulos. When Mitropoulos resigned at the end of that season, Bernstein became the first American-born conductor— and the youngest—to be the head of what New Yorkers consider the most important orchestra in the world.

He immediately instituted a number of reforms. For example, the Thursday night concert became a preview, that is, an informal dress rehearsal during which he addressed the audience in his dynamic way, explaining the music to them. This innovation meant that the newspaper critics reviewed the concert on Friday afternoon, when the performance was smoother and the critics could receive a better impression of what was being played. Even more important was the change in repertoire. For decades the public in Carnegie Hall had subsisted on a diet consisting chiefly of Beethoven, Brahms, Tchaikovsky, and other classics. Bernstein filled his programs with contemporary music, so that at his concerts the composers of the twentieth century—especially the Americans—finally came into their own. He is attuned to modern American music, he has the rhythm of it in his blood, and he conducts it with immense authority. Most important of all, he attracted an entirely new audience to Carnegie Hall, including thousands of young people who had never gone to symphony concerts before, but who went now because they were familiar with Bernstein through his Broadway and television shows. It soon became practically impossible to obtain tickets when Bernstein conducted. Those who got into the hall were treated to electrifying performances by one of the most exciting stage personalities of our time.

Bernstein differs in one important respect from the other composers whom we have discussed. For most of them, composing has been the central activity of their lives, to which all their other tasks were subordinate. For Bernstein, on the other hand, composing is only one outlet among several, his other activities being equally necessary to his musical personality. For this reason he has written considerably less than have other composers. The most important among his earlier works is the *Jeremiah Symphony* (1942). The final movement of this work, a Lamentation in Hebrew that is sung by a mezzo-soprano, found a splendid interpreter in his friend, the singer Jennie Tourel. The ballet *Fancy Free* (1944) served as the basis for *On the Town*, a musical comedy hit with book and lyrics by Betty Comden and Adolph Green. The ballet *Facsimile* followed in 1946. In 1949 Bernstein wrote his Second Symphony, *The Age of Anxiety*, a work for piano and orchestra based upon a poem by W. H. Auden. Music from this composition was used in the ballet of the same name (1950). Two years later came *Trouble in Tahiti*, a one-act opera on a libretto by Bernstein himself, satirizing life in suburbia.

Wonderful Town (1951) was based on the play *My Sister Eileen*, which Joseph Fields and Jerome Chodorov derived from Ruth McKenny's stories in the *New Yorker* magazine. This diverting musical comedy, for which his friends Adolph Green and Betty Comden again supplied the lyrics, made a big hit on Broadway. Bernstein's later works include the Serenade for violin solo, strings, and percussion (1954); *Candide*, a musical comedy on a book by Lillian Hellman based on Voltaire's satirical novel (1956), which failed to attract the public; and *West Side Story* (1957), the sensational musical play about gang warfare in New York, which won enormous success both on Broadway and as a motion picture. We should also mention his book *The Joy of Music* (1959), which contains seven scripts of his television shows on the Omnibus program.

Bernstein's music is exuberant, warm, overflowing with movement and rhythmic vitality. He is a romanticist at heart. His orchestration is sumptuous and colorful. As for his music for the theater, he has been a leader in creating a sophisticated type of musical play, more subtle both in its lyrics and its music than the usual Broadway fare. In plays like *On the Town* and *Wonderful Town* he has been extraordinarily successful in capturing the hectic tempo, the excitement of life in New York. *West Side Story,* which contained stunning dance sequences by Jerome Robbins, transplanted Shakespeare's immortal tale of Romeo and Juliet to the slums of New York, and did so with a poignance and poetry that no one who saw either the play or the movie is likely to forget.

The music for *Fancy Free* offers a good introduction to Bernstein's style. This ballet centers about the adventures of three sailors on shore leave. 1. *Opening Dance; Scene at the Bar.* The action takes place in a New York street on a summer night. The three boys enter, all set for a good time. The music—jaunty, full of swagger and gay rhythms—mirrors their mood. The piano teases the ear with a little phrase that is repeated over and over high in the treble. Then the orchestra takes over with brash, vigorous sounds. This is real ballet music. It suggests movement and gesture so vividly that you can almost see the dancing figures. The Brunette enters, whereupon the sailors begin to show off in order to attract her attention. She walks down the street, followed by two of the boys. The third runs into the fiery Redhead. They strike up an acquaintance and go into the bar.

2. *Pas de Deux* (*Dance for Two*). The music becomes lyrical as the sailor dances with the Redhead to the strains of a broadly flowing "blues." The sailor's buddies return, bringing with them

the Brunette. Now there are five; that is, one boy too many. The sailors begin to compete for the girls, each in turn eager to show how well he dances. 3. *Competition Scene: Galop.* The dance of the first sailor is breezy and full of action. The music builds up tension through dissonant harmonies and rapid, exciting rhythms. 4. *Waltz.* The second sailor is a quieter type. He seems to have a romantic streak in him, for the sweet sound of the strings comes to the fore as he dances. After a brief interlude of jazz rhythms, the waltz returns. 5. *Danzón.* The third sailor exhibits his talents to the exotic rhythm of a Cuban *danzón.* Here is Latin-American grace and languor, with an undercurrent of emotion.

6. *Finale.* The girls join the sailors in a general dance, but the spirit of competition gets out of hand. Suddenly there is a free-for-all, in the course of which the sailors and their girls are knocked down. For a moment there is a pile of tangled bodies on the floor. Then the two young ladies pick themselves up and leave in a huff. The three sailors disentangle themselves, and realize that the girls have walked out on them. They shrug off this misfortune, saunter into the bar, and have another beer. The Blonde passes by and turns down the street. The sailors pretend that they are not interested. Suddenly they realize that they are fooling nobody, and go chasing wildly after her.

The music of the finale brings back themes from the earlier scenes. Through this kind of musical reminiscence a composer unifies his composition. There is a mood of tender remembrance as the familiar themes return. The piano holds forth with a jazzy passage. A final burst of animation—and the sailors are off on a new adventure!

This music is thoroughly American in its energy and breeziness. Leonard Bernstein expresses the American point of view in a fresh, exuberant way that is all his own.

16. LUKAS FOSS

Lukas Foss is known as one of the talented composers of the present-day American school. Yet he was not born in this country. His family lived in Germany, where he spent the first years of his life. He grew up in an environment of art and culture: his father was a professor of philosophy, his mother a painter. Lukas was born in Berlin on August 15, 1922. When he was three years old his parents gave him an accordion as a Christmas gift. Almost at once the little fellow began to pick out chords to accompany the German folk songs that his mother had taught him. His parents realized that Lukas was unusually musical, but they did not wish to burden him beyond his years, so they did not let him take regular piano lessons until he was seven years old. He made such rapid strides as a pianist that he could easily have become a child prodigy. But his parents wisely decided that it was more important for him to have a normal childhood and to develop into an all-around musician. Accordingly, Lukas was not allowed to drift into the exhausting career of giving concerts at an early age.

When Lukas was eight years old his mother told him a fairy tale that made a deep impression upon him. It was about Griffelkin, a little Devil who is sent on earth to do mischief. Griffelkin commits a terrible sin for a Devil: he does a good deed instead. For this he is expelled from Hell and is doomed to become a mortal; that is, he begins a new life as a little boy. Lukas was so taken with this story that he at once turned it into an opera.

The following year, when he was nine, he heard Mozart's *Marriage of Figaro*. He immediately asked for the score and learned the whole opera. Soon he was giving performances of the *Marriage of Figaro* for his parents and their friends, singing all the parts in turn—soprano, alto, tenor, bass—while he played the orchestral accompaniment on the piano. To this day one of his favorite pastimes is to play his choral works at the piano, while he manages all the vocal parts with an ease and an enthusiasm that must be heard to be believed.

When Hitler came to power in Germany in 1933 Lukas was eleven years old. His father realized that there was no place for German Jews under the Nazis, and decided to leave his homeland. He took the family to Paris, where Lukas continued his schooling. The boy studied piano, harmony, and composition with professors of the Paris Conservatory and made extraordinary progress.

Despite this, Lukas's parents realized that they had nothing more to hope for in Europe. During their four years in Paris they had but one dream—to come to America. This desire was fulfilled when Lukas was fifteen years old. Full of hope, the family set sail for the New World. Excitement filled their hearts as their ship sailed past the Statue of Liberty and they caught sight of their new homeland. In time Lukas's father was appointed professor of philosophy at Haverford College, a Quaker school in Pennsylvania; and Lukas entered the Curtis Institute of Music in nearby Philadelphia. Three years later he graduated from the school with honors.

Lukas, like his friend Leonard Bernstein, belongs to the group of gifted young musicians whom the conductor Serge Koussevitzky gathered about him when he founded the Berkshire Music Center at Tanglewood, Massachusetts. Lukas was one of the first to apply for admission when the school opened its doors in 1940. He was determined to enter Koussevitzky's class in conducting. Koussevitzky smiled when he caught sight of the slender blue-eyed boy whose curly brown hair and fair complexion made him look younger than his eighteen years. "Aren't you rather young to want to be a conductor?" Koussevitzky asked. But Lukas was not to be put off. "Just let me go through the audition," he said eagerly.

The audition consisted of his leading the student orchestra through a performance of Richard Strauss's symphonic poem *The Merry Pranks of Tyl Eulenspiegel*. Lukas was afraid that he might have a hard time convincing the Maestro that he should be admitted to the class. But as soon as he stepped onto the conductor's stand and raised his baton, his qualms disappeared. He went through the audition so brilliantly that Koussevitzky immediately began to take a deep personal interest in his new pupil.

At Tanglewood Lukas studied composition with Paul Hindemith, and he was one of several young musicians who subsequently followed Hindemith to Yale University, where the distinguished German composer was then teaching. Shortly afterward, Koussevitzky informed Lukas that he was appointing him pianist of the Boston Symphony Orchestra.

Lukas had developed a dazzling technique at the piano and could easily have embarked upon the career of a concert pianist. But his first love was composition. He had been writing music ever since he was a boy, and now devoted more and more of his time to composing. He soon won recognition in this field. When he was sixteen years old—shortly after his arrival in the United States— several of his piano pieces were published by G. Schirmer, one of our most important music publishers. He followed up this achievement by writing a suite for small orchestra to Shakespeare's magical play *The Tempest*, as a result of which he won a Pulitzer Scholarship.

During these years Lukas was discovering America. He had

191

come to love his adopted homeland. Not having grown up here, he was perhaps more sensitive to the American way of life than those who, having been born in this country, are inclined to take it for granted. Thus, when he read Carl Sandburg's poem *The Prairie*—he was then nineteen—he was profoundly moved. He had never seen the rolling prairies of the West. But as he read on, Sandburg's eloquent lines came alive in his imagination. They seemed to be waiting to be set to music.

Most composers limit themselves at the beginning of their career to fairly short and simple pieces. But *The Prairie* took shape in Lukas's mind as a fifty-minute cantata for four soloists, large chorus, and orchestra, an ambitious enterprise for a young man to undertake. He threw himself into the task with all his heart. It was only after he was deep in composition that he realized he had never received permission to use the poem. Without such permission all his work would be in vain. He wrote at once to Carl Sandburg, explaining that he had already begun the piece and imploring the poet to allow him to use the text. Sandburg replied that it was up to his publisher to decide. But he interceded on behalf of Lukas, asking his publisher to "give the young man a break." Permission was forthcoming and Lukas, enormously relieved at having hurdled this obstacle, was free to get on with the work.

The Prairie was completed when Lukas was twenty-one. Serge Koussevitzky had followed its progress with great interest. He asked Lukas to prepare a short symphonic excerpt that could be played by the Boston Symphony Orchestra. This was the first time that a major orchestra played a work by Lukas Foss. He was the youngest composer ever to have his work performed by the Bostonians. For this occasion he wrote an explanation of what he had tried to express in *The Prairie:* "The attempt to develop an oratorio style based on the American soil and spirit is not new, but Sandburg's epic poem, it seems to me, offers new possibilities in its earthy and almost religious approach. It is a new expression of an old faith drawn from the native soil. The protagonist, simply, is the prairie, but through this poem the prairie grows until it becomes the symbol for the all-embracing principle of *growth* itself."

Some months later Robert Shaw and the Collegiate Chorale gave the first complete performance of *The Prairie* at Town Hall in New York, and repeated the piece on the radio. Artur Rodzinski, who at that time was the conductor of the New York Philharmonic Orchestra, happened to tune in on the broadcast. The music had already begun. Rodzinski listened with mounting interest. This was obviously a major work by an important composer. But who could it be? Copland? Roy Harris? Rodzinski was more and more intrigued as the composition unfolded. He was charmed by the freshness and buoyancy of this thoroughly American music. When the announcer mentioned the composer's name at the end, Rodzinski was more puzzled than ever. He thought he was familiar with all the important American composers, yet he could not recall having heard the name of Lukas Foss among them. He sent a telegram to CBS requesting further details. The result was that in February, 1944, Rodzinski conducted an impressive performance of *The Prairie* in Carnegie Hall with the New York Philharmonic Orchestra assisted by famous soloists and the Westminster Choir. It was the most ambitious work by an American composer ever to have been heard in the famous hall. Lukas Foss was acclaimed by critics and public alike as a rising star on our musical scene.

That year was a memorable one for Foss. He appeared as soloist with the Boston Symphony in his First Piano Concerto, written in 1942, and made a strong impression not only as a composer but also as a pianist. He spent the summer at the MacDowell Colony, where he wrote his First Symphony. His next work, *Ode for Orchestra*, reflected the grim mood of the war years. (He himself was rejected for military service because of his asthma.) He dedicated the *Ode for Orchestra* "to those who will not return." With this work Foss tried to express his conviction that the artist does not live in a world of his own apart from his fellow men, but must be directly involved with the great issues of the world around him. "The artist," he stated, "who feels that his art is not an escape from the world but a direct expression of it, always has the urge to come to grips with the problems of his time and seeks their solution in this particular field of expression. There is no definite program in my Ode. I can suggest the general idea: crisis, war, and ultimately 'faith.' Anything beyond this the music should express better than words."

In 1944 Koussevitzky invited Foss to become the pianist of the Boston Symphony Orchestra. This was an ideal job for a composer, for it left him time enough for his own creative work. And it gave him an invaluable opportunity, by participating in the rehearsals and performances of a great orchestra, to become intimately acquainted with the character and the possibilities of the various instruments. A year later Foss won a Guggenheim Fellowship; he was the youngest musician to have received this honor. He now felt sufficiently sure of himself to undertake what is undoubtedly the highest form of instrumental music, the symphony. His Symphony in G, written in 1945, is a gay, sunny work that amply shows the young composer's adroitness in writing for the orchestra, his jaunty rhythms, and his spontaneous lyricism.

Foss next found inspiration in the Old Testament. He wrote two solo cantatas on Biblical texts. The first, *Song of Anguish,* for baritone and orchestra, was composed in 1945. Based on the Book of Isaiah, this is one of his most powerful works. It was followed a year later by the *Song of Songs,* for soprano and orchestra. In this work Foss captured the sensuous poetic quality and the fervent emotion of Solomon's immortal song. During these years he also produced two works of an altogether different character. His ballet *The Gift of the Magi,* based on O. Henry's tale, is a lively score. The ballet won success both in Boston and New York. Foss now turned to opera, which had attracted him ever since his childhood. He found an attractive subject in Mark Twain's well-known tale, *The Celebrated Jumping Frog of Calaveras County,* and asked Jean Karsavina to write a libretto for him. This highly entertaining one-acter soon became popular with opera workshops and student groups throughout the country.

In 1950 Foss was awarded a Prix de Rome, which meant that he could stay at the American Academy in Rome and devote himself to composing without having to think about earning a living. He resigned his position with the Boston Symphony and sailed for Europe. He spent two years in Rome, composing steadily. When he returned to the United States he appeared as conductor and pianist with various orchestras. His talent as a pianist never failed to arouse audiences to enthusiasm. Foss distinguished himself especially by his brilliant performances of contemporary works, and by his sympathetic interpretation of the music of Bach.

Despite his activities on the concert platform, Foss found time to continue composing. His Second Piano Concerto, which was written in 1951 and revised two years later, is a modern version of the grand virtuoso concerto of the past. Foss himself plays it most brilliantly. This concerto won the award of the New York Music Critics' Circle as the best instrumental work of that season. *A Parable of Death* (1952) was written for the Louisville Symphony. It is a moving tale based on a text fashioned from the writings of the German mystical poet Rainer Maria Rilke.

The NBC Opera Company asked Foss to write an opera that could be presented on television. He looked about for a subject that would be appropriate, but could not find any. Suddenly he remembered Griffelkin, the little Devil who had stirred his imagination twenty-five years before, when he was a boy of eight. Much had happened in the world since then, but the fairy tale of the kindhearted little Devil who was forced to become a mortal seemed as fresh and as charming as ever. And so Foss wrote a new work about Griffelkin, "a fairy-tale opera for children from eight to eighty." *Griffelkin* was presented by the NBC Opera Company in a coast-to-coast telecast in November, 1955.

In recent years Foss has developed a great interest in improvisation. The art of improvising—making up music on the spur of the moment—played an important part in the musical life of former times. Bach and Handel were famous for their improvisations on the organ. So too Beethoven dazzled the public with his wonderful improvisations at the piano. After Beethoven's time musicians were expected to play only what was printed on the page, without adding anything of their own. The art of improvising has found its last refuge in the jam session of jazz musicians, who will take a given melody or sequence of chords and then proceed to add fanciful embellishments of their own.

Foss has tried to bring the spirit of improvisation into the concert hall. He has formed a chamber ensemble consisting of four musicians besides himself (percussion, flute, clarinet, and cello); he directs the ensemble from the piano. This group plays without written or memorized music, creating melodies, harmonies, and counterpoint on the spur of the moment. As in the case of jazz musicians who are improvising, Foss's group works within an overall pattern that is decided on beforehand. But within that pattern each of the musicians is able to give free rein to his imagination.

Foss is professor of composition at the University of California in Los Angeles. He lives in Pacific Palisades with his wife Cornelia and their two children, Christopher, who was born in 1957, and Eliza, who was born in 1962. In the summertime he teaches at the Berkshire Music Center in Tanglewood, where his own activity as a composer and pianist began. Here he has an opportunity to pass on to new generations of young musicians all that he has learned about his art.

He is essentially a lyric composer. His music abounds in melody. His impetuous rhythms show his wholehearted response to American jazz. His orchestral works are notable for their bright, lustrous sound. He generates tension through powerful dissonances resulting from the clash of massed harmonies. He builds an effective climax by repeating a melodic or rhythmic idea over and over again in an "obstinate" pattern—what is known as an *ostinato*. His music communicates to the listener because it is rich in emotion and dramatic force.

Foss's effective handling of American folk style is well exemplified by his one-act opera *The Jumping Frog of Calaveras County*. The Mark Twain story is set in California in the days of the Gold Rush. The opening scene takes place in Uncle Henry's saloon. Uncle Henry and his niece Lulu listen raptly while Smiley holds forth on his prize pet—Daniel Webster, the Jumping Frog of Calaveras County. This trio, with its syncopated melody and catchy rhythm, establishes the atmosphere of a frontier town. Smiley takes Daniel out of his box in order to show off his talents. The "frog music" is full of suspense and wonder as Daniel's admirers watch him exhibit his prowess. The scene ends with a lively toast to Daniel.

The mood changes with the entrance of the Stranger. The music becomes more sophisticated, suggesting a charming but slick character. The Stranger orders a rye whiskey, and is altogether unimpressed by Smiley's boasting. "I don't see no p'ints 'bout that frog that's better'n any other frog," says he. Smiley, deeply hurt, offers to bet forty dollars that Daniel will outjump any living frog in Calaveras County. The Stranger retorts that he would gladly take up the bet if he had a frog; whereupon Smiley offers to find one for him. The two men deposit forty dollars each with Uncle Henry. In a tuneful quartet the Stranger exults that he will soon outsmart Smiley, while the other three affirm their faith in Daniel.

Smiley leaves in order to catch a frog for the Stranger. Uncle Henry goes off to spread the news about the forthcoming contest. Lulu takes out a mirror from her purse and begins to make up. The Stranger catches sight of a shotgun hanging above the bar. He conceives the bright idea of emptying it of its buckshot and filling Daniel with same. After a brief flirtation with Lulu, she invites him to dinner and goes off to prepare the meal. The Stranger takes down the rifle, removes Daniel from his box, pries open the frog's jaws, stuffs him with buckshot, and puts him back in the box. He sings a vigorous aria, somewhat in the style of a "blues," which fulfills a dramatic function: it is not only interesting for the sake of the music, but also furthers the story line and reveals the Stranger's villainous character. "Each time I hit a town, turn on the charm . . . Each time I fool 'em, take what they got, but this time, by golly, I hit the jackpot! Forty dollars U.S. money, that's a good day's haul. Grab it up and kiss my honey, and good-bye all!"

Scene II is laid in the village square. On the porch of the general store two men are engaged in a crap game, while a third sits on the railing strumming a guitar. "Oh don't you remember sweet Betsy from Pike," he sings, "who crossed the big mountains with her lover Ike . . ." The use of this famous song of the West, like the opening number of Scene I, suggests the locale and sets the proper atmosphere for the action. At the same time the variations on *Sweet Betsy* show how ingeniously a traditional tune can be decked out with modern harmonies and rhythms.

Uncle Henry rushes in with the news that the Stranger is taking bets on the forthcoming contest. In a jazzlike episode the men discuss the contest and express their conviction that the Stranger will lose. They also voice their disapproval of Lulu's evident interest in him. This lively interchange is marked by incisive rhythm and a steadily mounting tension that finds expression in a *crescendo* (getting louder).

Lulu arrives with the Stranger, with whom she seems to be quite friendly. A brief romantic interlude follows, in the style of a folk song. The Stranger regrets that he must soon be on his way. But Lulu hopes that, now that he knows where she lives, he will come back frequently.

Smiley arrives with the Stranger's frog. The onlookers place their bets amid much excitement. Lulu, understandably, is torn between her warm feelings for the Stranger and her loyalty to Daniel. The contest begins. We hear the "frog music" of the opening scene. The Stranger's frog makes a few small jumps. But Daniel, despite the exhortations of his admirers, "is planted as solid as a church." In an ensemble of consternation Smiley, Uncle Henry, and their supporters plead with the Jumping Frog: "Don't let us down, Dan'l!" The Jumping Frog, despite all his huffing and puffing, is unable to budge an inch. His admirers mourn the defeat of their champion to the strains of a doleful "blues." The Stranger, triumphant, pockets all the money, and is gallant enough to present Lulu with a twenty-dollar bill. Then he quietly clears out.

Suddenly Smiley notices that Daniel is not feeling well. He picks up the frog, discovers that his pet is abnormally heavy, and turns him upside down. Daniel vomits up the buckshot. The men realize that they have been tricked, and rush off to catch the Stranger. The "blues" is transformed into an *allegro vivace* (fast and lively) as the Stranger is brought back. "Two of the men have their guns trained on him. Firm hands have him by the collar, and he is being propelled by knees in the backside."

In derision they cry, "So you don't see no p'ints 'bout that frog that's better'n any other frog!" They maul the Stranger until they have recovered all the money. "If you show your face in this town again we'll tar and feather you and draw and quarter you and string you up and ride you on a rail and truss you up like a Christmas goose!" They kick the Stranger out. And the opera ends with a triumphal ensemble saluting Daniel, the pride of Calaveras County.

The composer of this delightful one-acter has known how to combine many strains, both European and American, in his music. He has succeeded in fusing them into a personal style. Lukas Foss has firmly established his position as one of the fresh lyric voices of our time.

A Glossary of Musical Terms

Key: *Fr., French; Ger., German; Gr., Greek; It., Italian; Lat., Latin. The words in the definitions that are printed in* SMALL CAPITALS *are defined in their own alphabetical order in the Glossary. Look up these cross-references.*

ABSOLUTE MUSIC. Music without literary or pictorial associations; the opposite of PROGRAM MUSIC. Main forms of absolute music: SONATA, SYMPHONY, CONCERTO, CHAMBER MUSIC.

ACCELERANDO (It., *ak-sheh-leh-ran'-do*). Gradually getting faster. See TEMPO.

ACCENT. Emphasis or stress on a specific TONE or CHORD.

ACCOMPANIMENT. The HARMONY that forms the background of the MELODY. As in a SONG with PIANO accompaniment.

ADAGIO (It., *at ease*). (1) At a slow or leisurely TEMPO. (2) A piece or a MOVEMENT in this tempo.

ALLEGRETTO (It., *a little allegro*). Not as fast as ALLEGRO.

ALLEGRO (It., *happy*). At a quick pace; lively. See TEMPO.

ALTO. (1) A woman's VOICE of lower range than SOPRANO. The second highest PART in a four-part CHORUS. See CONTRALTO. (2) An INSTRUMENT in this range; e.g., alto SAXOPHONE.

ANDANTE (It., *going*). (1) At a moderate pace; fairly slow. (2) A piece or MOVEMENT in this TEMPO.

ANDANTINO (It., *a little andante*). Slightly faster than AN-
DANTE.

ANTHEM. A piece of sacred music usually based on Biblical
words, with or without instrumental ACCOMPANIMENT.

ARIA (It.). An extended SOLO song with instrumental ACCOMPANI-
MENT, either a separate piece or PART of an OPERA, ORATORIO,
CANTATA, etc.

ARPEGGIO (It.). A broken CHORD whose TONES are played in
succession instead of together.

ART SONG. A musical setting of a literary text. See LIED.

A TEMPO (It., *in time*). A return to the original TEMPO.

ATONALITY. Absence of relationship to a KEYNOTE or KEY center. Associated with Arnold Schoenberg and his disciples.

BALLAD. (1) A narrative poem, often of a popular kind. (2)
The musical setting of such a poem.

BALLET. A dance spectacle that is presented with costumes,
scenery, and music. It may be an independent work or a PART
of an OPERA.

BAND. An ENSEMBLE composed mainly of wind instruments. It
may be a brass, jazz, or symphonic band.

BARCAROLLE. A boat SONG or a piece in the style of one, in 6/8
TIME.

BARITONE. (1) A male VOICE higher than BASS and lower than
TENOR. (2) An INSTRUMENT in this range, such as the baritone
HORN.

BAROQUE. The period from 1600 to 1750, marked by a style
of massiveness, grandeur, energy, and emotion. Produced a
rich literature of OPERA and ORATORIO, CANTATA, and INSTRU-
MENTAL forms based on COUNTERPOINT: CONCERTO GROSSO,
FUGUE, SUITE, PASSACAGLIA, CHORALE PRELUDE, TOCCATA, etc.
Composers: Monteverdi, Lully, Purcell, Vivaldi, Bach, Han-

del. Painters: Tintoretto, Veronese, Rubens. Writer: John Milton.

BASS. (1) The lowest VOICE. (2) The lowest PART in a four-part CHORUS. (3) The lower REGISTER: in PIANO music, the left-hand part. (4) The lowest member of a family of INSTRUMENTS, such as the bass CLARINET.

BASS DRUM. A drum of indefinite PITCH, used mainly to accentuate RHYTHM. In the jazz BAND the bass drum is fitted out with a device that makes it possible for the drummer to accentuate the BEAT with his foot.

BASSOON. The BASS of the WOODWINDS, a flexible and highly useful INSTRUMENT. Its TONE is thick and weighty in the low REGISTER, dry and sonorous in the middle, reedy and intense in the upper. A double-REED instrument.

BATON. The stick used by the CONDUCTOR of an ORCHESTRA.

BEAT. The pulse of the meter; the unit of TIME.

BRASS INSTRUMENTS. The brass choir of the ORCHESTRA includes the TRUMPET, FRENCH HORN, TROMBONE, and TUBA. These have a cup-shaped mouthpiece; the TONE is produced by a column of air in the tube that is made to vibrate by the tightly stretched lips of player. Other brass instruments: CORNET, BUGLE.

BUGLE. A BRASS INSTRUMENT that is not equipped with valves, and is therefore able to sound only certain TONES of the SCALE, which accounts for the familiar pattern of military duty calls. Has a powerful tone that carries in the open air.

CADENZA. (1) An elaborate passage for SOLO instrument introduced into a work for ORCHESTRA in order to display the resources of the instrument or the capacities of the player. (2) A similar passage in vocal music.

CANCAN (Fr.). A gay Parisian dance in rapid 2/4 TIME.

CANTATA (It., *cantare*, to sing). A vocal work on a religious

203

or secular text, including RECITATIVES, ARIAS, DUETS, CHORUSES: usually with instrumental ACCOMPANIMENT. Is shorter than an ORATORIO.

CASTANETS. A pair of small clappers of ivory or wood, held in the hand. Used by dancers to accentuate the RHYTHM, especially in Spain.

CELESTA. A kind of GLOCKENSPIEL operated by a KEYBOARD. Its steel plates are struck by little hammers and produce a delicate, silvery sound. Looks like a miniature upright PIANO.

CELLO. A STRINGED INSTRUMENT larger than the VIOLIN and VIOLA, and lower in PITCH. Has a rich, mellow sound.

CHAMBER MUSIC. Music for small ENSEMBLES, with one performer to the PART, such as TRIO, QUARTET, QUINTET.

CHAMBER ORCHESTRA. A small ORCHESTRA consisting of twenty to thirty players.

CHORALE. A HYMN tune, especially of Lutheran origin. Also music in the style of a chorale.

CHORALE PRELUDE. An ORGAN piece based on a CHORALE.

CHORD. A group of three or more TONES conceived as an entity. The tones are generally sounded together. See ARPEGGIO.

CHORUS. (1) A large body of singers. (2) Music for such a group, written in four basic PARTS: SOPRANO, ALTO, TENOR, BASS.

CHROMATIC HARMONY. HARMONY based not only on the seven TONES of the KEY but also on the five extraneous tones, that is, on the twelve tones of the CHROMATIC SCALE. Especially typical of Richard Wagner and his disciples. See DIATONIC.

CHROMATIC SCALE. The twelve SEMITONES (half-steps) of the OCTAVE arranged in consecutive order. On the PIANO, includes the white and black KEYS.

CLARINET. A single-REED, WOODWIND INSTRUMENT that possesses a beautiful liquid TONE, with a remarkably wide range from lowest to highest NOTE and from soft to loud.

CLASSICISM. A style in art characterized by clarity, balance, mastery of form, and control of emotion. The Viennese classical school (c. 1775–1825) perfected the SYMPHONY, CONCERTO, SONATA, DIVERTIMENTO, and CHAMBER MUSIC, especially the STRING QUARTET. The four masters of this school are Haydn, Mozart, Beethoven, Schubert. Painters: David, Reynolds, Gainsborough. In literature, classicism came somewhat earlier: Pope, Dr. Johnson, Voltaire. Classical art was largely under the patronage of the aristocracy.

CLEF. A sign written on the staff to indicate the PITCH of the NOTES. (1) G-clef or TREBLE clef, used for high range: VIOLIN, FLUTE, SOPRANO, and upper staff of PIANO music. (2) F-clef or BASS clef, used for low range: CELLO, DOUBLE BASS, bass voice, lower staff in piano music. (3) C-clef, used in several positions such as ALTO clef and TENOR clef.

CLUSTER CHORD. A CHORD consisting of TONES lying either next to or close to each other, giving the effect of DISSONANCE. Much used in modern music by Bartók, Henry Cowell, and other composers.

CODA (It., *tail*). A concluding section that rounds off a piece or a MOVEMENT.

COMPOSER-IN-RESIDENCE. A composer who lives for a semester or a year at a college or university, guiding a few advanced students more through personal contact than through regular classes.

COMPOSITION. The study of how to write a musical work, based upon the shaping of the sounds into a coherent, well-organized structure.

CONCERTINO. A small CONCERTO.

CONCERTO (It.). A piece for SOLO instrument and ORCHESTRA, usually in three contrasting MOVEMENTS.

CONDUCTOR. The leader of the ORCHESTRA who not only beats

TIME for the players and gives them their cues, but also shapes the whole musical conception.

CONSERVATORY. A music school.

CONSONANCE. A combination of two or more TONES giving the effect of completeness. Opposite of DISSONANCE.

CONTRABASSOON. Also known as double bassoon. The lowest in range of the BASSOON family. Produces the lowest TONE in the ORCHESTRA.

CONTRALTO. The female VOICE with the lowest range. In the four-part CHORUS, the contralto PART lies between SOPRANO and TENOR.

CONTRAPUNTAL. Pertaining to COUNTERPOINT.

CORNET. A BRASS INSTRUMENT with a shorter body and a rounder TONE than the TRUMPET.

COUNTERMELODY. A MELODY "against" the main melody, that is combined with it contrapuntally.

COUNTERPOINT. (1) The art of combining independent PARTS or VOICES into a single musical TEXTURE. (2) A vocal line so combined.

CRESCENDO (It., *increasing*). Gradually growing louder.

CYMBALS. A pair of metal discs which, when struck together, produce a variety of interesting TONE colors.

DA CAPO (It., *from the head*). Abbreviated D.C. Indicates that a piece or a section thereof is repeated from the beginning. *Da capo al fine:* repeat from the beginning to *fine* (the end).

DIATONIC (Gr., *according to the key*). Pertaining to the seven TONES of a MAJOR or MINOR key. Opposite of CHROMATIC.

DIRGE. A lament for the dead.

DISSONANCE. A combination of two or more TONES giving the effect of incompleteness, therefore requiring RESOLUTION to a CONSONANCE. Dissonance represents the principles of tension in music, just as consonance represents completion and rest.

DISSONANT COUNTERPOINT. A style of twentieth-century COMPOSITION based on maximum independence of the CONTRAPUNTAL parts, with emphasis on the harsher INTERVALS and impelled by a strong rhythmic impulse. Stravinsky, Bartók, Hindemith, Piston, etc.

DIVERTIMENTO (It., *diversion*). A piece of light entertainment music consisting of a series of brief MOVEMENTS, for STRINGED and WIND INSTRUMENTS, or mixed ENSEMBLE, with one or two players to a PART.

DO. First and last TONE of the *do-re-mi-fa-sol-la-ti-do* SCALE. The KEYNOTE or central tone.

DOT. A dot after a NOTE prolongs its TIME value by half its original length: $\downarrow. = \downarrow + \downarrow$

DOUBLE BASS. The largest in size and lowest in range of the STRINGED INSTRUMENTS. Also known as contrabass. In the ORCHESTRA, the double basses carry the foundation of the HARMONY.

DOUBLE FLAT (♭♭). Lowers the PITCH by two SEMITONES. See FLAT.

DOUBLE SHARP (♯♯). Raises the PITCH by two SEMITONES. See SHARP.

DOUBLE-STOP. In VIOLIN playing, to STOP two strings together, thus obtaining two-part HARMONY.

DUET. A piece for two performers, in which both PARTS are of equal importance.

DYNAMICS. The volume of sound, the degree of loudness or softness. Ranges from PIANISSIMO through PIANO, MEZZO-PIANO, MEZZO-FORTE, FORTE, to FORTISSIMO.

EAR-TRAINING. A course of graded exercises designed to strengthen the student's ability to recognize individual TONES and CHORDS.

EIGHTH NOTE (♪). Receives half the TIME value of a QUARTER NOTE. In 4/4 TIME, there are two eighth notes to a BEAT (♫).

EMBOUCHURE (Fr., *ahm'-boh-shoor*). (1) The mouthpiece of wind instruments. (2) The position of the player's lips, tongue, etc.

ENGLISH HORN. An alto OBOE.

ENSEMBLE (Fr., *together*). (1) A team of vocal or instrumental performers. (2) In OPERAS, a piece for more than two singers, or for soloists and CHORUS.

EXOTICISM. A tendency in music and painting to exploit the glamor of the East, or the color and gaiety of the sunny South. Rimsky-Korsakov, *Scheherazade*. Mendelssohn, *Italian Symphony*. Aaron Copland, *El Salón México*.

FANTASY (It., *fantasia*). A fanciful piece that follows no set FORM.

FINALE (It., *fee-nah'-lee*). (1) The last MOVEMENT of a SONATA, SYMPHONY, CONCERTO, STRING QUARTET, etc. (2) In OPERA, the final number of an act.

FIVE-TONE SCALE. A SCALE of great antiquity found in different parts of the world, from Scotland to China, also known as *pentatonic scale*. Can be sounded on the PIANO by playing either the black KEYS or C-D-F-G-A. *Auld Lang Syne* and *Comin' Thru the Rye* are pentatonic melodies.

FLAT. (1) The sign (♭) that lowers a NOTE by a SEMITONE, as from B to B♭. (2) Off PITCH, too low.

FLUTE. The SOPRANO of the WOODWINDS. A cylindrical tube made of silver alloy rather than wood, stopped at the upper end and held horizontally. The player blows across a mouth hole (EMBOUCHURE) cut in the side of the pipe. A most agile INSTRUMENT.

FOLK MUSIC. Folk art figures in human society from the most primitive level on, and is a valid expression of the artistic impulse that lies deep in human nature. This impulse finds expression in folk songs and dances that reflect every aspect of life. The treasury of folk songs includes work songs, love songs, drinking songs, cradle songs, patriotic songs, dance songs, songs of mourning, marching songs, play songs, story-telling songs. A folk song originates with an individual, perhaps on the spur of the moment. It is taken up by others, a detail is changed, a stanza is added, another version is created, and in the course of its wanderings the folk song becomes the collective expression of a group.

FORM. The arrangement of the material in a work of art so as to achieve maximum effectiveness. Musical form aims for balance and symmetry, unity and variety, and a significant relationship of the PARTS to the whole. The musician achieves *unity* and *variety* through a judicious use of *repetition* and *contrast*.

FORTE (It.). Loud. Abbreviated *f*. See DYNAMICS.

FORTISSIMO (It.). Very loud. Abbreviated *ff*. See DYNAMICS.

FOUR-FOUR TIME. A metrical pattern of four BEATS to a measure, a QUARTER NOTE receiving one beat. See QUADRUPLE METER.

FRENCH HORN. One of the most useful of the BRASS INSTRUMENTS. Can be mysterious and remote in soft passages, noble and sonorous in loud. Also known as *horn*.

FUGUE (Lat., *fuga*, flight). A POLYPHONIC COMPOSITION in which a THEME or subject is stated at the outset in one VOICE and is imitated in close succession in the other PARTS or voices. The theme reappears throughout the piece now in one voice, now in another, against COUNTERPOINT in the other voices. A fugue is generally in three or four parts or voices. May be vocal or instrumental. Masters of the fugue: Bach, Handel.

GLOCKENSPIEL (Ger., *a set of bells*). A PERCUSSION INSTRU-

MENT of definite PITCH, consisting of a series of horizontal steel plates of various sizes that are struck with two hammers and produce a bright, metallic sound.

GONG. A PERCUSSION INSTRUMENT in the form of a large round metal plate that is struck with a stick and produces a low reverberating sound.

GRACE NOTE. An ornamenting NOTE that has no TIME value of its own but is attached to the longer note that follows it. Printed in small type. See ORNAMENTS.

GREGORIAN CHANT. The liturgical chant of the Roman Catholic Church, named after Pope Gregory the Great, who reigned 590–604. Pure unaccompanied MELODY in free RHYTHM. See MONOPHONIC.

HALF NOTE (♩). Equivalent to two QUARTER NOTES. In 4/4 TIME a half note receives two BEATS.

HARMONY. (1) The sounding of TONES in CHORDS simultaneously. (2) The background of chords that accompany and support the MELODY. (3) The study of chords, their movements and relationships.

HARP. A plucked-string INSTRUMENT that produces a clear, crystalline TONE.

HARPSICHORD. The main KEYBOARD instrument of the BAROQUE. Its strings are plucked by little quills. Incapable of the gradations from soft to loud that are possible on the PIANO, the harpsichord, however, brought out the CONTRAPUNTAL lines of baroque music with luminous clarity.

HOMOPHONIC (Gr., *single-voiced*). Music in which a single line of MELODY is supported by HARMONIES in the ACCOMPANIMENT. Opposite of POLYPHONY.

HORN. See FRENCH HORN.

HYMN. A SONG in praise of God.

IMPRESSIONISM. A refined style in painting and music that centered about Paris in the late nineteenth and early twentieth century. Marked by flowing RHYTHM and shimmering ORCHESTRATION, with use of WHOLE-TONE SCALE, CHORDS moving in parallel motion, medieval MODES. Influenced by impressionist painting and symbolist poetry. Composers: Debussy, Ravel, Griffes. Painters: Monet, Manet, Degas, Renoir, Seurat. Poets: Baudelaire, Mallarmé, Verlaine, Rimbaud.

IMPROVISATION. The art of making up a COMPOSITION or embellishing a THEME on the spur of the moment, while it is being performed.

INSTRUMENT. A mechanism that produces musical sounds: STRINGED, WOODWIND, BRASS, PERCUSSION.

INTERVAL. A combination of two TONES, named according to the difference in PITCH—that is, the distance between them. *Do-re* or C-D, a second; *do-mi* or C-E, a third; *do-fa* or C-F, a fourth, *do-sol* or C-G, a fifth, etc. The tones may be sounded in succession or together.

JAZZ. A style of American popular music influenced by Negro dance RHYTHMS and based on SYNCOPATION.

KETTLEDRUM. A PERCUSSION INSTRUMENT of definite PITCH. Consists of a copper shell shaped like a hemisphere, across which is stretched a "head" of calfskin held in place by a metal ring. Also known as *timpani*. In the ORCHESTRA, kettledrums are used in sets of two or three.

KEY. (1) A group of TONES related to a common center or KEYNOTE, to which they all gravitate. A COMPOSITION is identified by its key: Symphony in A major, Concerto in D minor. (2) On KEYBOARD instruments, the part of the action pressed down by the finger in order to sound the required PITCH.

(3) On wind instruments, a lever pressed down by the finger.

KEYBOARD. A set of KEYS in PIANOS, ORGANS, HARPSICHORDS, etc.

KEYNOTE. The first TONE of a SCALE. The central tone of a KEY, the DO.

KEY SIGNATURE. The SHARPS or FLATS written at the head of a COMPOSITION in order to identify the KEY.

LARGO (It.). Very slow and broad.

LIBRETTO (It.). The book—that is, the text—of an OPERA, ORATORIO, CANTATA, etc.

LIED (Ger., *song*). The German ART SONG of the period of RO-MANTICISM, marked by heartfelt MELODY and appealing lyricism.

MAJOR (Lat., *greater*). Larger. Said of INTERVALS, CHORDS, SCALES, KEYS, MODE. A major interval is a SEMITONE larger than a MINOR interval. C-E, major; C-E♭, minor.

MAJOR-MINOR SYSTEM. The twelve MAJOR and twelve MINOR keys, with their respective SCALES and CHORDS, that made up the HARMONY of our music from the seventeenth to the twentieth century. See MAJOR SCALE, MINOR SCALE.

MAJOR SCALE. The basic SCALE of Western music, the familiar *do-re-mi-fa-sol-la-ti-do*. A succession of WHOLE TONES and half tones (SEMITONES), the half tones occurring between steps 3–4 (*mi-fa*) and 7–8 (*ti-do*). The major scale may be built from any one of the twelve TONES of the OCTAVE (from C, C♯, D, D♯, etc.) giving twelve major SCALES and KEYS. Each key has another KEYNOTE or DO to which the other tones gravitate, and another KEY SIGNATURE, i.e., another number of SHARPS or FLATS. Each key therefore has another group of seven tones out of the possible twelve. G major has one sharp, F♯; D major has two sharps, F♯

and C♯; A major has three, F♯, C♯, G♯; E major has four, F♯, C♯, G♯, D♯; F major has one flat, B♭; B♭ major has two flats, B♭ and E♭; etc. The only key that has neither sharps nor flats is C major. The C major scale is, consequently, the only major scale that can be played on the white keys of the PIANO. See MINOR, DIATONIC, CHROMATIC.

MARCH. A piece to accompany marching, often in 2/4 or 4/4 TIME.

MARIMBA. A XYLOPHONE of African and South American origins, associated with exotic dance music.

MASS. A musical setting of the chief rite of the Roman Catholic Church, for VOICES, with or without instrumental ACCOMPANIMENT.

MELODY. A succession of TONES perceived by the mind as a significant unit.

METRONOME. A device that translates musical TIME into physical time by indicating how many NOTES are to be played per minute. If the composer writes ♩ = 60 on his SCORE, the player is able to set the metronome at that number and it will click sixty times per minute, thereby indicating to the player the exact TEMPO that was in the composer's mind, sixty QUARTER NOTES per minute.

MEZZO (It., *meh'-tso*). Half. *Mezzo piano* (*mp*), medium soft. *Mezzo forte* (*mf*), medium loud. See DYNAMICS.

MEZZO SOPRANO. The female VOICE whose range lies between SOPRANO and CONTRALTO.

MIDDLE-C. The C in the middle of the KEYBOARD of the PIANO; the NOTE between TREBLE and BASS staffs.

MINOR (Lat., *lesser*). Smaller. Said of INTERVALS, CHORDS, SCALES, KEYS, MODE. A minor interval is a SEMITONE smaller than the corresponding MAJOR interval: C-E♭, minor; C-E, major.

MINOR SCALE. Differs from the MAJOR SCALE in that certain of its TONES are flatted. *Harmonic minor scale,* third and sixth steps flatted: C, D, E♭, F, G, A♭, B, C. *Melodic minor scale,* third and sixth flatted ascending; third, sixth, and seventh flatted descending: C, D, E♭, F, G, A♭, B, C, B♭, A♭, G, F, E♭, D, C. See MAJOR SCALE.

MINUET (Fr.). (1) A stately French dance at the court of Louis XIV, in 3/4 TIME. (2) The third MOVEMENT of the classical SYMPHONY.

MODE. (1) The manner of arranging TONES in a SCALE or KEY. Each mode represents another arrangement of whole steps and half steps. Thus, the twelve MAJOR SCALES and keys represent the *major mode;* the twelve MINOR SCALES and keys represent the *minor mode.* A scale can also be built according to the WHOLETONE mode, or any one of the medieval church modes.

MODULATION. The act of moving from one KEY to another.

MOLTO (It.). Very. *Allegro molto,* very fast.

MONOPHONIC. Said of pure single-line MELODY without HARMONY. Either without ACCOMPANIMENT or with an accompaniment that duplicates or varies the melody. The music of the ancient world was monophonic, as is to this day the music of Asia and Africa. GREGORIAN CHANT is monophonic. See TEXTURE, POLYPHONY, HOMOPHONIC.

MOVEMENT. A separate PART in a larger work such as a SYMPHONY, CONCERTO, SONATA.

MUTE. A device attached to an INSTRUMENT in order to muffle or alter the sound.

NATIONALISM. A tendency in music to emphasize national elements by basing COMPOSITIONS on FOLK MUSIC and dances; by associating music with a national hero or historic event, with national myths, legends, folklore, with a beautiful spot in the homeland, or with the writings of a national poet. Tchaikovsky, *1812 Overture*. Smetana, *The Moldau*. Dvořák, *Slavonic Dances*. J. Strauss, *Blue Danube Waltz*. Copland, *A Lincoln Portrait, Billy the Kid, Appalachian Spring*. Douglas Moore, *The Devil and Daniel Webster*.

NEO-CLASSICISM. A movement in twentieth-century music to revive certain elements of the eighteenth century and earlier. (1) "Back to Bach" and COUNTERPOINT. (2) Emphasis on AB-SOLUTE MUSIC—SYMPHONY, SONATA, CHAMBER MUSIC, etc. (3) Revival of certain forms of the BAROQUE such as TOCCATA, PAS-SACAGLIA. (4) Rejection of romantic PROGRAM MUSIC and NA-TIONALISM. (5) Sober ORCHESTRATION, clarity of TEXTURE; e.g., Stravinsky, Piston.

NEO-ROMANTICISM. A movement in twentieth-century music to revive a simple, direct, expressive style; e.g., Virgil Thomson, Barber, Menotti, Dello Joio.

NOCTURNE (Fr., *a night piece*). A short lyric piece marked by expressiveness of a highly personal nature. Especially Chopin's Nocturnes for the PIANO.

NOTE. The written symbol for a musical sound, indicating its PITCH and duration. See WHOLE, HALF, QUARTER, and EIGHTH NOTES.

NUANCE. Subtle shadings in TEMPO, DYNAMICS, phrasing, and touch that add character and distinction to a performance.

OBOE. A double-reed, WOODWIND INSTRUMENT with an intense, reedy TONE. The PITCH of the oboe does not easily change, for which reason it is used to sound the A for the other INSTRUMENTS when the ORCHESTRA is tuning up.

OCTAVE. (1) The INTERVAL from a TONE to the one above or below that bears the same name, as from C to C. (2) The distance from the first to last tone of the MAJOR or MINOR SCALE. In Western music the octave is divided into twelve equal SEMITONES, represented by the seven white and five black KEYS of the PIANO.

OCTET. (1) A COMPOSITION for eight VOICES or INSTRUMENTS. (2) A group performing such a work.

OFF-BEAT. The weak or the unaccented BEAT of the measure. In duple meter, which is counted *one*-two *one*-two, the second pulse is off-beat.

OPERA. A drama that is sung, presented with scenery, costumes, and acting, and accompanied by an ORCHESTRA.

OPERETTA. A play with music, of a light romantic character. The dialogue is spoken.

ORATORIO. An extended musical work on a dramatic text of sacred or serious character, for SOLO voices, CHORUS, and ORCHESTRA. Performed without scenery, costumes, or acting. The emphasis is on the chorus. Handel's *Messiah*.

ORCHESTRA. A large ENSEMBLE of instrumentalists with a number of players to each PART. Consists of four sections or choirs: STRINGED, WOODWIND, BRASS, and PERCUSSION INSTRUMENTS. The modern symphony orchestra consists of about a hundred players.

ORCHESTRATION. The art of arranging music for the ORCHESTRA.

ORGAN. A wind instrument whose pipes are controlled by two or more KEYBOARDS and a set of PEDALS. Air is fed to the pipes by mechanical means.

ORGAN POINT. A TONE sustained in one PART while the HARMONIES change in the other parts. The organ point is usually in the BASS. Also known as *pedal point*.

ORNAMENTS. Traditional figures used to embellish a MELODY: TRILLS, ARPEGGIOS, GRACE NOTES, etc.

OVERTURE. (1) A piece for ORCHESTRA that serves as an introduction to an OPERA, ORATORIO, drama, BALLET. (2) An independent piece for orchestra on a picturesque or dramatic subject. Tchaikovsky, *1812 Overture.* Mendelssohn, *Hebrides Overture* (*Fingal's Cave*).

PART. (1) The music executed by a VOICE or INSTRUMENT, either alone or with others: *viola part, tenor part.* (2) A section of a piece.

PASSACAGLIA (It.). A CONTRAPUNTAL piece in moderately slow TRIPLE METER; a short THEME is repeated over and over again in the BASS while the other VOICES weave VARIATIONS above it.

PEDAL. (1) An action operated by the feet, as on the PIANO, to change DYNAMICS and tone color; or on the HARP, in order to change the PITCH. (2) On the ORGAN, the pedals constitute a KEYBOARD.

PERCUSSION INSTRUMENTS. Instruments made to sound by striking or shaking. Definite PITCH: KETTLEDRUMS (timpani), GLOCKENSPIEL, XYLOPHONE, CELESTA, chimes. Indefinite PITCH: BASS DRUM, SNARE DRUM, TAMBOURINE, CASTANETS, TRIANGLE, CYMBALS, GONG.

PIANISSIMO (It.). Very soft (*pp*).

PIANO (It.). (1) Soft (*p*). (2) An INSTRUMENT whose strings are struck by little hammers controlled by a KEYBOARD mechanism. Its full name, piano-forte (soft-loud), indicates its wide range of DYNAMICS. The piano is extremely useful because of its self-sufficiency: one is able to play on it both MELODY and HARMONY.

PICCOLO (It., *piccolo flauto*, little flute). A WOODWIND INSTRUMENT of the FLUTE family, half as long as the flute and playing an OCTAVE higher. Highest in PITCH of all the instruments of the ORCHESTRA.

PITCH. The location of a TONE in the musical SCALE, in reference to its being high or low. Pitch depends on the rate of vibration, which in turn depends on the length of the vibrating body (also the width, density, tension, etc.). The longer a string, the more slowly it vibrates and the lower the pitch. The shorter a string, the more rapidly it vibrates and the higher the pitch.

PIZZICATO (It., *plucked; pih-tsih-cah'-to*). Plucked instead of played with the bow. An effect much used in playing STRINGED INSTRUMENTS.

POLKA. A lively dance in 2/4 TIME.

POLONAISE. A stately march-dance at the court of the Kings of Poland, in 3/4 TIME.

POLYPHONY (Gr., *many-voiced*). Music in which two or more independent MELODIES are combined simultaneously in a unified TEXTURE. See COUNTERPOINT.

POLYRHYTHM. The simultaneous use of two or more contrasting RHYTHMS.

POLYTONALITY. The use of two or more KEYS at the same time. An effect much used in twentieth-century music.

PRESTO (It.). Very fast.

PROGRAM MUSIC. Music inspired by a "program," that is, a literary idea or a poetic mood specified in the title or in a "program note" appended to the SCORE. The opposite of ABSOLUTE MUSIC. Main forms: SYMPHONIC POEM, incidental music, OVERTURE. Also the program symphony. Liszt, *Les Préludes.* Berlioz, *Symphonie fantastique.* Grieg, music for Ibsen's *Peer Gynt.*

PSALM. A musical setting of one of the Psalms of David.

QUADRILLE. A square dance that alternates between 3/8 TIME and 2/4.

QUADRUPLE METER. A metrical pattern of four BEATS to a measure, as in 4/4 TIME, with the main ACCENT on the first beat and a secondary accent on the third beat.

QUARTER NOTE (♩). Equivalent to two EIGHTH NOTES. In 4/4 TIME a quarter note receives one BEAT.

QUARTET. (1) A vocal or instrumental COMPOSITION for four performers. (2) A group performing such a piece.

QUINTET. (1) A vocal or instrumental COMPOSITION for five performers. (2) A group performing such a piece.

RECITAL. A concert devoted to one performer. We speak of a SYMPHONY concert, a PIANO recital, a SONG recital.

RECITATIVE (It., *reh-tchee-tah-teev'*). A style of vocal declamation that presents the plot or action of an OPERA, ORATORIO, etc., by imitating the inflections of speech. At the lyric moments the action stops and recitative gives way to ARIA (or DUET, etc.).

REED. A small elastic piece of cane that sets the air vibrating in the mouthpiece of certain WOODWIND INSTRUMENTS. In single-reed instruments like the CLARINET and SAXOPHONE, the reed is fastened against a chisel-shaped mouthpiece. In double-reed instruments like the OBOE and BASSOON the two reeds are so shaped as to leave between them an extremely small passage for the player's breath.

REGISTER. (1) A portion of the range of the VOICE, as *head* or *chest register*. (2) A portion of the range of an INSTRUMENT, as high, middle, or low register.

REQUIEM. A musical setting of the Mass for the Dead.

RESOLUTION. The movement of DISSONANCE to CONSONANCE, of tension to response. The gravitation of an active TONE, INTERVAL, or CHORD to one of rest.

RHAPSODY. A piece in very free style with abrupt changes of mood, emotional intensity, and technical brilliance.

RHYTHM. The controlled flow of music in respect to TIME.

ROMANTICISM. A period in art marked by subjective emotion, individualism, emphasis on expressiveness, and revolt against tradition. Especially nineteenth-century romanticism, the aftermath of the French Revolution. Musical developments during the Romantic Period (c. 1810–1900) included: (1) Growth in size of the ORCHESTRA and a rise in the level of instrumental TECHNIQUE. (2) Founding of CONSERVATORIES in the main cities of Europe. (3) Growth of the middle-class public and concert life. (4) Emphasis on virtuosity and the personality of the performer. (5) NATIONALISM and EXOTICISM. (6) Emphasis on brilliant ORCHESTRATION and sensuous tone color. (7) Development of PROGRAM MUSIC, especially the SYMPHONIC POEM and the OVERTURE. (8) Love of short lyric FORMS—the ART SONG (LIED) and the PIANO piece. (9) Idealization of the Middle Ages, as in the music dramas of Wagner. (10) Art is seen as an escape from reality, self-expression, intoxication, infinite longing. Composers: Weber, Schubert, Berlioz, Mendelssohn, Schumann, Chopin, Liszt, Wagner, Verdi, Franck, Smetana, Brahms, Bizet, Tchaikovsky, Dvořák, Grieg, Rimsky-Korsakov. Painters: Delacroix, Géricault, Turner, Corot. Writers: Wordsworth, Coleridge, Scott, Byron, Shelley, Keats, Heine, Balzac, Hugo, Dumas, Pushkin, Dickens, Emily and Charlotte Brontë, George Eliot, Thackeray, Hawthorne, Poe.

RONDO FORM. A pattern based on the recurrence of a principal THEME that alternates with contrasting material in symmetrical sections, such as A-B-A-C-A.

ROULADE. A florid passage in a MELODY consisting of rapid passages, runs, TRILLS, or other ORNAMENTS that show off the performer's TECHNIQUE.

SARABAND. A stately dance of the seventeenth and eighteenth centuries in slow TRIPLE METER, of Spanish origin.

SAXOPHONE. A single-REED, WOODWIND INSTRUMENT with a metal body.

SCALE. An arrangement of the TONES of a KEY in consecutive order. See MAJOR SCALE, MINOR SCALE.

SCHERZO (It., *a joke; sker'-tso*). (1) A MOVEMENT in a SONATA, SYMPHONY, QUARTET, etc. (often the third movement) which Haydn and Beethoven substituted for the classical MINUET. Usually in quick 3/4 TIME, strongly rhythmic and whimsical. (2) An independent piece of this type, such as Chopin's Scherzos for the PIANO.

SCORE. The arrangement on a page of all the instrumental and/or vocal PARTS of a work. The different parts appear under each other on different staves (staffs), giving a complete picture of what is happening in the ORCHESTRA at any point.

SEMITONE. Half of a WHOLE TONE, as from C to C♯. A half step, the smallest INTERVAL in the music of the Western world. See OCTAVE.

SERENADE. (1) An "evening song" of romantic character. (2) A piece of social music of the late eighteenth century.

SEXTUPLE METER. A metrical pattern of six BEATS to a measure, as in SIX-EIGHT (6/8) TIME.

SFORZANDO (It.). A sudden ACCENT on a TONE or CHORD (*sf* or *sfz*).

SHARP. (1) The sign (♯) that raises a NOTE by a SEMITONE, as from C to C♯. (2) Off-PITCH, too high.

SICILIANA (It., *sih-tchih-lyah'-nah*). A peasant dance of Sicilian origin, in a moderately slow 6/8 or 12/8 TIME. Also a MOVEMENT in this style.

SIDE DRUM. A drum consisting of a cylindrical body of wood or metal and two heads. The upper head is beaten with two drumsticks. The drum is slung over the left thigh.

SINFONIETTA. A small SYMPHONY, usually written for a small ORCHESTRA.

SIX-EIGHT TIME. A metrical pattern of six BEATS to a measure, an EIGHTH NOTE receiving one beat.

SNARE DRUM. A SIDE DRUM that has gut strings or *snares* stretched across its lower head. These give it a crisp, rattling sound.

SOLFEGGIO. Vocal exercises designed to give the student facility in singing INTERVALS and RHYTHMS in all CLEFS and KEY SIGNATURES.

SOLO (It., *alone*). To be played or sung by one performer.

SONATA (It., *suonare*, to sound). A piece for one or two INSTRUMENTS, in three or four MOVEMENTS that contrast in character and in TEMPO. The first movement is generally an ALLEGRO of epic-dramatic character. The second is apt to be the "slow movement," of a soulful or meditative character, marked ANDANTE, ADAGIO, or LARGO. The third is generally the dance movement, marked allegro or ALLEGRETTO. In the classical symphony the third movement is a MINUET: in the nineteenth-century sonata, generally a SCHERZO. The fourth movement, in the sonatas of Haydn and Mozart, is generally a lively FINALE in the character of an allegro vivace, frequently in RONDO FORM. In the ROMANTIC PERIOD it is apt to have a dramatic ending of a triumphal nature. The four-movement cycle, when written for one or two instruments, is called a sonata. When intended for small groups it is known as a TRIO, QUARTET, QUINTET, etc., as the case may be. For SOLO instrument and ORCHESTRA it is a CONCERTO; for full orchestra, a SYMPHONY. Most ABSOLUTE MUSIC of the past two hundred years is cast in the form of the sonata cycle.

SONG. A short piece for solo VOICE with instrumental ACCOMPANIMENT.

SOPRANO. (1) The highest woman's VOICE. There are three types, dramatic, lyric, and coloratura, which is a very brilliant type of soprano. (2) The highest PART in a four-part CHORUS.

(3) The highest in range of any family of INSTRUMENTS: soprano SAXOPHONE.

SPIRITUALS. Religious folk songs of the South. The Negro spirituals are especially popular.

STOP. On STRINGED INSTRUMENTS, to bring down the finger at a certain point in order to produce the desired PITCH.

STRINGED INSTRUMENTS. Produce sound by means of stretched strings that are either played with a bow or plucked. The string section of the ORCHESTRA includes four bowed instruments: VIOLIN, VIOLA, CELLO, DOUBLE BASS. Plucked-string instruments: HARP, guitar, banjo, etc.

STRING QUARTET. (1) CHAMBER MUSIC for four STRINGED INSTRUMENTS: first and second VIOLINS, VIOLA, CELLO. See SONATA. (2) An ENSEMBLE of four musicians who play such a work.

STYLE. The characteristic manner in which the material of art is presented. May refer to: (1) A period in history: BAROQUE, CLASSICAL, or ROMANTIC style. (2) An artist's personal manner: Haydn's or Beethoven's style. (3) Purpose, function, or type: INSTRUMENTAL or VOCAL style; OPERATIC or ORATORIO style; SYMPHONIC or CHAMBER-MUSIC style.

SUITE. (1) A form of baroque instrumental music consisting of a set of dance-forms all in the same KEY, such as Bach's Suites. (2) A set of MOVEMENTS extracted from a longer work such as an OPERA, BALLET, or music for a play: Tchaikovsky, *Nutcracker Suite*; Grieg, *Peer Gynt Suite*. (3) A work in several movements that are connected by a central idea. Ferde Grofé, *Grand Canyon Suite*.

SYMPHONIC POEM. A work for ORCHESTRA in one MOVEMENT that suggests a story, a scene, or a mood. This is specified in the title of the piece or in a "program note" that the composer writes in the SCORE. Liszt, *Les Préludes*. Strauss, *The*

223

Merry Pranks of Tyl Eulenspiegel. Also known as *tone poem.*

SYMPHONY. An extended work for full ORCHESTRA, in three or four MOVEMENTS. See SONATA.

SYNCOPATION. A shifting of the ACCENT so that it falls on the OFF-BEAT, that is, the weak BEAT of the measure. The basis of JAZZ.

TAMBOURINE. A small drum consisting of a shallow circular hoop of wood or metal with one head of parchment. Metallic jingles are fastened at several points in the hoop. The player strikes the tambourine with his fingers, palm, knuckles, and elbow. Used to accompany dancing in Spain, southern France, and Italy.

TANGO. A slow, graceful dance of Argentine origin, in syncopated 2/4 TIME.

TARANTELLA. A lively Italian dance in 6/8 TIME.

TECHNIQUE. The mastery of the technical means of expression. We speak of a pianist's technique, a composer's technique, etc.

TEMPO. The rate of speed of a piece or a section thereof. Tempo markings range from slow to fast: LARGO, ADAGIO, ANDANTINO, ALLEGRETTO, ALLEGRO, vivace, PRESTO.

TENOR. (1) The high male VOICE, lyric or dramatic. (2) In a four-part CHORUS, the voice above the BASS and below the ALTO. (3) An INSTRUMENT in this range: tenor TROMBONE.

TEXTURE. The "weave" of the music, the distribution of the elements of MELODY and HARMONY. Three types of texture: MONOPHONIC, POLYPHONIC, HOMOPHONIC.

THEME. A musical idea or subject that serves as the basis for a COMPOSITION. Musical works are fashioned out of themes and motives.

THEME AND VARIATIONS. A musical FORM that presents a basic idea or subject in a number of transformations, each of

224

which explores a fresh aspect of the theme and constitutes a VARIATION.

THREE-FOUR TIME. A metrical pattern of three BEATS to a measure, with a QUARTER NOTE receiving one beat. Associated with the WALTZ. See TRIPLE METER.

TIE. A curved line joining two NOTES of the same PITCH, prolonging the first by the value of the second: ♩♩ = ♩.

TIMBRE (Fr., *tahm'-br*). The distinctive tone color of an INSTRUMENT; the quality that differentiates a NOTE on this instrument from the same note on any other instrument.

TIME. Musical time refers to meter, TEMPO, and/or the duration of a NOTE.

TIME SIGNATURE. Placed at the beginning of a piece or section to indicate the meter. The upper numeral shows the number of BEATS in the measure. The lower indicates the kind of NOTE that receives one beat. 4/4 TIME: four beats to a measure, a QUARTER NOTE receives one beat.

TIMPANI. See KETTLEDRUM.

TOCCATA. (It., *toccare*, to touch, i.e., the keys). A KEYBOARD piece that exploits all the resources of an INSTRUMENT—rapid SCALES, ARPEGGIOS, CHORDS, TRILLS, OCTAVES, etc.

TONE. (1) A musical sound possessing four properties—PITCH; duration (see RHYTHM); volume (see DYNAMICS); and TIMBRE. (2) An INTERVAL of two SEMITONES or half-steps, as from DO to *re* or C to D. A WHOLE TONE.

TONIC. (1) The first and principal TONE of the SCALE and KEY, the KEYNOTE or DO from which a musical MOVEMENT grows and to which it ultimately returns. (2) The CHORD based on this tone. The Tonic is the point of repose and completion to which all the other tones and chords resolve. See RESOLUTION.

TRANSCRIPTION. An adaptation of a piece for INSTRUMENTS or VOICES other than those for which it was written.

TRANSPOSE. To shift a piece from the KEY in which it is written to a higher or lower key.

TREBLE. (1) The upper part of the REGISTER as distinguished from the BASS or lower. In PIANO music, the right-hand part. (2) The highest PART in a choral COMPOSITION, the SOPRANO.

TREMOLO (It., *trembling*). On STRINGED INSTRUMENTS, the repetition of a TONE through a rapid up-and-down movement of the bow. An effect much used in orchestral music for building up tension and an atmosphere of suspense. (2) On the PIANO, the rapid alternation of a tone with its OCTAVE or other tones of the same CHORD. (3) In vocal music, a quavering tone.

TRIANGLE. A PERCUSSION INSTRUMENT consisting of a steel rod bent into triangular shape, that is struck with a metal wand.

TRILL. A musical ORNAMENT produced by rapidly alternating a TONE with its upper neighbor.

TRIO. (1) A piece for three players or singers. (2) The group performing such a piece.

TRIPLE METER. A metrical pattern of three BEATS to a measure, ACCENT on the first, as in 3/4 or 3/8 TIME.

TROMBONE (It., *large trumpet*). A BRASS INSTRUMENT fitted with a movable U-shaped slide that changes the length of the vibrating air column in the tube, hence the PITCH. Possesses a grandly sonorous TONE.

TRUMPET. The SOPRANO of the brass choir, possessing a brilliant TIMBRE that is associated with martial pomp and vigor.

TUBA. The BASS of the BRASS INSTRUMENTS. Has a dark resonance that ranges from velvety softness to a growl.

TUTTI (It., *all*). Those PARTS in a work for ORCHESTRA that are played by the whole orchestra.

TWO-FOUR TIME. A metrical pattern of two BEATS to a measure, a QUARTER NOTE receiving one beat.

VARIATION. A TECHNIQUE of transforming a musical THEME or subject through changes in the MELODY, HARMONY, RHYTHM, meter, and TEMPO; DYNAMICS, ORCHESTRATION, REGISTER, KEY, MODE; type of ACCOMPANIMENT; CONTRAPUNTAL combination with other themes; etc. As a result of all these changes the basic idea is presented in ever fresh guises. See THEME AND VARIATIONS.

VIBRAPHONE. A PERCUSSION INSTRUMENT that combines the principle of the XYLOPHONE with propellers, one to each NOTE, that are driven by an electric motor, giving an unusual TONE marked by a slow VIBRATO.

VIBRATO (It.). On STRINGED INSTRUMENTS, a slight wavering of PITCH obtained by an oscillating movement of the left hand in order to enrich the TONE. Also said of the VOICE.

VIOLIN. The SOPRANO of the STRINGED INSTRUMENTS, universally admired for its singing TONE, which brings it of all instruments closest to the human VOICE.

VIOLA. The ALTO of the string section of the ORCHESTRA. See STRINGED INSTRUMENTS. It is somewhat larger than the VIOLIN: its strings are longer, thicker, heavier; it is lower in range.

VIRTUOSO (It.). A master of instrumental TECHNIQUE.

VOICE. (1) The singing voice, the most personal and expressive of INSTRUMENTS. There are six types: Female: SOPRANO, MEZZO-SOPRANO, CONTRALTO. Male: TENOR, BARITONE, BASS. (2) A vocal line or a PART in CONTRAPUNTAL music: a FUGUE in four voices.

WALTZ. A popular dance in THREE-FOUR TIME.

WHOLE NOTE (𝅝). Is equivalent to two HALF NOTES. In 4/4 TIME, a whole note receives four BEATS.

WHOLE TONE. An INTERVAL equal to two SEMITONES, such as *do-re* or C-D.

WHOLE-TONE SCALE. A SCALE of six NOTES consisting only of WHOLE TONES, such as C-D-E-F♯-G♯-A♯-C.

WOODWIND INSTRUMENTS. A group whose TONE is produced by a vibrating column of air within a tube that has holes in its side. When one or another of these holes is opened, the length of the air column is changed, and with it the rate of vibration, consequently the PITCH. The air is set vibrating in one of three ways: (1) The player blows across an EMBOUCHURE, as in the FLUTE family. (2) By a single REED, as in the CLARINET and SAXOPHONE families. (3) By a double reed, as in the OBOE and BASSOON families. See WOODWINDS.

WOODWINDS. A section of the ORCHESTRA consisting of four principal INSTRUMENTS, each supplemented by another member of the same family. (1) FLUTE and PICCOLO. (2) OBOE and ENGLISH HORN. (3) CLARINET and bass CLARINET. (4) BASSOON and CONTRABASSOON. See WOODWIND INSTRUMENTS.

XYLOPHONE. A PERCUSSION INSTRUMENT consisting of tuned blocks of wood that produce a dry, crisp sound when struck. The player uses two mallets.

Books for Further Reading

GENERAL

This Modern Music by Gerald Abraham. A fine introduction to the subject for those who have some musical background.

America's Music, from the Pilgrims to the Present by Gilbert Chase. The complete story of music in America from its earliest beginnings to our own time. Especially good on the little-known composers of Revolutionary and pre-Civil War times.

Modern Music-Makers by Madeleine Goss. Compact biographies of thirty-seven modern American composers, with full-page photographs and a listing of each composer's works.

Modern Music by John Tasker Howard and James Lyons. A lively account, in a popular vein, of the main currents in twentieth-century music.

Introduction to Contemporary Music by Joseph Machlis. A comprehensive survey of the musical scene of our time, with discussions of important composers and their representative works.

BOOKS BY AMERICAN COMPOSERS

The Joy of Music by Leonard Bernstein. A collection of the television scripts that Bernstein presented on the Omnibus programs. They delighted the country and make interesting reading.

Our New Music by Aaron Copland. One of the finest introductions to the music of the twentieth century. It has been re-issued as a paper-back.

Essays before a Sonata by Charles Ives. Thoughts, fancies, and impressions by one of the most original figures our country has produced. A fascinating book.

The Musical Scene by Virgil Thomson. A collection of Thomson's reviews in the *Herald-Tribune*. Every page reveals Thomson's wit, his skill as a writer, and his perception as a critic.

BOOKS ABOUT AMERICAN COMPOSERS

Samuel Barber by Nathan Broder. An informative account of Barber's life and music.

Leonard Bernstein by David Ewen. A spectacular success story told with relish.

Aaron Copland by Julia Smith. A detailed study of Copland's music, preceded by an account of his life.

George Gershwin: A Study in American Music by Isaac Goldberg. *A Journey to Greatness: George Gershwin* by David Ewen. Two books that give a vivid picture of Gershwin's life and times.

Charles Tomlinson Griffes: The Life of an American Composer by Edward M. Maisel. A sympathetic account of Griffes' life and the world he lived in.

Charles Ives and His Music by Henry and Sidney Cowell. A thorough study of the "grand old man" of American music.

Edward MacDowell, A Great American Tone Poet by John F. Porte. *MacDowell* by William H. Humiston. Both books are written in a spirit of admiration for the first American who won a European reputation as a composer.

William Schuman by Flora R. Schreiber and Vincent Persichetti. A compact description of Schuman's career and his music.

Virgil Thomson by Kathleen Hoover and John Cage. Describes not only Thomson's life and music but also the intellectual-artistic world of Paris and New York that shaped his outlook and his art.

Index

231

ABOUT THE AUTHOR

Joseph Machlis's early training as a pianist and his study of English literature provided an excellent background for his major interest: lecturing and writing about music.

Professor Machlis received his B.A. and M.A. at City College in New York and Columbia University, respectively. He studied at the Institute of Musical Art of the Juilliard School, from which he graduated with the Certificate for the Artist Course in Piano. Mr. Machlis also received a Steinway Scholarship at the Conservatoire Américain at Fontainebleau, France, where he studied with Isidor Philipp.

At Queens College, where he is Professor of Music, Mr. Machlis has directed one of the largest music appreciation projects in the country. He is the author of *The Enjoyment of Music: An Introduction to Perceptive Listening* (which is used as a text by hundreds of colleges throughout the country) and, more recently, *Introduction to Contemporary Music.*

Professor Machlis is well known as a translator of operas. A number of his English versions have been presented on coast-to-coast television by the NBC Opera Company, among them: *La Bohème, La Traviata, Rigoletto, Fidelio, Cavalleria Rusticana,* and Prokofiev's *War and Peace.* His English version of Manuel de Falla's dramatic cantata *Atlantida* was presented by the Metropolitan Opera Company during the week of gala performances that celebrated the opening of Lincoln Center's Philharmonic Hall.